WHAT DO JAMAICAN CHILDREN SPEAK?

WHAT DO JAMAICAN CHILDREN SPEAK?

A Language Resource

Michele M. Kennedy

THE UNIVERSITY OF THE WEST INDIES PRESS
Jamaica • Barbados • Trinidad and Tobago

The University of the West Indies Press
7A Gibraltar Hall Road, Mona
Kingston 7, Jamaica
www.uwipress.com

A catalogue record of this book is available from the National Library of Jamaica.

ISBN: 978-976-640-630-1 (print)
     978-976-640-631-8 (Kindle)
     978-976-640-632-5 (ePub)

Cover illustration: Photograph by Lara Dayes of *Weave Jamaica* designed by her using colour-and-weave effects on the loom.
Cover design by Richard Rawlins
Typeset by The Beget, India
Printed in the United States of America

To my grandsons, Tyrell and Finn

Contents

Tables

Acknowledgements

There are so many to thank. Without them, I could not have written this book.

Pauline Christie introduced me to linguistics. After that theory course, I took every linguistics course offered at the University of the West Indies at the time, including those taught by Mervyn Alleyne, whose passion for linguistics was equally contagious. My life took many turns: I spent years teaching high school French and Spanish, and then more years as a small business owner, creating computer applications; but it is these two icons that I have to thank for a love of linguistics that has never left me.

I returned to the University of the West Indies in 2000, with linguistic theory still in my veins, to do my doctorate on aspects of quantification in Jamaican Creole. Silvia Kouwenberg took up the baton as another icon who shaped my thinking as a linguist.

But I wanted more. As a teacher I had been fascinated by how the students acquired language. That would be my area of post-doctoral research – first- and second-language acquisition, using theory to inform analysis and to provide insights into how students may better learn language.

Without exception, all principals and all teachers involved in the project on which this study is based facilitated it beyond all reasonable expectations. And of course, many thanks also to the children, the future of our country, and to their parents, such willing participants.

Trecel Messam-Johnson functioned as investigator, transcriber and supervisor of transcribers, truly the backbone of the project. Thanks also to the teams of graduate and undergraduate students – investigators, transcribers and native speaker consultants – for their dedication and hard work.

Funding and institutional support from the University of the West Indies were crucial. Funding took the form of a New Initiatives Grant covering all fieldwork expenses and, subsequently, a year's sabbatical leave. Special thanks go also to the help of administrators: Peter Watson, IT officer in the Faculty of Humanities and Education, for managing the videos on the university's intranet and advising me throughout, and Yvette Mundy-Whyte in the Department of Language, Linguistics and Philosophy for processing invoices and liaising with the bursary.

I have been blessed with the generosity of my colleagues. During my sabbatical, Christian Mair and Véronique Lacoste facilitated a month of me interacting with linguists with fresh insights at the University of Freiburg in Germany. Andrew Radford, both before and after our meeting at the University of Essex during the sabbatical, promptly and in great detail responded to my email messages, always making me think that much more. He also read and commented on a pre-final version of the manuscript, comments always on point. Pauline Christie has been with me throughout the writing of this book, reading and rereading chapters, always only a phone call away.

I am grateful also to other colleagues who read and commented on at least one chapter: Hugues Peters, Silvia Kouwenberg, and my colleagues in education Beverley Bryan, Zellynne Jennings-Craig and Yewande Lewis-Fokum. Material in this book was also used in the article "Systematicity in the Acquisition of Determination by Three-Year-Old Jamaican Children: Implications for Education", *Caribbean Journal of Education*, Department of Language, Linguistics and Philosophy Special Issue, 38, no. 2 (2017): 18–42. Many thanks to the *Caribbean Journal of Education* for having facilitated this.

Thanks go to Wayne, who in the early days of this project was always excited about my work and, though not a linguist, always managed to ask a relevant question. My friends Elinor, Cecille and Mary always believe in me and offer support. Robert put in hours helping to prepare the files for data manipulation, tedious tasks for him, perhaps, but reaping such valuable benefits for me.

Thanks to Tony, who, with his gift of an eye for detail, so generously helped with proofing.

I end with pride and thanks for the contributions of my own children for their love and encouragement, as well as for the tangible ways in which they helped – Lara with the editing of an earlier version of the manuscript, and Sean with pre-final editing. In addition, talented weaver that she is, Lara provided the picture of the hand-woven sample she created especially for the cover on her floor loom.

So very many thanks, all.

Abbreviations Used in the Presentation of Data

Glosses

x.y	y morpheme incorporated in x
x-y	y morpheme attached to x
1 2 or 3	first, second or third person
AGT	agentive morpheme
COMP	complementizer
COP	copula
DEF	definite article
DEM	demonstrative
EMPH	emphatic marker
FOC	focus marker
FUT	future marker
HAB	habitual marker
IMP	imperfective marker
IMPER	imperative
INCL	inclusiveness marker
IND OBJ	indirect object (function)*
INDEF	indefinite article
INF	infinitive
ITER	iterative marker
LOC	locative
MOD	modal
NEG	negator
NUM	number
Ø	null
OBJ	object (function)*

PAST	past tense
PERF	perfective marker
PL	plural
POSS	possessive (function)*
PREP	preposition
PRES	present tense
PROG	progressive
PTL	particle
REFL	reflexive
S	singular
SUBJ	subject (function)*
WH	'wh-' question word

*Note: Normally, glosses such as these mark overt case distinctions; here, .IND OBJ, .OBJ, .POSS and .SUBJ are used to differentiate functions. This is for clarity, since different functions for first, second or third person have the same form in Jamaican Creole.

Child Language Data Exchange System (CHILDES) Symbols

word [/]	repetition of preceding word (or <string>)
word [/-]	preceding word (or <string>) replaced
child form [: target]	for example, *kluoaz* [: *kluoz*] 'clothes' corrected form in square brackets
[?]	preceding word (or <string>) heard, but its meaning or relevance is unclear
#	pause
+	indicates a compound, for example, *lonch+pan* 'lunch-pan'
+...	at the end of an utterance indicates it was incomplete or interrupted
<string> [>]	
<string> [<]	indicates overlapping speech
xxx	indistinct speech

Other Symbols

*	at the beginning of a string, indicates that it is ungrammatical
??	acceptability of the string is questionable; would not be accepted by all speakers
( )	indicates optionality
≠	does not mean
~	indicates variants, for example, *famili* ~ *fambili* 'family'
INV	Investigator
##;##.##	the representation of age in YEARS;MONTHS.DAYS

File sources of utterances by the children are referenced in the following way:

[V# (Visit #)-ABC (three-letter code for the area): l.# (line number, ll #ff line numbers)-##;##.## (Age as above)]

For an explanation of visits, and details of three-letter codes for areas, see Methodology in section 1.2.1.

Other Abbreviations

AOA	age of onset of acquisition
CHILDES	child language data exchange system
CLAR	child language acquisition research
CR	consciousness-raising
CS	code-switching
DP	determiner phrase (D = determiner)
E, R, S	event time, reference point, speech time
FHC	functional head constraint
H (variety)	high variety
INV	investigator
JC	Jamaican Creole
JE	Jamaican English
JES	Jamaican English segment
JLU	Jamaica Language Unit
L (variety)	low variety
L1(A)	first language (acquisition)
L2(A)	second language (acquisition)
LO	loan word
MLU	mean length of utterance
NP	noun phrase (N = noun)
P&P	principles and parameters
SH	form regularly used in both JC and JE
UG	universal grammar
VP	verb phrase (V = verb)

1 | Laying the Foundation

DON: *mi a go a dakta nou.*[1]

DON: *"dakter shi iz sik."*

DON: *no . . . "shii" mi fi se.*

[V6-KN1:l.99ff-3;11.12]

his book seeks to paint a picture of the language of three-year-olds in their first year of formal schooling in Jamaica. It is intended to serve as a resource for creolists and acquisitionists, for academics in education, for teachers of literacy and language education, as well as for intermediary and advanced tertiary-level linguistics and education students. Its significance for educators lies in the fact that teachers' familiarity with learners' linguistic resources is considered essential to the task of supporting learning (Zapata and Roach 2011). This becomes particularly important in a Creole context such as that in Jamaica, referred to by Patrick (2004, 202), among others, as a complex linguistic situation characterized by extreme variability.

We explore the complexity and discover how the language of the children can inform our understanding of it. Data used as the bases of analyses, are drawn from a research project fully funded by the University of the West Indies, Mona, Jamaica, and designed and executed by the author and her team of student assistants. The project was entitled "Child Language Acquisition Research (CLAR): What Do They Speak?" The children who participated in the research are referred to as the CLAR children and, as the title of the project suggests, we will be looking at their speech.

It is often claimed that there are two languages or *codes* in the country:[2] Jamaican Creole (JC), also referred to as Patwa, and Jamaican English (JE).[3]

JC's lexicon (vocabulary) was originally based on that of English. For this reason, English is referred to as the lexifier language. JC is spoken natively by the vast majority of Jamaicans, yet English is the official language. The existence of an official language that is the lexifier of a Creole language, spoken by the vast majority of the population, is common in societies such as Jamaica, with socio-historical (sugar) plantation backgrounds. Problems arise due to the superficial similarities in vocabulary and pronunciation resulting from lexification by English. These similarities conceal differences between the languages at a deeper syntactic level (Craig 1980, 2), and have the further consequence that some speakers believe that they are speaking JE when in fact they are not.[4]

Since the early 1960s, the notion of the *continuum* has been applied by some scholars to the language situation in such Creole communities, with the lexifier language and the Creole at the opposing poles, and intermediate varieties linking them.[5] In the Jamaican situation, JE and JC form the poles; while in Guyana, for instance, Guyanese English and Guyanese Creole, or Creolese, do. The codes at either end of the continuum are seen as idealizations since, given the extreme variability which exists, it is unlikely that any one speaker would use only forms belonging exclusively to one code or the other.

The approach taken in this work is to view an individual's speech forms as being composed of *features*, which may in turn be identified as belonging to either (an idealized) JC or JE. Variation in speech is analysed, then, in terms of the feature-composition of the forms. This is done within a lexically based minimalist framework where words are seen as bundles of features, and features drive structure.[6]

The term *code-weaving*[7] is used in acknowledgement of the nature of the variation in speech communities across the island and in the speech of the children: speakers draw from linguistic repertoires with forms ranging from those most like what has been called the Creole to those most like the English lexifier. Guided by the distinction made explicit by Craig (1980), I differentiate between what I call *superficial weaving*, that is, the mixing of phonological[8] features at the level of the word, and *structural weaving*, the mixing of morphological and syntactic features in constructions.

Patterns of language choice by the children are investigated and the findings are used as a basis for recommendations for the expected benefit of language and literacy classrooms. One may say that linguistic analysis is used as a platform, a basis on which to understand the nature of the language that has been acquired by the children and used by them, leading to an informed picture of a possible way forward in English language education. It is argued that an understanding of the characteristics of the language that has been acquired by the children, an understanding, in effect, of what it is the children speak, will allow the language and literacy teacher to transform what are frequently considered hindrances into opportunities for learning the English language.

The sections which follow in this chapter lay the foundations for the study. As background, the characteristics of the Creole speech situation are explored in section 1.1 and the research project on which the study is based is outlined in sections 1.2 and 1.3. The chapter closes with an indication of the organization of the book in section 1.4.

1.1 The Language Situation in Jamaica

The particular concern here is with the Jamaican language situation. There is historical evidence from the eighteenth century of "extensive variation (among speakers and within individual usage) in features of basilectal and acrolectal models of Jamaican speech" (Lalla and D'Costa 1990, 98). This has been said to have evolved over the years into what Patrick (2004, 202) refers to as a complex linguistic situation, characterized by the "extreme variability of contemporary Jamaican speech".

I investigate in this section the link between historical phenomena and present-day issues, on the basis that, as pointed out as early as Alleyne (1971, 170), Creoles demonstrate the influence of social context on language change, language structure and language usage. Thus, the section begins with a note on the socio-historical foundation of the language situation in Jamaica, and then continues to review the linguistic consequences of this, leading to the basis of a characterization of an approach to the situation.

Britain imported hundreds of thousands of enslaved Africans to expand and sustain the plantation economy.[9] It is important to note, however, that it was not the case that all the enslaved spoke the same language – they were not a linguistically homogeneous group at all. It was their need to communicate with the Europeans and with each other that led to the emergence of JC. The slave masters, a small group on the plantations, did not themselves speak the same varieties of English – they were a mix of Scots, Welsh and speakers of a number of dialects of English. In addition, relatively few of the large majority of the enslaved population came into direct contact, on an ongoing basis, with the tiny minority who spoke these different varieties of English. Problems in communication would indeed have been great; this was by no means a straightforward case of migrants to a new country, where speakers of one language may learn one homogeneous target language spoken by all those with whom they come into contact outside of their family circles.

Despite this difficulty in communicating, linguistic communication became possible. This means of communication became known as Creole, derived from the term used originally to refer to the descendants of Europeans born in the colonies.

How Creoles emerged continues to capture the interest of linguists, and has resulted in a rich body of literature on their genesis. Early views held that Creoles emerged from Pidgins, structurally deficient auxiliary languages that expanded as a result of their acquisition by native speakers. As Kouwenberg and Singler (2011, 284) point out, such views have been largely abandoned in the field, on all counts: Pidgins are not structurally deficient auxiliary languages, and there is no evidence that every Creole started as a Pidgin or that linguistic expansion necessarily requires nativization.

The study of Creole genesis in the 1980s and 1990s resulted in hypotheses generally referred to as superstratist, substratist and universalist, differing fundamentally with regard to the mechanisms presumed to have produced these languages (Aboh 2015, 60). In broad terms, superstratists hold that Creole languages are distant varieties of the lexifier language (the superstratum), resulting from imperfect approximations of approximations of the target (see, for example, Chaudenson 2001, 125; his chapter 5). Substratists contend that it is the native language grammars of enslaved Africans which primarily formed the basis of Creole development (see, for example, Lefèbvre 1998). Universalists argue that children, confronted with extremely impoverished and chaotic language *input* on the plantation, created, in essence, a new language guided by their innate language capacity[10] (see, for example, Bickerton 1981).

Aboh (2015, 60) suggests that these proposals, though fundamentally different in their points of departure, are all based on the idea that creolization involves unsuccessful or incomplete learning of the target. He makes reference also to a more recent proposal by Plag,[11] the Interlanguage Hypothesis, based on the term coined by Selinker (1972). Interlanguage refers to the systematic knowledge of language which is independent of the second language learner's native language, as well as the target system she is trying to learn. In this view, Creoles are taken to be "conventionalized interlanguages of an early stage" (Plag 2008, 115), a view thought by Aboh (2015, 61) to be a rather extreme interpretation of the concept of Creoles as incomplete or a failed acquisition of a second language.

Building on work by Mufwene (1986, 2001, among other publications), DeGraff (2005, 294–99, for example) and his own earlier works, such as Aboh and Ansaldo (2007), Aboh (2015, 136) develops an account of the emergence of Creole languages in terms of the competition between and subsequent selection of features and patterns of the languages in contact. For Aboh, competition and selection take place at two levels: "the structuring of the input, and the combination of variants selected from the input into a coherent syntactic system" (ibid., 137). Such an approach to genesis, adopting an analysis of languages in contact as resulting in a recombination of formal features, is compatible with the pre-theoretical notion of the weaving of such features in contemporary speech in a Creole environment, as presented and developed here.

Within any contact situation, the nature of linguistic change is that it proceeds at different rates and at different levels of language structure (Trudgill 2011, 2). In contact on the plantations, however, rapid linguistic change would be predicted, given the urgent need for communication to take place. Trudgill continues: "it is widely agreed that syntactic change proceeds more slowly than lexical change" (ibid.). So, we would expect more rapid change in vocabulary than in structure. This would explain the large number of English-based words in JC, and the reason for it being commonly identified as an English-lexified Creole.

The language of the colonizers was associated with power and wealth, and that which the slaves developed was generally perceived to be malformed, since English words could be recognized in their speech but it was not *really* English. The colonizers' thinking was that it fell short because the complexities of the European language were beyond the grasp of the Africans. As Pollard (2002, 2) states, the status of a language is determined by the status of its speakers.

Speaking in this way of the language of the colonizers on the one hand, and the Creole which the enslaved developed on the other, might seem to suggest that there exist discrete languages. This is not the case in the Jamaican situation. Instead, there are several overlapping varieties, often referred to by linguists as codes. These codes are so finely articulated that they cannot even be divided into a finite number of discrete codes (Patrick 2002), but are characterized as a continuous spectrum of speech varieties (DeCamp 1971b, 350), with individuals occupying a span of the spectrum.

In this work, we will explore how the weaving of codes is manifest in the regular speech of Jamaicans, and we will suggest how a minimalist approach might be useful in its analysis.

The discussion turns, in the following section, to the functions of and attitudes towards the codes in contemporary Jamaican society.

1.1.1 The Creole and the "Standard" in Jamaica Today

Over the centuries, English has maintained its unique position, since it remains the only official language of Jamaica, and is expected to be used in the conduct of government business, in the law courts, in schools as the language of instruction, in the mass media, in religious worship and in all other contexts where written language is required. This official language is referred to loosely as "English". It is not the vernacular, the language of the majority, yet it is still, to a large extent, associated with high status in the society. JC is the vernacular language. It is the expected language for use in private and informal interactions involving friends. Though many educated Jamaicans do use JC at home, it continues to be associated largely with the poorer and less educated members of the society, and many parents feel that their children will only get ahead if they speak "English".

For these reasons, the language situation in Jamaica and other Caribbean territories is thought by some linguists[12] to be *diglossic*. This term is used in language situations where there are two often closely related languages, one of which is a so-called H(igh) variety generally used by the government and in formal contexts. It is learned and taught in formal situations by most of the population, and so students will tend to focus on its use in the formal domain only. The other language is of low prestige – the so-called L(ow) variety which is the vernacular used by most people in informal situations. The L variety is not generally used in the formal domain, is not traditionally taught in schools, and may have no accepted orthography associated with it. Importantly, given that the two varieties have these very distinct functions in the community, the prevailing view is that the H variety is the language of social mobility.

Devonish (2003, 158) uses the term *conquest diglossia* to characterize language situations such as those in Jamaica and typically those across the Caribbean. Conquest diglossia is a subtype of diglossia involving an "external" H variety owing its status and functions to imposition by colonial powers. In countries such as Jamaica, the vernacular varieties used by the majority of the population share vocabulary with English, resulting in the lack of a clear distinction between those varieties and English. Devonish (ibid., 159) refers to this lack of distinction as a gradual shading off from the most English varieties towards those most deviant from English. This is a result of what Ferguson (1959, 332) describes as a kind of linguistic convergence, said to be characteristic of diglossic situations.

Another consequence of the social history of Creole communities is that attitudes towards language are very complex. It is commonly expressed, for example, that JC is what we use when we are passionate about something, when we are being humorous, when we are upset, when we let our guard down or when we react impulsively to pain or fear. We have the notion that it is "more expressive", and that there are jokes that really would never "come off" if they were delivered in the official language. As reported by Rickford (1985) in his study of how Guyanese feel about so-called standard and non-standard language varieties in their speech community, it is the language of friendship, identity and solidarity.

In other words, JC does have value, but it "has its place". Because it is a "lesser" language, for instance, it is considered inappropriate for use as a medium of personal prayer: the Lord must be respected, and so He must be spoken to in English.[13]

It is also, still today, the prevailing view, even among native speakers of JC themselves, that JC is nothing but "bad English" or "broken English", and parents and grandparents are known to chastise the younger generations when they speak it. We may call this a *culture of correction*,[14] indicating the perceived need and resulting insistence that children be able to *taak prapa* 'speak properly'.

Irvine (2005, 45–47) suggests that when language is being assessed in this way in spoken interaction, attention usually focusses on phonology and lexis, causing phonology rather than grammar to inform a listener's judgement of standardness. She cites Beckford-Wassink (1999, 66) as evidence that Jamaicans perceive accent and vocabulary to be the primary difference between JC and JE: only 18 per cent of Beckford-Wassink's fifty-one informants identified any aspect of morphosyntax as distinguishing the two languages, with 82 per cent mentioning either accent ("how they sound their words") or accent and vocabulary as determinants.

A category of phonological variables that appears to be salient for producing JE is identified by Irvine (2005, 307–8). Using a construction analogy, she terms these variables *load-bearing*. This means that the variants are indexical, seeming to function primarily to define the variety the speaker is using: without producing them in significant quantities, a speaker will not be considered in the Jamaican speech community to be speaking English. Nine variables characterizing speech as English were identified (ibid., 307); they are as follows:

- [h] word-initially in words like 'hand' (vs *h-dropping*[15] in JC *an*)
- the voiceless TH consonant as in 'thin' (vs [t] in JC *tin*)
- initial aspiration [k̲ʰa:] in words like 'calf' (vs palatalized [k̲ya:f] in JC)
- [ɔ] in words like 'pot' (vs [a] in JC *pat*)
- rhoticity following [ɔ] before [+ coronal] consonants such as [t] as in 'for̲t̲y' (vs [a:] in JC *faati*)
- [ɔr] in words such as 'poor' (vs [ʊɔ] in JC *puor*)
- [o] in words like 'goat' (vs the diphthong [uo] in JC *guot*)
- word final phonological cluster [nt] before a vowel, as in 'wan̲t̲' (vs a nasal vowel in JC *waahn*)
- word final morphophonemic cluster such as [kt] resulting from the past-tense inflection, as in 'looked' (vs uninflected root in JC *luk*)

What takes place, in effect, is that when switching from an informal to a formal situation, speakers do not switch from some L variety to a H variety, as in a typical diglossic language situation. Instead, they signal a shift by manipulating load-bearing phonological variables (ibid., 311).

Irvine's (2005) claim that pronunciation differences between the languages trigger language associations in the minds of speakers is important to this work. Recall that Craig (1980, 2) referred to pronunciation and lexical differences between a Creole language and its lexifier as superficial, and those in the morphosyntax as existing at a "deeper level". This is the motivation behind using the term superficial weaving to refer to the manipulation of options provided by JC and JE, phonologically with regard to the pronunciation of words, or lexically with regard to the words themselves. Superficial weaving is distinguished from structural weaving; the latter involves a mix of JC and JE features in syntactic constructions.[16]

Pollard (2001, 103) provides an interesting perspective on the perception by Creole speakers of what differentiates English from Creole. It is that wherever a JE form is identical to a JC one, it runs the risk of not being considered English by the Creole speaker. She gives an example of a grade 6 student questioning the teacher with 'I am to *wrote* everything from the board?' For a form to qualify as English, then, it would seem that it must be different from what one would "normally" say.

Forms considered closer to JE have become associated not only with social advancement and social status, but also with personality traits. Christie (2003, 5) speaks of the use of JC as being perceived in the society as an indication of poor moral standards and coarse behaviour as well as a lack of intelligence. Such perceptions affect interactions, even in the service industry where favourable treatment would be assumed. For example, Walters (2016) studied the differing treatment by public agency service representatives of JC versus JE-speaking callers. She found that when callers spoke JC they were twice as likely to be ridiculed and to be treated dismissively than when they spoke JE.

Yet, attitudes towards JC are not straightforwardly negative by any means. Kouwenberg (2011, 389) indicates that among first-year university students at Mona, JC speakers invariably score higher on qualities such as "honesty" and "friendliness" than do JE speakers. She speaks about the language of choice at the Mona campus being JC, not only for informal exchanges, but also for more academic discussions. This indicates that there is, perhaps, growing prestige associated with JC among the more educated who are proficient in JE and who are destined for more privileged positions in the society.

In addition, there is growing acceptance of the use of JC in the public arena in domains where, not so long ago, in colonial Jamaica, it would have been frowned upon, that is, domains such as radio talk shows and speeches in parliament.

Zellynne Jennings-Craig (pers. comm.) points out that this growing acceptance of JC and the increase in its use make it more difficult for children to learn English: the models are becoming fewer and fewer, reducing possible sources of input. This is underlined by Devonish and Walters (2015, 231), who indicate that it is with political independence in 1962 that the awakening of Jamaican political and popular cultural expression came. Along with this came a cementing of JC as the symbol of national identity in these domains, and an acceptance of its legitimacy as the main language of private and informal expression across all social groups.

Walters (2016, 236) takes such linguistic trends as support for the existence in Jamaica of what she terms *transitional diglossia*. By this she means "a change in the attitudes towards the functions which the H and L languages formerly performed and a desire to see the L language being used in public formal domains", that is, in the domains formerly reserved for the H language.

Even so, attitudes remain ambivalent: as Christie (2003, 2) points out, for example, it would likely be cause for surprise, if not outrage, if speeches in parliament were delivered entirely in JC. I note that such attitudes tend to be characteristic not only of Jamaicans, but also of the wider West Indian community, who, as Nero (2015, 346) indicates, "also hold deeply entrenched and ambivalent views towards Creole".

Whether the status of JC is favourably or ambivalently regarded, it is still commonly believed that, as a "bastardization" of English, it cannot be considered to be a language. It inevitably solicits a chuckle when mention is made of the rule systems governing JC, or when it is suggested that it is possible for there to be ungrammatical JC utterances. Instead, it is thought that JC does not *have* a grammar, and therefore could not be considered to be a language.

That JC is "bad" is not sanctioned by linguists, who do not place value judgements on language. That it is a language, has long been upheld by linguists. From as early as the 1960s, DeCamp (1968, 31) wrote, "A Creole is inferior to its corresponding standard language only in social status." In 1966, syntactician Beryl Bailey, in her seminal work *Jamaican Creole Syntax: A Transformational Approach*, created a grammatical account of JC by applying the then-groundbreaking work of Chomsky (1957) in the transformational analysis of grammar. She cited the following as one of the three goals of her work: "To explode once and for all the notion which persists among teachers of English in Jamaica, that the 'dialect' is *not* [her emphasis] a language, and further that it has no bearing on the problem of the teaching of English" (p. xiii).

I look now at some of the reasons that would cause linguists to conclude that JC and JE are different languages,[17] and that JC is, therefore, a language in its own right.

1.1.2 Are JC and JE Really Different Languages?

Christie (2003, 25) points out that as a form of communication in regular use for interaction by the community for at least three hundred years, and as a form of communication which uses a consistent set of sounds, words and sentence structures, JC is considered by linguists to be a language.

Devonish (2003, 172–74) answers the question in two parts. First, he establishes that linguistic differences between two languages are not the sole basis on which to make such a determination. He cites, on the one hand, dialects of Chinese which include varieties that may be as different linguistically from one another as English is from German, and on the other, languages such as Spanish and Portuguese which are very similar, but which are considered by their speakers to be different languages.

Having established this professional disclaimer, Devonish continues to argue that it is quite common for languages which are considered by their speakers to be distinct, to be linked by dialect continua. So, for example, (standard) Dutch and German lie at polar ends of such a continuum, with dialects in between, ranging from more Dutch to more German. In such language situations, there may be varying degrees of mutual intelligibility between the languages at either pole. Mutual intelligibility is of importance, since it is considered to be a basic test of languagehood: if speakers of two languages are not able to understand and communicate with each other, then the codes they speak may be said to be distinct languages rather than dialects of the same language.[18]

The second part of the answer is to establish whether the linguistic distance between languages considered to be distinct can be said to be similar to that between JE and JC. To address this, Devonish (2003, 174) outlines distance measurements between Creoles and their lexifiers:

1. for the lexicon or vocabulary, about the distance between the lexicon of Spanish and Portuguese;
2. for phonology or pronunciation patterns, at least the same distance as that between the phonology of French and Spanish;
3. for morphology or word construction patterns, about the same distance as between the morphology of English and German; and
4. for syntax or grammatical structure, depending on the Creole in question, ranging from about the distance between the syntax of French and Spanish to the distance between the syntax of English and German.

It is on the basis of these estimates of linguistic distance that Devonish offers his personal opinion that Caribbean English-lexicon Creoles are languages other than English. This is supported by social trends which appear to be taking place in these societies. In Jamaica, for example, we have seen that the functions of JC are gaining ground and "invading" the traditional domains of English.

That JC is a language in its own right, a language with sounds, lexical items, word formations and grammatical structures distinct from JE is the position adopted in this work.

The fact is that, nonetheless, there are similarities between the two languages. The vocabulary of JC is largely derived from English, and JC words can readily be seen to be related to their JE counterparts – JC *bwai* JE 'boy'; JC *gyaadn* JE 'garden', for instance. Noting the many similarities in vocabulary, speakers believe that the languages are similar in other respects as well, resulting in a lack of awareness of the differences between them and, often, in surprise that it is not understood by non-JE speakers.

Yet another consequence of the superficial similarity between JC and JE is that speakers often believe that they are using JE when they are not. Vintenko (2016, 10, 51) reports, for instance, that in a school setting outside a primary school classroom, when asking a nine-year-old child to repeat what she had said in English because it had not been understood, the child replied *bot mi a spiik Ingglish* 'but I am speaking English'. Mair and Lacoste (2012, 89) ascribe this to the general population in the following way: "most speakers on the island do not draw a rigid line of division between S[tandard]JE and JC. Even speakers who show strong and obvious influences from JC still consider themselves as speakers of English, if of a more or less highly stigmatised variety."

Perceptions of what it means to speak English become an important consideration, then. Clues to perceptions may be discerned through hypercorrected forms. Hypercorrection takes place when there is an awareness of a difference between the native and the non-native language, causing the non-native form to be over-applied, that is, used in contexts where it is not used in that language. An example is the (hypercorrected) pronunciation of JC *bait* 'bite' as /bɔit/. This can be explained in the following way: the JE diphthong /ɔi/ as in 'boy' does not form part of the inventory of sounds in JC. The JC segment which corresponds to the JE sound is /ai/ as in *bwai*. The hypercorrected version /bɔit/ arises from a recognition that in JC /ai/ is pronounced where JE would pronounce /ɔi/, alongside an over-application of that knowledge.

Often, what arises is that English is associated with the so-called high society, as we have seen, but also with foreignness. As a result, when an attempt is made to speak English, there may be a perceived need to *sound* either American or British, often involving hypercorrection.

The reality is that although English is referred to as the official language of the country, what is actually spoken is a Jamaican variety of English, much in the same way that other English-speaking Caribbean people, Americans and the British themselves speak their own Englishes. American and British Englishes are foreign to Jamaica; we have our own Jamaican English. It is internationally recognized as a distinct variety: for example, it is one of the fourteen currently available Englishes of the world forming part of the International Corpus of English (ICE), with a body of one million spoken and written words.[19] Strictly speaking, then, JE is a variety of English.

JE is commonly referred to as Standard Jamaican English by linguists and others. The label "Standard" is, in fact, a misrepresentation, since no formal determination of what pronunciations, lexical items and grammatical structures would actually constitute a Standard in Jamaica has been made. Instead, the informal presumption seems to be that at any linguistic level, the form which would be chosen would be that which is closest to some internationally accepted norm.

The situation may not be as simple as this. Shields (1989) was perhaps the first to classify speakers of English in Jamaica, in terms of whether they acquired the language natively, that is, as a first language (her Group 1 speakers), or whether they learned it as a second language in school, say (Group 2 speakers). A syntactic example is the preposition 'from' and what may follow it. For Group 1 speakers, 'From a child I learned the skill of tatting' can only mean "A child taught me", that is, "with child as a source". In contrast, for Group 2 speakers 'From a child' may also signal a beginning time, expressed in the Group 1 model as 'from childhood', using an abstract noun (ibid., 48–49). I note that Group 2, but not Group 1, speakers also allow a clause to follow the preposition, as in 'from I was a child'. The question becomes, *Which forms would we consider to be Standard?* Research would need to be conducted to determine the answer to such a question.

As a result, I avoid the designation Standard Jamaican English, and refer instead to the variety, abstract and idealized though that may be, as JE, Jamaican English.

Discussions of how JC and JE differ syntactically will be a focus of this work. In the chapters on the nominal and verbal domains, before analysing the children's acquisition of their native language JC, and how JE features are incorporated into their speech, details of the differences between the two languages will be presented. We shall see throughout this study that similarities that exist in words exist only at the surface, and that the ways these words are used to form structures are often fundamentally different. To characterize the mixing of structures from the two languages, I use the term structural weaving. An example is the question *Wat yuu aar duin?* 'What are you doing?' This structural weave consists of the JE progressive construction *are duin* within a JC interrogative structure, that is, no inversion of the subject 'you' and auxiliary 'are'.

We shall see also that the weaving of JC and JE features is not random, but that patterns exist, allowing us to predict the kinds of mixing likely to occur, and those tending to occur less frequently.

What now follows is a discussion of the approach taken in this work to the continuum, with JC and JE at the poles, and the "space" between them where features are woven.

1.1.3 The Creole Continuum

The existence of a "continuous spectrum of speech varieties" (DeCamp 1971b, 350) in language situations in Creole-speaking communities inspired the term Creole continuum.[20] Patrick (2002) indicates that the term was developed specifically by DeCamp (1961, 1971a, 1971b) to account for Jamaica. The continuum is a theoretical construct which "locates all variation, including socially conditioned variation on a unidimensional scale that extends from the most English-like to the most Creole-like" (Kouwenberg and Singler 2011, 293). The notion is foundational to this work, since the presumption is that the input which children hear as they acquire language is characterized by this variation.

In Continuum Theory, the language considered to be the official language is termed the *acrolect*. The language at the other end, comprising the most Creole forms of the Creole, is known as the *basilect*. These are the forms which are considered to be "very" Creole, often referred to as broad Creole, and here, as JC. Given their history, these are also the forms which carry more negative social significance than others. As examples, in the sound system the use of the palatalized velars (as in *kyaad* 'card') would be considered to be basilectal, and in the syntax, so would the formation of the possessive using *fi* as in *fi di bwai* 'the boy's' (lit. possessive preposition + the boy).

It has traditionally been assumed that communities in rural areas would be more likely to have speakers of more basilectal forms.[21] This is thought to be the case since such areas are isolated in both geographic and socio-economic terms. As a result, they exhibit networks that are generally confined to the community in question, and therefore remain relatively immune to more mainstream developments,[22] including, it is assumed, linguistic behaviour.

From the early 1970s, however, DeCamp identified Jamaica as what he called a *post-creole* community, undergoing decreolization. The status of post-creole is possible only when the dominant official language is the same as the Creole vocabulary base, and when the social system provides for sufficient social mobility and sufficient corrective pressures from above in order for the standard language to exert real influence on Creole speakers (1971a, 29). Factors such as radio, television, internal migration and education contribute to the pressures. DeCamp notes that these pressures do not operate uniformly, but act on individual speakers pulling them in differing degrees towards the standard end of the continuum (ibid.).

DeCamp was speaking about a Jamaica of over forty years ago. It is assumed that the post-creole status of which he spoke would have progressed over the years, with boundaries between the two language systems becoming more blurred, as speakers continue to acquire so-called standard forms to varying degrees.

As a result, speakers do not fit so neatly into labels or categories. As Nero (2014, 225) puts it, "[i]n everyday language use in Jamaica, 'pure' forms of JC or S[tandard]JE are rare. Rather, there is a seamless mixing of both forms." Thus, instead of consistently using only forms which are considered to be either basilectal or acrolectal, forms reflecting more or less "Creole-ness" are regularly used as well. People using such "midway" forms have been termed mesolectal speakers. Winford (1997, 236) indicates that for Jamaica, the *mesolect* is used to refer to an area of interaction between a relatively basilectal Creole and the local standard, and appears to have no distinct status as a system. The term "area of interaction" was perhaps originated by Craig (1971, 372), who refers to it as such because "its existence has been, and continues to be, dependent on the cross influences from the two extremes".

An example of mesolectal speech would be the use of neither the basilectal JC past-tense marker (*b*)*ehn* nor of the JE past-tense inflected verb form ('walk<u>ed</u>'), but of a form such as 'did' as in 'He <u>did</u> walk.' In such a sentence, 'did' has been borrowed from JE, but functions in much the same way as the JC past marker *behn*, and not as an emphatic form as it would in JE. Similarly, mesolectal speakers might use a sequence such as *Jan singin*. Here, the form of the verb 'singin' corresponds to that following the auxiliary 'be' in the expression of the progressive aspect in JE ('John is <u>singing</u>'). Differences include, however, the use of the final alveolar nasal /n/,[23] where JE uses its velar counterpart /ŋ/, as well as the absence of the auxiliary, that is, neither the JC pre-verbal progressive marker *a* (*Jan <u>a</u> sing* 'John is singing') nor the JE 'is'.

In this work, the mesolect will be viewed from a feature-based minimalist perspective. I will speak in terms of features which are associated with JC, and would be viewed as being basilectal using continuum terminology, as well as features which are associated with JE, viewed as being acrolectal. There is no intention in so doing, to imagine that any one speaker would have in her linguistic repertoire only those features which we might ascribe as being JC or as JE, necessarily. Following early accounts such as DeCamp (1971b), neither is there a possibility of deciding the point on the continuum at which any speaker might be placed. Instead, in theory, a speaker will have at her disposal all the features in the input.

Variation, then, is characteristic of speech in Jamaica, and not reserved only for speakers who may be identified as mesolectal. Instead, it is a part of the input to which children are exposed, even in the most rural communities. Even so, despite extreme variation in the input, it is possible to ascribe features as "belonging to" JC or JE. What will concern us are the ways in which these JC (basilectal) and JE (acrolectal) features are merged and the detection of patterns in which they combine, or are woven, in the speech of the speaker.

It is against this background that the CLAR research was conducted. The project is presented in the next section.

1.2 Methodology

The CLAR "What do they speak" project had as its primary aim, the determination of the language structures used by Jamaican three-year-olds from communities across the island in the school environment.

The interest was in the language spoken by children as they enter the public school system, and as a result, only children in their first year of basic school were chosen. Elicitation sessions took place in such schools in western, central and eastern parishes. The school was chosen as a setting, and sessions were conducted during the school day, so as to associate them in the children's minds with their education, and in an effort, therefore, to capture the language spoken at school.

The assumption of the Ministry of Education is that the communities feeding such schools are mainly JC-speaking, and that the children are monolingual speakers of JC. The 2001 *Language Education Policy*, for instance, states explicitly that JC is the language most widely used in Jamaica (p. 23). In addition, the *Literacy 1-2-3 Manual* (p. 4) accompanying the language education curriculum for grades 1 through 3 contrasts JC as the language used in the home and on the street, with JE as the language of school and written texts, thereby indicating not only the same assumption concerning students' native language, but articulating also that they are in the process of acquiring JE as a second language in schools. The implication is that children enter the school system speaking only JC.

The language situation as outlined in the preceding sections would suggest far more complexity than this, however. Indeed, Devonish and Carpenter (2007, 26) refer to "another language of the school", the language variety used among the children themselves, described as being largely similar to the *home language*, but subject to the levelling process of peer group pressure at school. It is the question which arises – "What is it that our children really speak?" – that the project seeks to answer.

In what follows, details are provided of the participants (section 1.2.1), of how the interviews were structured (section 1.2.2), and of the transcription and coding conventions (section 1.2.3).

1.2.1 The Participants

The study aimed to arrive at a linguistic profile of three-year-olds. A virtual year of data was collected over a six-month period. This was achieved modelling Meade (2001) in the following way: the age of half of the children at the start of data collection was $3;0^{24} \pm 2$ months; and the other half, $3;6 \pm 2$ months. In effect, the percentages of children belonging to these groups were 45.3 and 54.7 respectively. The resulting age range of all children interviewed was 2;9 to 4;2.

There were a total of eighty children interviewed in a maximum of six sessions each. Of these, twenty-eight (or 35 per cent) attended all six sessions, fifty-three (or 66 per cent) attended at least four, and sixteen (or 20 per cent) attended only one session. The sixteen children who were interviewed only once

Table 1.1. Children interviewed by region, area, community type and sex

Region	Area	School Code	Community Type	# girls	# boys
West	St Elizabeth	SER	Rural	4	5
	St James	MOB	City	3	4
Central	Clarendon	CLA	Town	6	7
	St Ann	AN1	Rural	1	1
		AN2	Rural	2	2
East	St Andrew	ADR	Rural	2	2
		ADT	Town	1	4
	Kingston	KN1	City	2	2
		KN2	City	2	3
	St Mary	SMR	Rural	3	3
		SMT	Town	5	4
	St Thomas	STR	Rural	2	3
		STT	Town	4	3
			Total:	37	43

Table 1.2. Children interviewed by community type and sex

Community Type	# Girls	# Boys	Total
Rural	14	16	30
City	7	9	16
Town	16	18	34
Total:	37	43	80

included those whose starting age was too high; others had subsequently moved away from the district. Data from these interviews are included nonetheless in analyses. The total number of interviews was 214, with 51,650 utterances by the children. It is on these utterances that the analyses in this work are based.

Consideration of possible gender effects on the speech of children was not an aim of the study; however, an attempt was made to have equal representations of boys and girls from each school.

Eight areas across the island were chosen as follows: two from western, two from central and four from eastern Jamaica. This was intended to replicate in a general way, the distribution of the population across major divisions.

The distribution of participants by region, community type and sex is presented in table 1.1, and by community type and sex in table 1.2.

Care was taken to have representation from schools in rural areas, in the two major cities, Kingston and Montego Bay, and in towns, with no attempt to include a range of social classes, despite the suggestion in previous sections that social class is an important determinant of language use. I note, however, that the basic school system was created to cater mainly to the lower socioeconomic groups (Miller 2015). In 2012, 74.2 per cent of children aged three to five years attending early childhood education institutions in the country were enrolled in basic schools (SABER Country Report 2013, 15, table 12).

1.2.2 The Interviews

Interviews were conducted between September 2009 and April 2010, with the permission of school principals and parents. Each interview lasted for half an hour. Children were interviewed once a month over a six-month period by JC native-speaking graduate students at the University of the West Indies, Mona, who had received at least a B+ grade in our undergraduate language acquisition course.

There were two teams of investigators, each comprising two members and responsible for interviews at its own set of schools, as shown in table 1.3.

Each set of monthly interviews was named a *visit*; there were six visits. In areas where only one school was visited, a larger number of children was interviewed than in other schools.

All interviews were video-recorded using a Sony camcorder with a hard drive, and audio-recorded backups were done using a Sony handheld recorder. Team members alternated roles as investigator or camera operator in the course of the day.

The decision to video-record was based primarily on the importance of observing contextual clues for the understanding of interactions with children. As Eisenbeiβ (2010, 16) indicates, video-recordings provide information regarding object, deictic and temporal references, and links among speech, gestures and actions.

In approximately half of the sessions (108/214), only one child was interviewed. For the remainder, interviews were of two children. The rationale for choosing to interview two children at a time was to allow for the possibility of analyses of children as they interacted with each other. In addition, there were non-linguistic reasons such as attitudes, fair-play and dominance. In some cases, particular children who appeared to be shy were paired to encourage conversation.

The store of materials used for elicitation included laminated picture flash cards, storybooks, toys, colouring books with crayons, and scrapbooks with markers. To allow for role-playing, there was a range of cooking utensils, including a wooden stove, pots and food items, as well as telephones. As expected, individual children quickly revealed their own preferences, and requested their preferred toys in subsequent sessions.

The flash cards centred around the elicitation of tense and aspect, adjectival and prepositional predication, argument structure and derivational morphology. Books were used for the naming of animals, foods and fruit, and for general picture description or storytelling. New word formation was elicited

Table 1.3. Areas visited each month for six months

Week	Team 1	Team 2
1	St Mary – 2 schools	St Ann – 2 schools
2	Kingston – 2 schools	St Thomas – 2 schools
3	Clarendon – 1 school	St James – Montego Bay 1 school
4	St Andrew – 2 schools	St Elizabeth – 1 school

using objects such as a nut cracker and a tea-infuser with a ball inside, chosen on the presumption that the children would not be familiar with them. Guided conversation was used throughout the interview to elicit other structures such as possession, plural formation, including the use of numerals, pronominal reference and negation, as well as tense and aspect (*Wa yu jos du?* 'What did you just do?' *A wa yu a du?* 'What are you doing?').

The aim was for the children to interact naturally, and data were elicited primarily via conversation during play. Sessions were loosely structured as follows:

- An initial ten-minute segment intended to put the child at ease and to set the scene for the session. This typically included a discussion of events and activities relating to the child's own home-life and experiences. In cases where the child was less talkative, discussion was encouraged through books or pictures.
- Ten minutes using laminated flash cards or objects chosen especially for the elicitation of specific structures. Discussion around these materials was encouraged.
- Ten minutes involved in various activities such as free play, role-playing or colouring to encourage discussion and interaction.

After the first interviews, when the children had become more familiar with the format and the investigators, time devoted to free play and role-playing activities was extended on the children's urging, allowing for conversation through play to be captured.

Interviews were conducted primarily in JC.[25] The intended effect which this would have on the speech of the children relates to what is known as the language mode. In this, I draw on work which has been done in the field of bilingualism. Grosjean (1989, 2008 and elsewhere) defines this as the state of activation of a bilingual's languages and language processing mechanisms at any given point in time. *Activation* is a neural modelling term for calling upon a language when it is determined by the speaker, normally quite unconsciously, that it is needed, given numerous psychosocial and linguistic factors (Grosjean 2008, 38). Importantly, activation levels of the languages available to bilinguals may differ, but a language is never totally deactivated, even in monolingual speech mode. In bilingual mode, the bilingual speaker chooses a base or main language. This is defined by Grosjean in psycholinguistic terms as the more activated language, taken to be the language of the conversation, and considered to be fully active, since it is the language which governs language processing (2001, 4). The speaker activates the other language and calls on it from time to time by way of code-switches and borrowings.

We might expect, then, that since the children were interviewed primarily in JC, that would be their base language of choice, and they would therefore make less use of JE. Given the status of the languages in the society, and attitudes such as those discussed previously, however, it is reasonable to assume that there would have been conflicting sociolinguistic considerations. In particular, it was expected that the children would believe that the language appropriate for inter-actions with strangers introduced to them by their teachers would have been JE, and that they would have made efforts to use JE, most particularly in Visit 1 when they had just met. We see in chapters 3, 4 and 5 that mixing prevailed throughout, although as discussed in section 6.2, the *dominant* language used by the children was indeed JC.

In Visit 6, the final visit, JC was the language of the investigators to start with, as had been the practice in the first five visits and, therefore, as the chil-dren would have expected. After the first fifteen minutes, however, investigators seamlessly began speaking JE, so as to determine what influence, if any, there might have been on the children's speech. Conducting interviews in a language other than the preferred language of interviewees is expected to lead to a situa-tion where both languages are highly activated for all those involved in the con-versation (Gawlitzek-Maiwald and Tracy 1996, 911). The dominant language of the children in those sessions tended, nonetheless, to be JC.

1.2.3 Transcription and Coding

Interviews were transcribed from the videos for manipulation in CHILDES, a child language data exchange system which provides online tools for transcrip-tion and data analysis (MacWhinney 2000a, 2000b).[26] More than four of the six visits, or approximately 70 per cent of interviews, were transcribed during the academic year by teams of six undergraduate linguistics students meeting as a group in the linguistics computer lab at the University of the West Indies, Mona. Video files were stored on the university's intranet, with password pro-tection. The sessions were supervised by a graduate student research assistant who served also as one of the investigators. The remainder of the interviews were transcribed by individual students during the summer, and checked by the supervisor or the author, or both.

All the variables discussed previously (age, sex and provenance) appeared in an identification header line assigned by CHILDES in the order: languages|project name|name of participant|age| sex||area|role of participant||, as shown in (1) below. This allowed for queries on any of these variables.

(1)   @ID: jam, eng|clar0910|BIA|3;1.|female||town|Child||

Transcriptions were orthographic, using the Cassidy-JLU (Jamaica Language Unit) writing system[27] for all utterances, including those in JE. Since the children used vowels existing in JE but not in JC,[28] the inclusion of additional representations was required (see table 1.4).

Another difference between the Cassidy-JLU orthography and the representation of data here is the use of 'z' to represent plurality regardless of actual pronunciation: *kyatz* 'cats' and *dogz* 'dogs' versus Cassidy-JLU transcriptions *kyats* but *dogz*.

All transcriptions were checked for CHILDES-system codes and were verified by at least two different JC speakers against the videos as being true representations of actual speech. Checks included accuracy in orthography.

Formats of videos were changed from .mpg to .mp4 to accommodate the linking of all transcriptions to videos, allowing for full interaction between the two. This greatly facilitated the checking process.

All transcriptions were tagged using the MOR and POST facilities provided by CHILDES. Lexicon files were created (4,282 entries in thirty-nine files)[29] for this purpose, following, for the most part, word categories in use by CHILDES.[30] The report *mor +xl *.cha* provided by CHILDES was run to ensure that all words in transcribed files were included in the lexicon.

Coding for tagging was adapted to suit the purposes of the analysis. For example, all entries in the lexicon files, except communicators such as *ye* 'yes',

Table 1.4. Orthographic representations of JE vowels

Segment	English Example	Orthography
/e:/	play	ee
/o:/	goat	oo
/ɔ:/	paw	aw

Table 1.5. Language codes for tagging

Code	Meaning	Explanation	Example
&JC	Jamaican Creole	Regularly used by JC speakers; considered to be JC by native speakers.	*bwai* 'boy'
&JConly	Jamaican Creole only	These words are not used in JE. The JE counterpart has a very different form.	*nyam* 'eat'
&JES	Jamaican English segment	Once a JE segment not associated with the JC inventory of sounds appears in a word, it is considered to be a JES form. Some JES words may in fact be the JE form, but JES variants do not necessarily have all JE segments; they may also mix JE and JC segments.	The JES variants *boi* (the JE form) and *bwoi* (a mixed form) are used regularly by JC speakers alongside the JC form *bwai*. Other words may have multiple variants, mixing JE and JC segments, e.g., JC *aas* 'horse', with JES variants *haas, aars, ars, aws, hars, ors, hors*. Of these, only *hors* is a JE form.
&JE&LO	JE loan	A word borrowed from JE, not forming part of regular use in JC.	*wind* (JC *briiz*)
&JE&CLO	Creolized JE loan	A JE loan incorporating a JC vowel or consonant segment, but not forming part of regular use in JC.	*win* (JC *briiz*; incorporated into JC phonology using word-final cluster reduction)
&SH	Shared form (cognate) – referred to as SHared	A form shared by both JE and JC in form as well as meaning.	*wiik* 'week'
&SH&SE	SHared with semantic differences	A shared form which has taken on a different meaning in JC.	*tii* 'tea'. Refers in JC to various drinks; often modified to signal which drink, e.g., *mailo tii* 'Milo'.

Notes: See section 3.1, and especially table 3.1 for a listing of JC and JE segments. Details of the superficial weave in JC and JES variants of 'horse' are discussed in section 3.1.1.

and fillers such as *aahm* were coded for language, using the three major categories JC, JE and SH. Language codes are presented in table 1.5.

With regard to SHared words, it is acknowledged, as Kroll et al. (2012, 234) note, that pronunciations are almost never precisely the same in any two languages. To determine classification as a SHared form, I follow Gooskens and van Bezooijen (2006, 554): there are to be no sounds which would need to be inserted, deleted or substituted in order to transform them into the corresponding words in the other language.

All words were assigned a language code in the lexicon initially by the author.[31] Three native speaker consultants verified these assignments. The judgements of the first consultant, made by line item for all nouns, verbs, adjectives and adverbs, were used as the working document. The second consultant also judged language codes in the lexicon files by line item, and the third was used as arbiter for those words where there was disagreement between the first two. There was overall agreement of 96 per cent, indicating near uncontroversial decisions with regard to language-membership. This included judgements on which forms "belonged" to JC, on which would be considered to be variants closer to JE, though used regularly, and those which would be considered loans, not in regular use in JC. These language codes formed the basis of the analyses of the mixing of JC and JE. Other codes used for tagging are summarized in appendix 3.

The entry for *brook* 'broke' in the lexicon serves as an example of how tagging works. It is coded in the v.cut lexicon file as a verb ([scat v]), a JE Loan (&JE&LO),[32] past (&PAST), irregular (&IRR), with the translation enclosed within "=" signs.

(2)   brook {[scat v]} "brook&JE&LO&PAST&IRR" =broke=

When run, the CHILDES *mor* command uses the lexicon files as a look-up, resulting in the creation of a new data file with the addition for each utterance of a tagged line labelled %mor:, a morphological tier. An example of the information drawn from the lexicon is shown in (3) below.

(3)   *ANT: *mi brook di plien.*
       %mor: pro|mi&JC&1S&PERS=I_me v|brook&JE&LO&PAST&IRR=broke
       det|di&JC&DEF=the n|plien&JC&BA=plane.   [V5-CLA:l 894-3;3.27]

Automated tagging allows for one-time changes in the lexicon to be reflected in all data files, and facilitates more fine-grained analyses should the desirability of further manipulation become apparent.

The coding conventions used for the CLAR data, as briefly outlined in this chapter, allowed for extremely flexible interrogation of the data by any code, or combination of codes. In addition, CHILDES output was exported to Microsoft Excel for further manipulation, as needed.

1.3 Limitations of the Study

There were limitations in data collection and in the system developed for transcription which are worthy of mention and discussion. The idea behind conducting the data collection sessions at the schools was primarily that there was an interest in seeing how the children spoke not in a class with the teacher, but in a school setting nonetheless. As a result, children were taken out of their classrooms and interviewed elsewhere on the compound. The schools accommodated us as best they could: in one school, we were given the sick bay, and in another, a section of the assembly hall, for instance. In some of the schools, however, there was no one area within the building where ambient noise was at an acceptable level. It was decided that outdoors in the playing field would not be suitable in those schools, since it would be more difficult to keep the children from wanting to run freely. Though the study was a syntactic one, and not dependent on laboratory-quality audio, background noise levels did interfere at times with unambiguous interpretations of the children's speech. Such speech was transcribed as 'xxx', as recommended by CHILDES. The effects of this could have been minimized, perhaps, with the use of lapel microphones.

That interviews took place in a school setting had the consequence, of course, that speech was only gathered in that one setting. That was the aim of the research. Perhaps future research can supplement the findings of this study, by gathering data in other settings.

Interviews were transcribed initially by a team of six final-year undergraduate linguistics students who were native speakers of JC. Transcription sessions were held in the linguistics computer lab at the University of the West Indies, Mona, and led by a graduate student supervisor who was also one of the investigators. They met for two three-hour sessions a week. It was determined that final-year students would have the most experience with the writing system, and would bring more linguistic maturity and expertise to the task. The system worked very well for the first semester and a half, after which the students felt they needed to devote the time to preparing for final examinations. Only two were able to continue during the summer, since others had secured jobs. Thus, the plan to have transcriptions completed by the end of the academic year did not materialize, and after the first year, new transcribers had to be chosen and trained. This also meant that these transcriptions were not done immediately or even shortly after the interviews; that they were done from video recordings reduced possible negative consequences of this delay.

The multifunctionality of JC words made the margins of error very high in assignments of word categories by the automatic tagging provided by CHILDES. To resolve this, the decision was made to distinguish, at the level of the transcription, between words having a single form but multiple functions. An example is *a*, where in JC this same form is used for the focus marker (coded as *afc*), the progressive marker (*ag*), the habitual marker (*ab*), the iterative marker (*ai*), the preposition (*app* translated into JE as 'of', 'at', 'in', 'on', or 'to'), the JE indefinite article (*ad*), a variant of the first-person singular subject pronoun (*ap*), the copula (*ac*) and the lexical verb (*av*) (see section 3.2 for a discussion of multifunctionality in Creoles). This could be seen to compromise, at least to some extent, the readability of the transcribed files.

An alternative might have been to manually tag the corpus, as was done by De Lisser (2015, 43). However, as explained in section 1.2.3, tagging involves creating a %mor: line for each utterance. Given this, and taking into consideration the size of the corpus (51,650 utterances by the children alone),[33] it was determined that automatic assignment of codes entered (once) and stored in the lexicon master files would be preferable to manually typing such a line for every utterance (see [3] above for an example of a %mor: line).

Yet another alternative, adopted by Yip and Matthews (2007, 71) for their Cantonese data, would have been to run the CHILDES automated tagging, and then to manually disambiguate, checking for incorrectly assigned word classes in all %mor: lines. A disadvantage of this solution was thought to be that if there were need to rerun the automated tagging,[34] the corrections previously made would be overwritten, and would therefore need to be re-done.[35]

The transcription process itself could have been helped significantly if the facility provided by the CHILDES "F5 insertion mode" had been used. This allows for the insertion of links to the video files at the point of transcription, and the ability to replay a segment of text quickly and accurately for checking while transcribing. Links were created, but only after the transcriptions had already been completed. At that point, linking of videos with transcriptions is a tedious, time-consuming process of replaying videos and linking line by line. It did however, provide an opportunity to conduct yet another verification of data files against recordings, and was considered well worth the effort, given the facility to instantly locate the exact position on a video, of any line of text. This is achieved simply by double-clicking on the relevant line either in the transcription file or in a generated report.

1.4 Aims of the Research and the Structure of the Book

As has already been stated, the primary aim of the research was to provide a linguistic profile of aspects of the grammar used by children across the island in their first year of entry into the public school system, the basic school. It was guided by the following research questions:

1. How can the language structures used in certain syntactic constructions by three-year-olds from JC-speaking communities across Jamaica be described?
2. How do the two linguistic systems JC and JE interact in the speech of these children in these constructions?
3. How can the mixing of JC and JE in the children's speech be accounted for theoretically?
4. How can this be instructive to the teacher of language and literacy in Jamaica and in the diaspora?

Select language structures were targeted, but conversation through play allowed for the collection of rich data. Not all of the language structures targeted are reported in this work. The lexicon is the focus of chapter 3. It includes a look at the inventory of sounds making up words, an overview of type–token counts,[36] the categorial composition of the children's vocabulary, adjectival modification and word-formation strategies. Aspects of the nominal domain are addressed in chapter 4, specifically the count–mass distinction, the expression of plurality, (in)definiteness and possession. Chapter 5 investigates aspects of the verbal domain, specifically tense and aspect, and their interaction.

For each linguistic phenomenon investigated, the linguistic differences between the two language systems are outlined, and the mixing is addressed in terms of the presence of features which may be said to belong to JC and to JE, allowing for research question 2 to be addressed.

Because the basis of analyses is just over one hundred hours (107) of data collected, and because interviews have been transcribed and tagged using the (computerized) CHILDES data manipulation system, analyses enjoy the benefits of corpus linguistics. As will become apparent, frequency of occurrence and the range and frequency of possible combinations of JE and JC forms play an important role in the interpretation of the data. This allows for trends to be detected, and for patterns which may not be immediately obvious to be easily confirmed by looking at the speech of children of both genders, of different age groups, in different major regions (western, central, eastern), in different parishes, and in communities of different rural/urban status.

The framework used for addressing research question 3 is a feature-based minimalist approach, which is outlined briefly in section 2.5. Discussions on the mixing of the two languages is in terms of features, and an analysis of the interaction of *interpretable* and *uninterpretable* features is applied to findings in section 6.3.2.

The idea behind the fourth and final research question is to make the linguistic insights gained available to language and literacy teachers. The value of the insights is addressed in some detail in chapter 6, where, given the nature of the linguistic profile of the children emerging in chapters 3, 4 and 5, it is argued that there is a compelling case for the promotion of language awareness as a tool for increasing the proficiency in JE of children from Creole-speaking communities. The intention is to provide the linguistic base on which to make pedagogic decisions.

The work presumes a background understanding of how language works, such as that gained in introductory tertiary-level linguistics courses. It is grounded in linguistic theory, but does not require advanced linguistic knowledge. The most theoretical discussion appears in section 2.5 by way of an introduction to aspects of how features regulate syntax. The reader already familiar with these linguistic concepts may find it useful, nonetheless, for the application of the concepts to JC. This discussion in 2.5 leads the way to an understanding of the analysis of language choice in sections of chapters 4 and 5 and in section 6.3.2. Outside of these sections, terminology is explained as it is presented or, where it is deemed that lengthier explanations might be useful, supplemental material is provided in appendices.

2 | Theoretical Bases of the Study

> "If we are in the right environment, we will grow language the way we grow arms and legs. We can't do anything about it."
>
> —Noam Chomsky (1994)

In this chapter, I discuss aspects of the acquisition of language, and of minimalism, the approach used for the analysis of the way features of JC and JE as idealized varieties[1] combine in the speech of the children.

Crucially, I speak about "acquiring" a language. Implicit in this approach is an acknowledgement of a difference between *acquisition*, a natural process, and *learning*, which implies the involvement of instruction of one form or the other. Krashen (1981, 1982, among other publications) hypothesized that the basis of the distinction is that there are two types of knowledge. Learning is a conscious process, producing knowledge that is conscious and can only be used consciously. Learning typically takes place in an instructional setting, and applies to the learning of a second language. In contrast, acquisition is a subconscious process resulting in acquired competence, or implicit knowledge. This requires meaningful interaction in the target language and takes place in natural or informal environments. It is similar if not identical to the way children develop ability in their first language (Krashen 1982, 10).

This is not to say, however, that informal environments alone may provide the necessary input for acquisition, nor that the classroom is expected to only increase learned competence. Instead, the classroom can accomplish both learning and acquisition simultaneously: to the extent that the target language is used realistically, acquisition will occur (Krashen 1981, 47).[2]

The discussion of the value of consciously learned knowledge is developed in section 6.3.4 and its application to the literacy and language education classroom in 6.4.

Section 2.1 looks at the enormity of the task of first language acquisition, a task accomplished by the child in only a few years. It does so by considering what must be acquired, and continues to outline how the Nativist Theory is able to explain this feat. The acquisition of a second language is discussed in section 2.2, where it is determined that the acquisition of JE by native speakers of JC must be viewed as what has been termed *successive bilingualism*. Section 2.3 explores the role of input, relevant to both first and second language acquisition. Section 2.4 considers the linguistic and non-linguistic factors influencing the mixing of languages in speech, a natural phenomenon of bilingual speech. Finally, minimalism is presented in section 2.5, with a discussion in section 2.5.1 of how this might be applied to the analysis of Creole languages.

2.1 The Acquisition of a First Language

The task which the child faces in the acquisition of a first language (L1A) is indeed a formidable one. The miracle of what she accomplishes may easily be overlooked, since language is so much a part of our everyday lives. She will need to acquire the inventory of sounds which are relevant for the particular language, as well as the system of rules governing the combination of these sounds. The child must also acquire morphemes which regulate grammatical relations such as subject-verb agreement as well as those involved in new word formation. Lexical items, or words, are the basic units which are manipulated by the syntax. Children must learn which parts of the strings of sounds they hear are words, and having determined what they are, know how they may be combined into phrases in order to form sentences in the language. They must come to know also, the various types of sentences, such as statements and questions, how those are related, and the principles which govern their use. Children must acquire knowledge of the meanings of words and phrases and how these meanings are related to one another. Children achieve all this through exposure to speech, including speech directed at them, as well as opportunities to observe and, as they begin to speak themselves, to engage in communication through speech.

It would be virtually impossible to show how children could learn all this unless it is assumed that they have a considerable amount of innate cognitive machinery in place before they start. Noam Chomsky formalized the notion of innateness, by referring to what he calls a language acquisition device (LAD).[3] The LAD is an inborn, biologically endowed capability which all normally developing humans have, giving them a predisposition to learn a language and ensuring that, if they are in a normal linguistic environment, they will be 100 per cent successful in learning to speak their first language.

In addition to this tacit knowledge of language structure, children must know the ways we use language to communicate appropriately, such as using language to affect others or simply to relay information (Owens 2001, 26), as well as non-verbal means of communication. This has been called *communicative competence*, conceived originally by Hymes (1972)[4] and defined as the competence of language use appropriate not only to participants of the interaction, but also to its social context and situation, including knowledge of "when to speak, when not . . . what to talk about, with whom, when, where, in what manner" (p. 277). Such is the task of children as they acquire their first language.

Heredity must be involved in language acquisition, since house pets do not learn language, but children do. In fact, this ability seems characteristic only of humans. As Pinker (1995, 136) puts it, no other animal "appears to have the combinatorial rule system of human language, in which symbols are permuted into an unlimited set of combinations, each with a determinate meaning". Since this cognitive machinery is uniquely human, we can speak about the human uniqueness of language.

The environment must also be involved in language learning, since a child growing up in Japan hearing Japanese around her will speak Japanese, for instance, but a child with a variety of Caribbean English as input will acquire that Caribbean English. Importantly, it is input in the form of speech which triggers the inborn LAD referred to above. Exposure to input is also crucial, of course, for the acquisition of a second language. The role of input in acquisition and its relevance to this study are explored in section 2.3.

With regard to how it is possible for all this to be achieved, the logical or nativist approach is adopted in this work. This is the theory mentioned above, as being associated with Chomsky. The belief, as we saw, is that children know innately whatever they could not have learned from observing and subconsciously analysing the language they hear. It is dubbed "logical", because those who hold this view are making a logical deduction – that children could not have inferred everything they know from the input, since this vastly underdetermines their linguistic knowledge. How else could we explain, for example, that children acquiring language are not deterred by errors in the input such as slips of the tongue or incomplete sentences; or the fact that no one sets out to teach them, so corrections are rare and unreliable, yet they know which forms are grammatical or acceptable and those which are not? So, they must come armed with some fairly intricate unconscious knowledge, which seems to be triggered, not created, by experience.

The insight here is that language is not a collection of utterances learned through imitation and repetition.[5] Instead, as children utter sentences they have never heard before, the creative use of language must go beyond the input they receive. The nativist approach explains this ability through the internalization of a rule system – a finite set of rules – which allows the child to generate all these previously unheard utterances. The child who says 'I eated my food', for example, has likely never heard the word 'eated' before. What has taken place is that she, having been exposed to forms such as 'rested' and 'wanted', has internalized the rule governing past-tense formation in JE to be that the morpheme /ɪd/ is suffixed to the bare form of the verb. Producing 'eated' is an example of what is termed over-regularization, or too extended an application of a general rule; it shows clearly that the child has internalized a rule. Later, further input will allow for the rule system to be amended to incorporate the notion of irregular past-tense formation.

Interestingly, in the process, children seldom receive correction from adults; when they do, they tend to be resistant, and to continue to make the same "mistakes" as they speak. Nonetheless, they somehow seem to be able to re-analyse the data they hear around them (the input), and all come to speak the language, having intuitions as native speakers as to what may sound correct, and what is unacceptable or ungrammatical in the language.

That definite patterns such as these can be detected as children acquire language follows logically from acquisition being a natural process, and is reminiscent of natural stages of other kinds of development in other animals.

The idea that children come to the learning task with this innate knowledge is captured by universal grammar (UG), a "powerful hypothesis-formulating system" (Kirby 2014, 427). The principles and parameters (P&P) approach is a version of nativism developed by Chomsky in the 1980s, which holds that UG consists of universal principles which all languages must follow. These constitute a finite set of principles or statements that account for all possible (or grammatical) linguistic structures, and statements that rule out impossible (or ungrammatical) structures. The system of principles is said to be generative, since it generates potentially infinite linguistic output.

In addition to there being universal principles, the theory must account for the fact that individual languages differ – in terms, for example, of whether or not they require overt subjects, or how questions are formed, or whether heads (such as verbs) precede or follow their complements (such as objects), say. These variations are also well-defined: they do not occur randomly but within certain parameters. We say, then, that parameters account for the differences between languages, hence "principles" and "parameters".

An example of how P&P might be applied follows. A universal principle concerning phrases is that every phrase has a head word which determines the nature of the overall phrase. For example, an expression such as 'in the kitchen' is a prepositional phrase, comprising the preposition as head, and its complement 'the kitchen'. Similarly, an expression such as 'close the door' is a verb phrase comprising the head verb 'close' and its complement 'the door'. Languages differ, however, in the order in which a head and its complement appear within a phrase. In English, heads normally precede their complements. In Korean, however, the opposite ordering is found. The Korean counterpart of English 'close the door', for instance, is *muneul dadara* (lit. door close).[6] This is known as the head position parameter.[7]

Importantly, UG is not a theory of language acquisition, but constitutes the "core theory of language" (Chomsky 2005, 4) which allows us to explain facts of acquisition such as the ability of children to acquire so much in such a short period of time. If children come to the language acquisition task equipped with the principles of UG, and if the process of the acquisition of syntax consists of setting parameters, then we should be able to find evidence that (1) children know principles from a very early age and (2) children's language changes in ways that conform to parametric variation in UG (Hoff [2005] 2009, 256). Theories of language are integrally related, therefore, to theories of language acquisition, their adequacy being dependent on their ability to explain the learnability of language, to model the learner's innate mental capacity to acquire language. The question which a theory of language must explain, then, becomes how language must work in order for a child to acquire it in such a short time with such accuracy and without instruction.

As part of the analysis in the chapters which follow, given the age of the children, their speech is compared to findings of the acquisition of a first language. Because of the universal nature of language and of language acquisition, research on acquisition in other language situations is considered, and compared to that of the CLAR children. For the acquisition of JC as a first language, De Lisser (2015) is referenced. This study comprised six children from Creole-speaking communities in western Jamaica, and focused on early acquisition, in the age range 1;6–3;4, with both lower and upper ages in the range far below those of the CLAR study. Nonetheless, it is the only work on the acquisition of JC syntax other than Stewart (2010b) on the comprehension of wh- questions by two-year-olds in urban Kingston. Meade (2001) on the acquisition of phonology by Jamaican children is the only work of its kind, and inspired the choice of age groups for the CLAR study (see section 1.2.1 for discussion). Earlier work by Youssef (1991a, 1991b, 1993) on the acquisition of Trinidadian English Creole is also referenced as relevant.

Given the assumption that the children in the study are native speakers of JC, and further that JC and JE are considered to be different languages (see section 1.1.2), it becomes important to consider the process of acquiring a second language. This is addressed in the next section.

2.2 The Acquisition of a Second Language

Another aspect of the study of language acquisition is the acquisition of a second language (L2A). I note that where aspects of L2A as investigated by scholars in non-Creole language situations are discussed, they are intended to serve as a knowledge-base for our investigations, and to allow us to consider the extent to which such findings can be instructive to or usefully applied in a Creole-speaking environment. It should be noted also that these studies are of situations where the L1 and the L2 may be clearly distinct, unlike the Jamaican case where they are not.

UG was presented in section 2.1 with specific reference to L1A. This has been said to be the innately determined mental architecture which humans have that is dedicated specifically to language acquisition (R. Hawkins 2004, 233 and 241). With regard to L2A, discussions of the end-state falling short of native speaker varieties, and of advancing age being a deficit in this regard, have led to research investigating the extent to which UG is available to and operative for L2 learners. This has resulted in different models claiming varying degrees of access to UG by the learner.[8] The model assumed here is Full Transfer Full Access (FTFA), as proposed by Schwartz and Sprouse (1996, 2007). The authors explain the differences between native (L1) and non-native (L2) development in the following way: "they have different starting points, but [they] are nevertheless epistemologically equivalent because they are constrained by the same domain-specific cognitive mechanisms" (Schwartz and Sprouse 2007, 315);[9] that is, they are both constrained by UG.

In L2A, teaching and learning can and do take place in the classroom, in what is commonly referred to as an instructional setting. Research in this area has shown definitively that patterns attested in the speech of L1 acquirers are also evidenced in the language of learners of an L2, despite varied sequences and strategies of instruction. Such patterns cannot be explained by what has been taught (and therefore learned), but must instead have been "acquired". As such, they are attributed to natural processes.

L2A is said to differ in many respects from L1A, however. Mention has already been made of adults finding learning a second language more difficult than children do as they acquire their L1. In fact, whereas given favourable conditions, children necessarily acquire full competence in their native language, a mere 5 per cent of adults learning an L2 reach a native speaker level of competence, even after years of exposure in either a naturalistic or an instructional setting.[10] Such considerations have led to a rich research agenda exploring the factors which might be said to account for this difference in the speed and the levels of proficiency of first and second language learners.

The age at which exposure to the second language begins is known as the age of onset of acquisition (AOA). This has long been identified as a major contributor to the degree of acquisition possible. A child who is exposed to two or more languages from birth would be expected to proceed through the same developmental stages as monolinguals of those languages. This is a case of simultaneous (bilingual) acquisition, and such a child can be expected to attain native competence in each of the languages (Meisel 2011, 212). McLaughlin (1984) proposed that acquisition be considered simultaneous, resulting in bilingual proficiency, as long as AOA is before three years.[11]

Following a rather exhaustive review of the literature on the maturational effects on ultimate attainment in second language acquisition, Hyltenstam and Abrahamsson (2005, 575) conclude that at least up to an AOA of six or seven, "all learners will automatically reach levels that allow them to pass as native speakers – provided that there is sufficient input and that the learning circumstances are not deficient". They continue to suggest the possibility that absolute native-like command of an L2 may never be possible for an older learner, since the language learning mechanism "inevitably and quickly deteriorates from birth if not continuously stimulated".

Although exact age ranges are still a matter of speculation, it has been observed that there will also be major maturational effects at around the age of four (Meisel 2011, 205). Meisel indicates that differences in particular between L1 and L2 morphosyntactic development – the concern of this work – emerge as early as an AOA of between 3;6 and 4;0 years. Further, if AOA is after six or seven years, the stages of acquisition as well as the grammatical knowledge acquired will increasingly resemble adult L2 acquisition, and so could not be considered to be bilingual acquisition. Instead, this would be referred to as child second-language acquisition. The age at which L1 acquisition ends and L2 acquisition begins, however, remains unclear, and so the question of whether the successive acquisition of language during the first three years of life, that is, up to age 3;0, can still be considered to be bilingual first language acquisition is difficult to answer (Meisel 2011, 212).

The key to successful acquisition must lie in Hyltenstam and Abrahamsson's (2005) provisos that there be sufficient input, and that the learning circumstances not be deficient. It would seem that, to use Montrul's (2005, 203) terms, our children may best be classified as early child L2 learners who are exposed to the second language early in childhood, well before the end of the critical period.

We shall see in section 6.2, however, that evidence points towards JE being the weaker language among the CLAR children. Given the age of onset and the levels of proficiency and fluency attained, a classification of successive bilingualism is applicable, with the second language, JE, being the weaker language, and the first language, JC, the dominant. This provides evidence that the input and learning circumstances do not suffice for full bilingualism.

Meisel (2007, 510) shows that in successive bilingualism, the use of grammatical L2 constructions alongside target-deviant ones is evidence that learners have the relevant grammatical knowledge of the L2. For example, problems with inflectional morphology, or the omission of obligatory elements such as subjects, objects or articles where the target language requires them, never occur systematically. This would indicate that the required grammatical knowledge has been acquired, but that the children seem to encounter problems when putting it to use (p. 500). Meisel suggests that in such situations, and most particularly where, as is the Jamaican case, one language is strongly dominant, children have difficulty establishing and developing the sets of mechanisms required for bilingual language use. Examples of required mechanisms are the ability to switch into the other language, or, conversely, to inhibit switches which may be inappropriate. Of course, knowledge of the L2 grammar will only be possible for those constructions which form part of the input.

Following Hyltenstam and Abrahamsson (2005) and Meisel (2011), as outlined above, our children, with exposure to JE at school at age three, if not before in the home through radio, television or the community, should be at an advantage for the successful acquisition of JE. Yet, it has been the common cry of teachers and education policy makers that our students perform unsatisfactorily both in English as a course, even at the tertiary level, and in other subjects, since performance in all is dependent on the comprehension and use of that language. This points to the importance of bearing in mind the particular language situation pertaining in Creole-speaking communities, when attempting to apply to those communities findings in the "mainstream literature". In a Creole-speaking environment, for instance, discrete language systems which may be defined separately as the L1 and the L2 do not exist. It is recognized, of course, that variation is a characteristic of natural discourse in any speech community, that it is inherent, and unable to be factored out in any analysis of language (Poplack 1993, 253). However, for the CLAR children, the input is characteristically extremely varied, and the L1 and L2 are very closely related lexically, to the extent where, as we have seen, members may believe they are speaking the L2 when in fact they are not.

When studies are cited, therefore, it is in an effort to situate our children in the field, rather than to suggest that the findings relating to them ought to align with those of children in different language situations.

2.3 The Role of Input in Acquisition

Input or "experience" is crucial in acquisition. It is one of three factors cited by Chomsky (2005) as interacting in language design, along with genetic endowment – the topic of UG – and principles that are language-independent, such as those associated with data processing, structural architecture and computational efficiency (p. 9). In fact, it is age of onset of exposure to the languages (already discussed in section 2.2) and the role of input which are said in the research on child bilingualism to account for differences in outcomes in acquisition (see, for example, Unsworth et al. 2014).[12] In exploring input, I consider both its quantity and quality.

The evidence that quantity of input influences bilingual development is robust and well-researched (see references quoted in Paradis 2011, 67–68): it is the language of greater exposure which becomes the dominant language, and generally, more input leads to greater rates of acquisition. There may be multiple sources of input including parents and siblings at home, depending on the extent to which the L2 is spoken at home, as well as peers, native speakers and the school (Unsworth 2016, 104–7). Input might also include time spent watching television. I note, however, that watching television is considered inadequate, since though it may make available an additional language model, it does not involve a communicative partner, making two-way communication impossible (Hoff 2006, 58), and thus does not allow for the children's participation in the language-based activities (p. 71).

Important for us is a consideration also of the quality of input. Measures of input quality include the so-called richness of the language in the environment, that is, in the home, community, and the school. This is determined by the degree of native-speaker contact experienced by children via, for example, playmates, the media and organized extracurricular activities (Paradis 2011, 69). Research supporting this includes Place and Hoff (2011, 1845–47), who show that among the Spanish-English bilinguals[13] they studied in their homes, after controlling for the amount of English exposure, the percent of exposure provided by native speakers was a significant correlate of the English vocabulary they acquired. This suggests that in the home, non-native input is less useful to language acquisition than native input.

In Jamaican communities, opportunities for native-speaker exposure may be inadequate. Recall the discussion of transitional diglossia in section 1.1.1 said to be resulting in fewer and fewer models of JE being available to children, as JC becomes acceptable in domains previously reserved only for JE. Given the Jamaican language situation as outlined, it seems reasonable to assume that speakers of JE as an L2 outnumber JE native speakers.

Jamaican teachers would also, of course, be included among these L2 speakers of JE. With regard to the school, research on the extent to which specific properties of teachers' speech relate to bilingual children developing school language skills is limited (Unsworth 2016, 107), but the need for teachers of English to be native speakers of English is considered a myth in need of debunking (see, for example, Kiczkowiak 2014). Instead, what matters more is considerations such as personal traits, qualifications, experience and demonstrable proficiency (ibid.).

Native speaker modelling is not the only variable affecting proficiency. Place and Hoff (2011, 1845) found new evidence in their study of twenty-nine Spanish-English bilinguals, that in addition to exposure provided by native speakers, the number of exclusively L2 conversational partners and the number of different sources of the L2 were also significant correlates of the grammatical complexity of the children's use of the L2.

Paradis (2011, 68) takes input quality to refer to "how much variation exists in the form and use of morphosyntactic structures in a child's linguistic environment". He explains that the result of variation in the form and use of a structure in the input could lead to "optionality [or 'errorful' usage] in the learner's use and processing of that structure and/or influence a learner's underlying linguistic representation for that structure, leading to non-convergence with the monolingual grammar" (ibid.). Byers-Heinlein (2009) also provides evidence[14] that exposure to mixed language impedes English vocabulary development at eighteen and twenty-four months, and suggests that this may be due at least in part to increased difficulty in language separation resulting from the mixed input.

Variation in the input and its role in L2A is of particular relevance to this study.[15] In the chapters which follow, how variation is manifest in the children's speech is investigated. The CLAR interviews took place in the school setting, but outside of the classroom, with no consideration of the children's speech in any other setting, so there is no possibility within this study to compare their speech in different domains. The expectation might be, given the diglossic nature of the language situation, that there would be intrusions of JE in their speech, in response to the relatively formal context of interviews at school by strangers. Interestingly, though interviews were to have been conducted in JC, variation also characterized the speech of the investigators, being members themselves of the Jamaican language community. Nonetheless, we find that, particularly after the first visit, the dominant language used by the CLAR children was JC.

Importantly, though it exists in the input, and therefore becomes the model in acquisition for the children, the variation exhibited is not random or chaotic. An understanding of the patterns in the weaving of forms in the speech of the children will allow for knowledge of what children do with the linguistic resources available to them.

This brings us to a consideration of *code-switching*, a linguistic consequence of languages in contact.

2.4 Code-Switching

Code-switching (CS) is the term used to refer to the ability of a bilingual to use both languages within a discourse or within an utterance (Cantone and Müller 2008, 811). It is said to be a typical or normal aspect of bilingual development, and is known to be a virtually necessary result in the language of children who grow up bilingually (Nicoladis and Genesee 1997, 259).

Meisel ([2004] 2006, 96) indicates that sociolinguistic factors play an important role in CS, which he defines as "a form of language use determined by a complex network of sociolinguistic variables and constrained by grammatical properties of the utterances". Both the sociolinguistic and the grammatical aspects of CS will be discussed in what follows.

Youssef (1991b, 1993) uses the term *varilingual* to label the emerging communicative competence of small children acquiring coexistent grammars along with sociolinguistic skills. She found that from age 2;10, children in the Trinidad linguistic situation not only produced variable grammatical features, but also exhibited stylistic variation in their use (1993, 258–59).

Sebba ([2009] 2012, 40) likens CS to playing two games at once, keeping to the rules of both in a way that is satisfactory to the participants. The assumption in this analogy is that there are no CS-specific rules, but that the rules of both "games" are obeyed. This is in line with the generative model where the possibility of the generation of an infinite number of utterances is said to be due to the internalization of rule systems. Each of the codes in CS comes, then, with its own internalized rule system.

Two types of CS have been identified in the literature: inter-sentential CS (between or among sentences), which occurs within a discourse, and intra-sentential CS, which occurs within a sentence.

Inter-sentential CS takes place when whole sentences are uttered in a language, and switching to another language occurs according to pragmatic constraints[16] such as the perceived language of the interlocutor (participant in the discourse), or the demands of a particular social situation.

With regard to CS among children, Meisel ([2004] 2006, 97) indicates that by age 2;0 bilingual children choose the language according to the addressee, and soon afterwards they begin to adapt to other sociolinguistic requirements.[17]

Fantini (1985) traces language choice in his Spanish-English bilingual son Mario to age ten years. Spanish, the child's first language, was spoken in his home. Active use of English, his second language, began at 2;6, when he was faced with the task of sorting out which linguistic code was appropriate for each situation. From age 3;0 he maintained a clear and consistent separation of the two.

Given the language situation in Jamaica as outlined above, we might predict a difficulty in maintaining a clear and consistent separation of the two codes. We shall see how accurate that prediction might be, as our story unfolds, but Fantini's (1985) account is instructive to us at least insofar as he identifies factors which allowed his son to change from code to code up to age 5;0; those most affecting choice were limited to interlocutor and setting (pp. 57–68).

The interlocutor variables which proved most significant were whether the interlocutor was known to the child and, if so, whether intimately or not; the role played in his life; whether the person "looked Spanish-speaking" or not (as judged by the child); and the degree of comprehension and fluency with which the person used the code.

Concerning setting, the child was sensitive to whether the event took place in a predominantly Spanish-speaking locale or not, and whether the gathering was obviously of Spanish speakers. In short, if the participant and the language spoken were both known to the child, the choice of code became obvious, and he was capable by his third year of making appropriate language choices, switching rapidly and naturally from one to the next.

Children do seem, then, to be able, even at early ages, to be sensitive to the social implications of using one code rather than another. We might expect this sensitivity to be compromised in a Creole continuum environment, however, where extreme variation is a characteristic of the input children hear. Blurred boundaries may mean that such children are often not able to correctly identify the code to which a form may belong, and therefore may not be able to successfully manipulate codes in this way. Youssef (1991a, 77), says of the Trinidad linguistic situation, that variation is characteristic also at the acrolectal end of the continuum: "Generally, in even the most formal settings, Creole rules have infiltrated and affected the supposed acrolect without speakers being aware of this."

CS also takes place within an utterance. This (intra-sentential) CS has been used to explain the speech of Jamaicans, as they manipulate the two languages at their disposal in everyday interaction. Christie (2003, 3) reports this to be very common in everyday informal interaction in Jamaica among persons of all social classes. She uses, as an example, a nurse who was overheard addressing no one in particular in a hospital room. Her exact words were (JC italicized):

(1) *Dem   a   kaal im   bot im*   can't be found.
     3PL.SUBJ PROG call 3s.OBJ but 3s.SUBJ can't be found
     'They're calling him, but he can't be found.'

As Christie explains, this phenomenon is widespread, evidenced in the speech of a member of parliament who uses a Creole word or phrase in a speech delivered mainly in JE, the writer who uses Creole for dialogue in his or her novel or play, or the talk show host on radio when addressing Creole-speaking callers.

In addition to the mixing of whole phrases within an utterance, also prevalent in intra-sentential CS is the mixing of particular features of one language with those of another within a phrase or construction. An example would be the following:

(2)   CHR: *a   mai   kaar dis   we   fi   shraiv* [: *jraiv*] *go op deso.*
              FOC 1S.POSS car   this COMP MOD drive   go up there
              'This is my car that's for driving up there.' [V3-SMT:l.1130-3;2.20]

What we have here is a noun phrase *mai kaar* consisting of two JE constituents "inserted" in an otherwise JC utterance.

Insertion is the term used by Muysken (2000), and adopted by many, as one of the three processes involved in the mixing of structures from one language with those from another. For Muysken, inserting an element is similar to lexical borrowing, except that insertion may also include larger structures (the insertion of a noun phrase, for example), whereas lexical borrowing is restricted to the insertion of lexical items (pp. 69–78). Insertion is said to be frequent in colonial settings and recent migrant communities, where there is considerable difference in the speakers' proficiency in the two languages (p. 9).

A second process in code-mixing is *alternation*. Alternation involves phrases from one language alternating with phrases from another. This takes place when there is structural equivalence between the two languages at the point of switching, allowing the introduction of the other-language phrase. This is what is involved in canonical CS, since both the grammar and the lexicon are involved, a case of "true" CS. Christie's example, cited in (1) above, is an example of alternation.

The third and final type of mixing proposed by Muysken (2000) is *congruent lexicalization*. This refers to a situation where two languages share a particular grammatical structure that can be filled lexically with elements from either language (p. 4). An example is provided in (3) below. JC and JE share the grammatical structure indefinite determiner+noun. In such a shared grammatical structure, the incorporation of material from different lexical inventories (that is, stocks of lexical items) into the shared grammatical structure is allowed.

(3)   TAS: *mi   waahn wahn   sooda.*
              1S.SUBJ want   INDEF soda
              'I want a soda.'   [V3-SMR:l.630-3;5.6]

This structure is found in typologically similar languages, or in cases of dialect–standard variation. The choice of material to be incorporated would be determined by sociolinguistic considerations such as what style or register is to be adopted, given particular social situations.

Muysken (2008, 154) indicates that there are language-related factors which play a role in furthering or constraining code-mixing. Matching word orders in the languages involved, for instance, are said to facilitate code-mixing, as are simple or absent inflectional morphology, lexical similarity or *cognate* status.[18] If an element is *functional*,[19] it will mean that a complement will be inserted with it, blocking its insertion by itself, and blocking also a switch immediately following (p. 163). An example is the English progressive auxiliary 'is', which must be followed by a progressive verb form, as in 'is playing', making a switch to a JC verb form unlikely, then, following 'is'. We shall see in chapters 4 and 5 how functional items and their complements are woven in the grammars of the CLAR children, and suggest in section 6.3 what factors might influence the mixes which occur.

Intra-sentential CS by bilinguals has been heavily researched in terms primarily of the constraints governing the occurrence of switched elements. Such studies assume that there must be specific CS-related rules which predict where switches may occur within a sentence, and where they must not occur. These studies were of adult bilinguals (see Poplack [2004] for a comprehensive overview).

Gawlitzek-Maiwald and Tracy (1996, 907) indicate that there have been at least two respects in which the mixing in child language has been argued to differ from that in adults. The first is that children may not have mastered grammatical concepts or categories that enter into the constraints proposed for adult code-mixing. The authors cite, as an example, the government constraint of Di Sciullo, Muysken and Singh (1986), which would predict, for instance, as in the sentence 'He said that he would go', that the complement clause (single underline) must remain in the same language as the verb (double underline). This would not apply to early acquisition: because of the complexity of the construction, it would not yet have been acquired.

The second way in which adult and child CS differ, according to Gawlitzek-Maiwald and Tracy, is that children lack the pragmatic knowledge, specifically, the control over whom to address in what language. Because intentionality of this sort is absent in the child, authors such as Meisel (1989) prefer to use the term *code-mixing* for children's bilingual speech.

However, we have already seen that Fantini's son (cf. Fantini 1985) was applying pragmatic principles from a very early age. Perhaps it is the case that such knowledge varies according to the sociolinguistic context in which acquisition is taking place. In a language situation such as that in Jamaica where, as we have seen, the input to which children are exposed often does not consist of two clearly separate codes, it may become difficult for them to correctly identify which forms belong to each code. This would have implications for language education, as is discussed in some detail in chapter 6.

Cantone (2007) found that the children she investigated mix at all boundaries which in the literature have been both allowed and rejected, though some boundaries are less violated than others, and though the children she studied differ in the types of mixing they used – some mix only nouns, for instance (pp. 172–73). The occurrence of mixing such that all constraints proposed in the literature may be violated, leads Cantone to a determination that the only constraints on CS are those required by the grammars of the two languages involved, and that any switch is possible as long as the rules of the languages are respected. In this, Cantone follows MacSwan's (1999, 2000) opinion on CS in adults, and concludes (p. 33) that child mixing is not different from adult mixing. This is, quite simply, language at work.

I move now into a discussion of the framework used in this study for the analysis of language.

2.5 Minimalism

The models proposed by Chomsky for the syntax of human language as introduced in section 2.1 above, have evolved since the mid-1950s, increasing in simplicity, economy and explanatory power. In the P&P model of the 1980s presented, parameters are language-specific and may pertain at the level of constructions. They are thought to be properties of the syntax – languages may require heads to follow or to precede complements, as we saw – with different systems of syntax, or computational systems, in use in different languages, but all following universal principles of language.

Chomsky's thinking further developed into another model, minimalism. Minimalism, as presented in Chomsky (1995, 1999), is the theoretical framework adopted here. As suggested above, it is more simple, more economical and has more explanatory power than its predecessors, seeking to investigate language in terms of principled explanations (Chomsky 2005, 2). It is introduced in this section, and constitutes the most theoretical discussion in this work. Only aspects of the theory deemed to be important for an understanding of analyses of the CLAR data in sections of chapters 4 and 5 and in section 6.3.2 are introduced, however. Radford's (1997) textbook may be consulted for a complete discussion of the Minimalist Program.[20]

It is important to note that minimalism is considered to be a programme rather than a theory, referred to also, therefore, as the Minimalist Program. As a programme, it has been applied to the study of language structure in different ways. The basis of the discussion here is features. Throughout the work, variation is viewed from a feature-based perspective, and is pre-theoretically referred to as the weaving of features from both systems at two levels: superficial weaving of phonological and lexical features and structural weaving of syntactic features.

In minimalism, the syntax is viewed as a computational system, conceived as being invariant across languages. But languages do differ. Variation, resulting in differences between languages, resides not in the syntax, but in the lexicon. The lexicon is essentially a store of all the lexical items (words) which we know; the store resides in our memory and is often referred to as the mental lexicon. All learning is lexical: words are taken to be bundles of features, and the features associated with a word will differ from one language to the next, causing structure to be built in different ways. Features include

- phonological features, relating to the sounds and sound systems of the language;
- morphological features, to do with how words may be formed;
- syntactic features, relating to principles concerning the grammatical relations which may or may not exist in a particular language;
- semantic features, relating to the interpretational possibilities of words; and
- pragmatic features, tied to the discourse context within which particular words may appear.

The core concepts needed for an understanding of the analyses in later chapters is that words and constructions are viewed in terms of features belonging to (idealizations of) JE, JC, or both, and that it is the interplay of these features which regulates the syntax. The remainder of this section is an extension of these basic concepts.

A feature is conceived in the Minimalist Program as a property of syntactic objects (words), and has the structure [attribute: value]. The feature [number: plural] refers to the real world morpheme /s/ in JE, say, in the same way that in chemistry, H represents hydrogen (Adger and Svenonius 2011, 28). What becomes important is to determine how feature structures may be formed, that is, to determine the properties of features which allow for relationships with other (properties of) features.

So, lexical items are syntactic objects, symbolic units which are bundles of phonetic, semantic and formal information in the form of features (Uriagereka 2000, 128). They reside in the (mental) lexicon. All relevant lexical items for the formation of a particular utterance to be processed are SELECTed from the lexicon. SELECT is a core process in the minimalist approach, and we shall see the ways in which it interacts with the lexicon in the creation of utterances, as our story unfolds.

When a lexical item is SELECTed and enters the computation, it is said to have MERGEd. The syntactic component is then responsible for deriving utterances, a process quite transparently known as the derivation, or the computation. The process involves taking objects already formed and combining them into a new structure via MERGE. MERGE yields a potentially infinite number of structured expressions and is therefore thought to be without bound (Chomsky 2007, 5).

Interestingly, in recent years, Chomsky has become concerned with the kind of evolutionary step(s) which have enabled humans to develop language. In the tradition of minimalism, the answer would serve to minimize recourse to constructs or principles which are not conceptually necessary, that is, principles which if a system failed it could not then be called a language. If there is a single evolutionary step which took place at some point in human evolution giving rise to language, it is likely not to have been a step in which a whole range of different properties idiosyncratic to language were acquired (Radford 2016, 28). This leads to an enquiry into the nature of the operation which would have given rise to language in this way. In Chomsky (2007), the operation is taken to be MERGE.

Where more than one language is involved, I assume in this work, following MacSwan (1999), that there is a different (mental) lexicon associated with each[21] – in the case of Jamaica, one associated with JC and the other with JE. SELECT will be responsible for taking items from one lexicon or the other, so that the utterance may be generated, but there will be one, invariant computational system (the syntax) operating according to the requirements of the features associated with the lexical items SELECTed.

There are two kinds of features which are of importance here – interpretable and uninterpretable features. Interpretable features are those which are able to be read ("interpreted") by the semantic component. They are associated with meaning, therefore, and are inherent to the understanding of the lexical item. The past tense is an example. It has meaning associated with it in any language – it means something different if we SAW something yesterday than if we SEE it now. This points to the involvement of an interpretable feature [tense: past].

In JE, the form of the verb may change to signal this change in meaning. Signalling a change in the morphosyntax is the responsibility of the second kind of feature – the uninterpretable feature. This type of feature is not associated with meaning, but has only (morpho)syntactic consequences. In our example, the JE verb SEE will be associated in the lexicon with an uninterpretable tense feature [uTense:]. At this stage, it is not known whether the value of the feature will be [past] or [present]; we say that it is unvalued. It is not until it is fed into the computation that it receives its value from the relevant interpretable (tense) feature.

Valuing takes place via a process known as AGREE(ment) in the following way: the interpretable past-tense feature carried by T values a hitherto unvalued uninterpretable [uTense:] feature on V as [uTense:past]. Having been valued, the uninterpretable feature is then deleted. The idea is that it is through AGREE that the tense affix becomes "attached" to the verb at *spell-out*.[22]

In order for an interpretable feature to value its uninterpretable counterpart, they must be in a structurally close relationship with each other. This sometimes requires that the relevant syntactic object MOVE closer to the object valuing it. An example is the movement in question-asking of the auxiliary 'is' in (4b) below to a position preceding the subject 'he', in order to have its Q(uestion) feature valued by the question word 'What':

(4a)   He is playing dominoes.

(4b)   What is he playing?

Movement in the computation, that is, the operation MOVE, is considered to be costly in terms of the computational load required. Costly operations are less economical, and therefore less desirable in theoretical terms; in the spirit of economy, movement must be seen to be a last resort (Chomsky 1995, 130).

We have seen how it is that in minimalism, features play a central role: it is through features associated with the word that structure is built. Importantly, morphosyntactic relations are realized or spelled out in different ways in different languages. In JE, SEE [tense: past] will be spelled out as SAW. Regular forms are spelled out with an inflectional ending (WALKED /wɔ:kt̪/, LIVED /lɪvd̪/ or RANTED /rant̪ɪd̪/). In contrast, there are no tense affixes in JC and, therefore, there would be no tense agreement, no uninterpretable inflectional feature that needs to be valued by (an auxiliary in) T. The result is an invariable, uninflected form, with the past tense being realized as either an independent morpheme BEHN or its variants, or a null T, without phonological realization but with a (default) tense interpretation nonetheless (see sections 5.1 and 5.3 for discussions of how tense works in JC).

I take the lexicon to consist of both lexical and functional categories. There are, obviously, differences in how languages label entities in the world to create lexical categories. In French, *la siège* is used to represent a seat, and *la chaise* refers to the piece of furniture, the chair. These labels are arbitrarily assigned by languages,[23] and must be learned.

Functional categories are the locus of variation within and among languages. This is because uninterpretable features are associated with functional morphemes consisting of formal features which regulate the syntax and the conditions on their expression (Lardière [2008] 2010, 114).

A source of the blurred boundaries between JC and JE (see sections 1.1.2 and 1.1.3) may be found if we consider that the functional features regulating the syntax are different in the two languages, even though the lexical items may appear similar. This may cause the speaker to conclude erroneously that these similar words function in a similar way. A speaker, for example, could be aware that the JE counterpart of the JC personal pronoun *im* is 'him', and simply use the JE form without internalizing that, unlike JC, the JE pronoun carries both gender and case features.

Though at the level of pronunciation there are strong correspondences between the two languages, it becomes clear that since the grammatical and semantic features associated with those words differ, it cannot be said that JC and JE share one lexicon. Instead, the task which faces the JC L1 speaker in learning JE is an understanding of the featural differences between the lexicons of the two languages, including but, very importantly, not restricted to phonological features.

Another type of feature is a selectional feature. A word such as 'the' requires a complement which contains a noun, so that it is not possible to have a sequence *'the write'.[24] Instead, 'the' must SELECT a nominal, such as 'the <u>book</u>'. An uninterpretable selectional feature on the determiner [uN] ensures that a complement with the (matching) feature [+N] is selected.[25]

We can now view in terms of features, the example 'from <u>I was a child</u>', introduced in section 1.1.2 as the structure chosen by L2 speakers of JE, versus 'from <u>childhood</u>' preferred by L1 speakers of JE: 'from' for the L2 speaker SELECTS a clause, whereas for the L1 speaker of JE, it must SELECT a nominal, that is, it must have a complement with the matching feature [+N]. Though the preposition itself differs phonologically in JE and JC (JE /from/ versus JC /frã/), this is more superficial than the difference in their syntactic features, which drive structure.

Belazi, Rubin and Toribio (1994, 228) assume that one of the relevant features associated with lexical items is LANGUAGE. This was formalized as the functional head constraint. As conceived by the authors, it was strictly grammatical, regulated solely by the syntax. It read (p. 229):

(5)   The Functional Head Constraint (FHC)
       The language feature of the complement (f-)selected by a functional
       head, like all other relevant features, must match the corresponding
       feature of that functional head.

The idea of the constraint is that it is operative in all speech, but its effects only become apparent in CS.

Applying this to the Jamaican language situation, a lexical item associated solely with one language or the other might be labelled *monolectal*:[26] in our case, either acrolectal [±ACR], or perhaps basilectal [±BAS]. If a functional head belongs to the JE lexicon, it could be taken to bear an uninterpretable selectional feature, [uACR], say, requiring it to SELECT a complement with a matching interpretable JE feature [+ACR]. A JC noun would not bear the interpretable feature [+ACR]. Instead, it would form part of the JC lexicon, and bear [-ACR] or perhaps BAsilectal [+BAS]. As such, it would not match and, therefore, could not be selected to satisfy the requirements of [uACR].

MacSwan (2014, 13–14) indicates that the FHC is a CS specific proposal, since the language feature as an identifier of a particular language plays a role in the grammatical system. He criticizes it as simply relabeling the descriptive facts of CS: it is a label representing a class of expression defined by the grammatical system, and so cannot itself be a part of the definition. In effect, it treats LANGUAGE as a grammatical feature. Instead, MacSwan's thesis is that, formally, CS must be the union of two lexically encoded grammars, where each lexical item imposes requirements on the syntax based on its features, and where syntactic operations need take no notice of what particular language a lexical item is associated with (MacSwan 2006, 299).

MacSwan himself admits, however, that the FHC is "much improved" if, as communicated to him by Jacqueline Toribio, the language feature is taken to be a variable for a bundle of features which formally characterize the language (2000, 41). This would mean for us that, to evaluate the FHC, particular hypotheses would be needed regarding which features of JE result in a conflict with features of JC.

If the FHC is correct, it would, in effect, be a constraint on weaving, as I have defined it (see chapter 1 for discussion). However, there are numerous counter-examples to the constraint, as shown by researchers, such as MacSwan, working in languages where switching language between a functional head and its complement is possible. Additionally, we see in section 6.3.2 that, given the nature of weaving as revealed in the data in chapters 3, 4 and 5, the FHC seems to be implausible. Instead, there is reason to believe that, in our case, sociolinguistic (or perhaps more specifically, sociophonological) and pragmatic constraints become more important in lexical choice, if only because patterns in mixing reveal tendencies rather than (im)possible combinations. As pointed out by Andrew Radford (pers. comm.), "if . . . formalize[d] . . . in terms of features, [mixing] predicts ZERO exceptions, not a statistical tendency".

To summarize, lexical items in the lexicon contain features which drive the computation that ultimately derives utterances. The assumption is that there is a JC lexicon which is different from the JE lexicon. Minimalism reduces the differences between languages to the choice of features which are associated with lexical items. Because the items are stored in the lexicon, it becomes central to our concerns. The lexicon resides outside the computational system (the syntax), and so therefore does variation within and between languages.

We will examine some cases where features of JC and those of JE differ radically from each other and consider what their different requirements in the languages are. The relevant constructions in which these features appear include plural, (in)definite and possessive noun phrases (chapter 4), as well as tense and aspect in the verbal domain (chapter 5). We will also examine the ways in which the different requirements of the features in the language combine in the speech of the children.

2.5.1 Minimalism and Creole Languages

It was indicated previously that JC does not mark tense using an inflectional ending. Neither does it mark the following by way of inflections: aspect or agreement with the subject on the verb; pluralization or possession on the noun; or case or gender on the noun or pronoun. Yet, these all form part of the domain of uninterpretable features which in other languages must be valued (by interpretable features), and which in turn are spelled out. Uninterpretable features form the basis of minimalism, yet seem not to play a significant role in JC, then.

We now explore whether this means that minimalism has no useful application for the analysis of a Creole language such as JC.

One approach to reconciling a system based on features with the analysis of JC is to call on the notion of the independence of the computational component. This component is said to be invariant across languages. Its independence means also that it is blind to the phonological component (PF) where features are spelled out: features exist in the lexicon, are introduced into the derivation and proceed regardless of whether there is any phonological realization for them. What this means is that they may exist, and may fulfil the requirements of the syntax without being expressed overtly, that is, without being uttered. We see, for example, that in JE, the marker of agreement of the subject with the verb is overtly expressed only for the third-person singular in the present tense: 'he/she/it eats'. No other forms are overtly expressed – 'I eat, you eat, we eat, they eat' – yet we consider that these forms too express the present tense. It may be, then, that such forms exist in JC, but are never expressed. Evidence of their existence is that the syntax is regulated, and that we know that they exist in other languages (where they are overtly expressed).

An alternative, proposed by Radford (2000), is very appealing. In exploring the nature of children's initial grammar, he uses Chomsky's (1998, 1999) argument that language is a (near) perfect system in which only what is conceptually necessary is projected in the syntax. This is in the spirit of the economy of language driving minimalism. If language reflects maximal economy, then perfection will be maximized and imperfection minimized. The expectation will be, then, that the innate system allowing for the acquisition of language would lead the child to construct a perfect grammar, excluding imperfections which would be acquired at a later stage of development.

In attempting to define what would constitute (im)perfections, Radford (2000, 3n12) quotes Chomsky (1999, 3): "the relation Agree and uninterpretable features are prima facie imperfections", and concludes that good design principles will require that uninterpretable features be projected only when necessary. It seems logical that not only redundant syntactic material but also phonological material would be avoided. As an example, number-marking is redundant when a numeral is present ('two cups'): since the numeral expresses plurality, it is not necessary to mark the plural on the noun. Indeed, children acquiring English are known to initially omit the plural marker, the spell-out of a valued uninterpretable number feature on the noun. Similarly, in a sequence such as 'Man drive truck', where tense and agreement features are absent,[27] it can be determined by the discourse (context) that the activity is in the present. Meaning can be assigned, since the event ('drive') has been defined in terms of its participants – 'man', the person responsible for initiating the event, and 'truck', the entity which is affected by the event.

It may be that, in initially producing perfect structures, children treat features which are uninterpretable in adult grammars, as being interpretable. Returning to the example 'two cups', in adult (JE) grammar there would be an uninterpretable feature on the noun, which, having been valued, would then be spelled out as /s/. In child grammar it could be misanalysed as interpretable.[28]

Since structures without number-marking and without agreement, case or tense marking exist also in adult Creole, it would seem to be a logical extension of Radford's proposal to apply it to Creole languages. In such a case, then, it may be that uninterpretable features which are never phonologically realized in JC, simply do not exist. This is not to say that uninterpretable features do not exist at all in (adult) JC, but they do not exist in the same form, or with the same functions as they do in JE. There is evidence that features operate differently for the possessive, for instance; that there exist features in JC such as inclusiveness (see section 4.2) which do not exist in JE; and that movement, triggered by the valuing of uninterpretable features in wh- question-asking and in focus constructions, as examples, does take place in JC. In learning JE, the child will need to learn what the differences involved are, in each case. She will need to learn, for example, that number is an obligatory uninterpretable feature of count nouns in JE, and that the indefinite article or some other constituent will be needed to value that uninterpretable feature (Radford 2000, 20). Note the differences between the two languages:

(6a)   MAU: *kaaz   im   <u>a   gorl</u>.
                because 3s.SUBJ COP girl
                'Because she is a girl.'   [V5-KN1:1 589-3;8.30]
                *kaaz im   <u>a   wahn gorl</u>.
                because 3s.SUBJ COP INDEF girl

(6b)   *Because she <u>is girl</u>
                Because she <u>is a</u> girl

This book seeks to highlight differences between JC and JE, to establish how the languages combine in the speech of the three-year-olds studied, and to lay the foundation for a way forward in the teaching of JE by providing a linguistic means of differentiating between these languages.

I look now at aspects of the vocabulary of the children.

3

How the Children Use and Create Words

INV: *wa i fan a du?*[1]
ANN: *it a briiz yu.*
[V6-KN2:1.301-3;4.21]

n this chapter, I look at words or lexical items residing in the mental lexicon. In the course of the discussion, a clear picture of the composition of the CLAR children's lexicon(s) will emerge. Acquisition of the lexicon is important in the theoretical tradition adopted in this study, in which the acquisition of syntax is fundamentally linked to the acquisition of features. In fact, lexical items are considered to be bundles of phonological, morphological, lexical, syntactic and semantic features (see section 2.5 for discussion). The presumption is that the different features associated with JE and JC words may combine under certain conditions and within certain constraints. Recall that the term *weaving* is used to refer to the resulting patterns evidenced in the speech of the children, with a distinction between superficial weaves, involving phonological and lexical features, and structural weaves, which combine syntactic features of the languages (section 1.1). In this chapter, I also look in some detail at superficial weaving.

Since JC and JE are considered to be two different languages, they would be expected to have two different inventories of sounds. First I look at differences between phonological features that are revealed in the inventories of sounds in JC and JE, noting the sounds which are absent in one, but present in the other. Those words which do not show differences in vowels or consonants are considered to be SHared. I use these differences and similarities as a basis for categorizing words by language, and in section 3.1 look at the relative representations of JC, JE and SHared words in the children's speech. The composition of the lexicon is considered from the point of view of the percentages of lexical versus functional categories in section 3.2. In section 3.3, the focus is on adjectives, and in section 3.4 on word formation strategies.

3.1 Inventories of Sounds in JC versus JE

Chapter 1 includes a rather detailed discussion of JC as an English-lexified language and the possible effects of this on the language situation. Here I look at the range of possible variants available to speakers, using as the basis the differences between the inventories of sounds in JC and JE.

I note that there is wide agreement in the literature that the earlier a second language is learned, the better (see section 2.2 for discussion). There is evidence, however, that regardless, L2 phonology is influenced by that of the L1, and that differences between the two languages can influence L2 speech development. Flege (1999) found, for example, that adult Italian-English bilinguals had lower pronunciation accuracy with vowels that are present in their L2 English but not in L1 Italian, when compared with vowels present in both languages. This was the case even though they had begun learning English as young children.

Differences between the vowel and consonant systems of JC and JE are shown in table 3.1. Sounds are illustrated using words in which they might appear, and some also using the relevant International Phonetic Alphabet (IPA) phonetic symbols. They are presented as those existing in JC only, those existing in JE only, and for vowels and diphthongs, those which are SHared.

Note that this account is linked to how words are spelled, and so would be dependent on a knowledge of spelling, typically not yet mastered by children of this age. Instead, of course, children model their pronunciation on spoken forms, hence an understanding of differences between the spoken forms of JC and JE is important, and independent of spelling forms which are learned later. Given that learning to spell and read is so linked to knowing the "sound" of words, knowing what children might know or not know of the JE sound system is essential for the literacy and language education teacher.

With regard to vowels, note that there are diphthongs which exist only in JC (line entries 1 and 2), and those which exist only in JE (line entries 10 and 11). Note also that although neither JE short [ɔ] nor long [ɔ:] is found in the JC counterparts of 'pot' and 'paw' (line entries 6 and 7), [ɔ] does exist in JC in different environments; an example is line entry 28, *dong* [dɔŋ].

Table 3.1. Inventories of sounds: JC and JE

Ref		Segment	JE Example	Translation	Possible JC	Example
	Vowels and Diphthongs					
1.	**JConly**	[ɪe]		play	*plie*	
2.		[ʊɔ]		goat	*guot*	
3.	**JE only**	[e:]	take		*tek*	[tɛk]
4.			play		*plie*	[plɪe]
5.		[o:]	pole		*puol*	[pʊɔl]
6.		[ɔ]	pot		*pat*	[pat]
7.		[ɔ:]	paw		*paa*	[pa:]
8.		[ʌ]	but		*bot*	[bɔt]
9.		[ə] unstressed	letter		*leta*	[lɛta]
10.		[ɔi]	toy		*tai*	[taɪ]
11.		[aʊ]	cow		*kau*	[koʊ]
12.	**SHared**	[i:]	teeth		*tiit*	[ti:t]
13.		[ɪ]	tin		*tin*	[tɪn]
14.		[u:]	pool		*puul*	[pu:l]
15.		[ʊ]	pull		*pul*	[pʊl]
16.		[ɛ]	bed		*bed*	[bɛd]
17.		[a:]	pass		*paas*	[pa:s]
18.		[a]	mat		*mat*	[mat]
	Consonants and Clusters					
19.	**JConly**	bw		boy	*bwai*	
20.		pw		spoil	*pwail*	
21.		gy		girl	*gyal*	
22.		ky		car	*kyaar*	
23.		ny		eat	*nyam*	
24.	**JE only**	[θ]	thing		*ting*	
25.		[ð]	that		*dat*	
26.		[ʒ]	television		*telivijan*	[dʒ]
27.	Sequence	[aʊn]	bounce		*bongks*	[ɔŋk]
28.			down		*dong*	[ɔŋ]
29.	Clusters: initial s+	s + m	smile		*sumail*	

(*Table 3.1 continues*)

Table 3.1. Inventories of sounds: JC and JE (*continued*)

Ref		Segment	JE Example	Translation	Possible JC Example	
30.		s + n	snake		*siniek*	
31.		s + p	spit		*pit*	
32.		s + t	stick		*tik*	
33.		s + k	skin		*kin*	
34.	medial changed	d + l	middle		*migl*	
35.		t + l	title		*taikl*	
36.	final dropped	cons+d	land, old		*lan, uol*	
37.		cons+p	crisp		*kris*	
38.		cons+t	must		*mos*	
39.	Special case of "r"					
40.	initial dr → j	[dʒɹ]	drum		*jom*	[dʒ]
41.	tr → ch	[tʃɹ]	truck		*chok*	[tʃ]
42.	medial	[aɹ]	marble		*maabl*	[aː]
43.		[əɹ]	bird		*bod*	[ɔ]
44.		[ɔɹ]	horse		*aas*	[aː]
45.	final -or, -ar, -er	[ə] or [əɹ]	dollar		*dala*	[a]

For consonants, initial s-clusters containing a nasal consonant undergo vowel epenthesis ('sm' and 'sn' in line entries 29 and 30) in JC, resulting in the reduction of the cluster, for example, *smail* > *sumail*. There is also a tendency in first language acquisition cross-linguistically to reduce consonant clusters in this and other ways, presumably since they appear to be more difficult to pronounce (see Clark 2003, 115, for instance). However, only one CLAR child (from rural St Mary) used the epenthetic *sumaal* 'small'. He used this form six times in the first four visits.[2] The only other word in the CLAR files with an epenthetic vowel was *sumail* 'smile'. This was used once, and the non-epenthetic counterpart *smail*, twelve times.

Similarly, the children often do not drop the initial /s/ in initial s-clusters where the consonant following /s/ is non-nasal ('sp', 'st' and 'sk', as in line entries 31–33), thus preserving the cluster, despite the JC tendency to reduce such clusters. There is even an instance in the CLAR data, known to exist in adult JC, where the initial s-cluster appears, though it does not exist in the JE counterpart: *stanjariin* 'tangerine'.

The sound [h] is absent from the table. It is of importance in a discussion of the differences between JC and JE pronunciation, however, since there are cases where it is used in JE, but absent in JC. This is commonly known as h-dropping.[3] As is typical also in dialects of English, the converse is equally true; that is, there are cases of the sound [h] occurring in JC in contexts where it is absent in JE. I now discuss this briefly from the point of view of the production of [h] in relation to written forms.

There is no [h] in the JC counterparts of some JE words where the sequence [h]+vowel begins an initial or medial syllable. An example of [h]+vowel appearing medially is 'behave' 'be-have'; [h] does not appear in JC *biiev*.

In the CLAR data, h-dropping occurs in all but 5.7 per cent of the words in which this sound would be pronounced in their JE counterparts. An example is JE 'house', JC *ous*. I note that h-dropping is said not to be characteristic of the JC spoken in St Elizabeth, a western parish in Jamaica. In line with this, CLAR children from St Elizabeth did not drop the initial /h/.[4]

There were only two instances of the converse, that is, initial [h] occurring in words, the JE counterparts of which have no [h]. These are *heg* 'egg', *haki* 'ackee'. It is likely that these forms were heard by the children, since they may form a regular part of the input; or it may be that these are examples of hypercorrection on the part of these child-learners.

The interest here in the similarities and the differences between the sound systems of JC and JE lies in their contribution to identifying blurred boundaries between the two languages. We now see that a wide range of variants occurs in the children's speech, indicative of this blurring.

3.1.1 Languages to Which Forms in the Children's Vocabulary Relate

As has been noted, the CLAR data are coded for language.[5] There are three major language codes: JC, JE and SH(ared). These major categories and their subcategories will be discussed in this section. Note that all words uttered by the children, including JE forms, were transcribed using the Cassidy-JLU orthography.

Setting aside words such as *alo* 'hello' and *babai* 'bye-bye' – termed *communicators* in CHILDES – and fillers such as *aahm*, 69.7 per cent of all occurrences of tokens used by the CLAR children are JC forms, 12.8 per cent are JE, and 17.5 per cent, SH. This indicates clearly that JC is the dominant language in terms of the lexicon. I begin with a discussion of the category JC.

As an English-lexified language, in many cases a JC word may have originated as an English word and later been incorporated into the JC phonological system. An example of such a word might be *bied* 'bathe'. Following table 3.1, we can predict how 'bathe' would incorporate into the JC phonological system: there is no consonant [ð] in JC, so this would be replaced by [d] (line entry 25). Similarly, there is no vowel [e:] in JC; instead, this would be replaced by the diphthong [ie] (line entry 4). These two changes would have resulted in the JC sequence *bied*.

There was a handful (twenty-five types) of words in the data thought to exist only in JC. Some, such as *frak* 'dress', may have been derived originally from English, but are no longer in use in contemporary JE, and therefore not readily associated with English. Others, such as *anansi* 'spider' are of African origin. These words belong to the subcategory of JC, "JConly".[6]

Several JConly words were used far less frequently than were their JE counterparts. JE *wai* 'why' was used eighty-one times, for instance, and its JConly phrasal counterpart *wa mek* (lit. what makes) only seven times. In addition, JConly *nyam* 'eat' was used only five times, while the JC variant *it* was used fifty-seven times and the SHared variant *iit* 464 times. JConly *gyal* was used three times, but the JE *gorl* 625 times, including twelve uses of the plural *gorlz*.

In some cases, these JConly words were used with distinctly different meanings. The contexts in which the JConly words *nyam* 'eat' and *gyal* 'girl' were used, for example, suggest that they were chosen for negative emphasis: *gyal* was used in a derogatory sense, suggesting that the girl is ill-mannered (as in [1] below),[7] while *nyam* was used more in the sense of 'gobble' (2). Note that in (2) AMA first used *iit*, and then corrected herself using *nyam*, presumably for dramatic effect.

(1) DON: *cho   mi   kyaahn bada   wid da   gyal ya.*
            forget it 1S.SUBJ can.NEG bother with DEM girl DEM
            'Forget it, I can't bother with this girl.' [V6-KN1-JE:l.376-3;11.12]

(2) INV: so, why will he fly from the dog?

     AMA: *&bikaaz i   daag aa &iit   nyam im.*[8]
             &because DEF dog FUT &eat eat.up 3S.OBJ
             'The dog is going to gobble him up.'   [V6-SMR-JE:ll 63ff.-3;8.26]

Other JConly words such as *juk* 'stab; inject', *pikni* 'child' and *tiif* 'steal' were the only variants chosen, without any occurrences of their JE counterparts.

The second category, JE, includes JES (JE segment) forms. For a word to be categorized as JES, it must have a JC counterpart which is recognizably derived from JE. It may not be the form used in JE, yet does contain segments which exist in JE (forms at the JE pole of the continuum), but not in JC (at the JC pole). The result is a word-internal superficial weave. I use 'bathe' again as an example. The JC form, as discussed above, is *bied*. A JES variant would be *beed*, containing the JE vowel [e:] but not the JE final consonant [ð].

This is not to suggest that the children's speech today has been influenced necessarily by JE, and that, as a result, they are creating novel forms with L2 interference. These are not child forms, but forms which may be used regularly in adult speech. As a result, the children would have been exposed to them in the input, given the extreme variation said to characterize the speech of Jamaicans (see chapter 1 for discussion).

Some of these words have many variants. The JC counterpart of the JE 'horse', for example, was pronounced in seven different ways by the children, involving variants of all four sound segments as seen in (3) below. The form in (3)1 is the JC form, and that in (3)7 is JE, spelled using the Cassidy-JLU orthography; all other forms vary with respect to a combination of the vowel and the presence or absence of the initial 'h' or the 'r'.

(3) 1. *aas*   (**JC**- h-drop, long vowel *aa*, no 'r')   58 occurrences

    2. *aws*   (JES- JC h-drop, no r; JE vowel)   2

    3. *aars*   (JES- JC h-drop, *aa*; JE 'r')   2

    4. *ars*   (JES- JC h-drop; JE short vowel, 'r')   13

    5. *haas*   (JES- JC *aa*, no 'r'; JE 'h')   1

    6. *ors*   (JES- JC h-drop; JE vowel, 'r')   6

    7. *hors*   (**JE**- all JE segments)   7   Total: 89

In the example in (3), there were eighty-nine tokens for the type 'horse', of which fifty-eight (or 65.2 per cent) were JC. This was a characteristic pattern of overall usage.[9] It is difficult to place some variants at points along a continuum between JC and JE with any certainty – should *aws* in (3) have been placed in third position instead of in second, for instance, and on what basis? To complicate matters further, [h] can be called on for emphasis by the JC speaker, so *haas* may not necessarily be a JES. In that case, might it be better to assign it to second position, classified as a JC variant?[10]

Another example is the JC temporal adverb *ye-si-de*, JE 'yes-ter-day'. Table 3.2 shows nine forms used by children, teachers and investigators; of these, children used seven, omitting the two bolded entries. I note the following trends: the first syllable 'ye-' is represented in all variants; the initial consonant 't' of the second JE syllable appears in all but the "most" JC *yeside*, but the vowel in this syllable varies between /i/ /u/ and /a/; the consonant beginning the third and final syllable appears throughout, but the vowel varies between /e/ /ie/ (JC) and /e:/ (JE).

Native speaker consultants have agreed that *yeside* is the regularly used JC form. I note that the JC variant *yesidie* was not used by the children.[11] Given the data presented here, it may be argued that *yestude* is a JC variant, since it is the most frequently occurring form. In addition, since /t/ appears in 71.8 per cent (or 28/39) of total variants, perhaps this is becoming a regular form.

Superficial weaves need not take place within the word only, but may involve the manipulation of the words themselves. This is superficial weaving at the lexical level. It may be the case, for instance, that a JC word is used within a JE construction as in (4), or the reverse, that is a JE word within an otherwise JC utterance as in (5). In (4a) and (5a), differences between the JE and JC lexical items lie in pronunciation: JC /lɪkl/, JE /lɪtl/ and JC /ya:d/, JE /ya:rd/, respectively.

Table 3.2. Variants of *yeside* 'yesterday'

Variant	Language	Tokens
yeside	JC	11
yestide		6
yestude		12
yestade		2
yestudie		2
yestadie		2
yestudee		1
yesterdie		1
yesterdee	JE	2

In addition, in (5a), there are semantic differences – 'yard' is not used in JE to mean 'house', but the land around the house, or perhaps a courtyard. In (4b) and (5b) the words in the two languages are very different one from the other: in (4b), the JC word (*bagi*) is chosen over JE 'panty', whereas in (5b) JES *ort* 'hurt' is chosen over its JC counterpart *bon* 'burn'.

(4a) NAT: *won iz   likl.*
              one COP little
              'One is little.'   [V1-MOB:l.325-3;5.3]

(4b) GAB: *laik   a   bagi tuu.*
              like   INDEF panty too
              'Like a panty, too.'   [V4-SER:l.579-3;9.27]

(5a) OSS: *op a ihn   yaard*
              up at 3s.POSS yard
              'Up at his house.'   [V5-MOB:l.651-3;7.14]

(5b) OSS: *mi* [/] *mi ed   wehn de   ort mi ...*
              1s.SUBJ   head PAST PROG hurt 1s.OBJ
              'My head was hurting me ...'   [V5-MOB:l.299-3;7.14]

The data are also coded for the JE subcategory "loan", &LO. A word is considered to be an LO if it is in common use in JE but not does not have an English-derived counterpart in JC. Together, they accounted for 0.1 per cent of all words. There were 91 LOs (types) used 455 times (tokens). Examples are *byuutiful* 'beautiful' and *sliipi* 'sleepy'. Loans which had then undergone phonological incorporation into JC are coded &CLO. There were 41 CLO types and 113 tokens. Examples are *udi* 'hoodie' and *ruobot* 'robot'.

The third and final category, SHared forms, consists of words used regularly in both languages, and having sequences of consonants and vowels which are shared by both. A consequence is that it is difficult to categorize them with any certainty as forming part of either the JC or the JE lexicon.

There are instances of SHared words which have taken on meanings in JC which differ from those associated with them in JE. These constitute 5 per cent of the SHared words used by the children.[12] An example is the verb *chat* 'chat'. In JE, this refers to engaging in a conversation which is friendly and informal, whereas in JC, it is used simply to mean 'talk', as seen in (6) below.

(6)   GAB: *im   n-   aa   chat tu mi.*
             3s.SUBJ NEG-PROG chat to 1s.OBJ
             'He's not talking to me.'   [V6-SER:l 64-4;0.0]

Table 3.3 summarizes overall variation among lexical words.

We see that of the 645 JC types[13] used by the children, 313 or 48.5 per cent had variants. Further, 257 or 82.1 per cent of all 313 words with variants contained JESs. All differences in JC/JE vowel and consonant segments and clusters listed in table 3.1 were involved in these variations. The great number of variants possible would all be potentially confusing for the JC learner of JE as a second language, in terms of which sequence "belongs" to JC and which to JE.

I note that it is not the case, however, that all words with these segment differences were susceptible to variation. The JC diphthong /ie/ in *tiel* 'tail' was preserved and the JC vowel /a/ in *blak* 'block' never varied with JE /ɔ/. This would likely be due to lack of sufficient evidence from the input, either because adults do not vary in their production of these forms or, perhaps more likely, because they are not words of high frequency use.

In sharp contrast, there is minimal variation among SHared words – only 8.1 per cent or thirty-three of all SHared types have variants. The use of eponyms, hypercorrections or JC variants account for this variation. Examples are the

Table 3.3. Examples of types of variants of JC lexical words

Words	# Types	%	Example of JC Word	Example of JES or SH Words
JC and SH forms exist; no other variants	56	8.7	*fambili* 'family'	*famili* (SH)
JES forms have variants	211	32.7	*uom* 'home'	*hoom ~ oom ~ huom*
JC and JES forms both have variants	46	7.1	*waata ~ wata* 'water'	*waator ~ waador ~ waater ~ water*
Subtotal	313	48.5		
JC with no variants	332	51.5	*se* 'say'	
Total	645	100.0		

eponym *lasco* used in addition to the SH *milk*, and *bog*, a hypercorrection of the SH *bag*. JC variants include lexical forms such as *frak* used alongside the SH *jres* 'dress', as well as phonological forms, such as JC *puun* alongside SH *spuun* 'spoon'.

SHared forms exist only for lexical categories, that is, nouns, verbs, adjectives and adverbs.[14]

In the discussion of the variants of JC *aas* 'horse', it was indicated earlier that the language of the majority of forms used by the CLAR children is JC, and that this is an overall characteristic of their speech. There are cases where JES variants outnumber their JC counterparts, however. Table 3.4 shows relative numbers of tokens for word initial and word final clusters of consonant+/r/.

It may be that the JES variants have been used to this extent under influence of the code-mixing evident in the investigators' speech.[15] Indeed, trends are similar in the investigators' speech: as an example, there were 481 occurrences of JES *berd* by investigators, with sixteen of the plural *berdz*, and only one instance of JC *bod*. This may point to changing trends in what ought to be considered JC for these forms, as well as for lexical items such as *gorl* 'girl' discussed above, though verification would be required from a far larger sample, including adult speech, before making such a claim.

Table 3.4. JES variants outnumbering JC: [consonant + /r/]

TOKENS	Translation	JC	JC Tokens	JES Tokens	JES Variant
481	drive	*jaiv*	9	472	*j**r**aiv*
187	truck	*chok*	86	101	*ch**r**ok*
111	drink (v)	*jingk*	3	108	*j**r**ingk*
67	tractor	*chakta*	21	46	*ch**r**akta* 37; *ch**r**aktor* 7; *chakt**or** 2
41	drink (n)	*jingkz˙*	1	40	*j**r**ingkz*
269	bird	*bod*	–	269	*be**rd***
100	work (v)	*wok*	2	98	*we**rk***
85	dark	*daak*	2	83	*daa**rk***
73	church	*choch*	1	72	*che**rch***
68	work (n)	*wok*	1	67	*we**rk***
33	dirt	*dot*	–	33	*de**rt***
31	shirt	*shot*	2	29	*sh**e**rt**

˙ *"z" indicates plurality regardless of pronunciation.*

3.2 The Categorial Composition of the Children's Vocabulary

Children usually produce their first words sometime between 0;10 and 1;3. After the appearance of first words, most add words to their vocabulary slowly at first, but with increasing speed as they approach the achievement of a fifty-word vocabulary, between ages 1;3 and 2;0 (Hoff [2005] 2009, 188). This results in the average two-year-old having a vocabulary of two hundred to three hundred words (Peccei 2006, 16).

Gentner's (1982) seminal work on the lexical acquisition of English and five other languages, shows for all languages that nouns are the predominant early forms. She calls this the *nominal bias* (p. 321), with the earliest occurrences consisting mainly of names for individual objects and beings. She suggests (p. 328) that nouns have a transparent semantic mapping to objects in the perceptual-conceptual world, and so are coherent and stable. Since the child has already formed object concepts, having spent much of the first year of life in social interaction around objects and in object exploration, she need only match words and concepts, when acquiring nouns. In contrast, verbs and other predicate words have a less transparent relation to the perceptual world and require more time to acquire, since their meanings cannot be learned independently of the semantic system of the language (Imai et al. 2006, 451).

Studies of children's early vocabulary differ with regard to the organization of word categories. By way of an introduction to issues surrounding that categorization, I now discuss the approaches of Gentner (1982) and, more recently, of Dhillon (2010), highlighting how they may inform an approach to the CLAR data. I also refer to De Lisser's (2015, 51–63) analysis of the lexical composition of her study of six JC-speaking children. I use the data of five of her children whose ages are comparable, though with a lower upper range than those of the CLAR children; the five children fall also into her highest mean length of utterance (MLU) [16] category of 4.5 or greater.

Gentner (1982, 305) divided words into four categories. The first, nominal terms, includes what would be classified in adult language as common and proper nouns. The second, predicate terms, include (adult) verbs, prepositions and modifiers (adjectives and adverbs). Gentner (1982, 302n1) justifies creating the umbrella category predicate terms with the claim that the distinctions among predicate classes are rather fluid compared to the distinction between nominals and predicates. The third category, expressive terms, includes forms which function to express a feeling in a direct way (for example, "ouch"), or

Table 3.5. Make-up of the CLAR lexicon: Lexical vs. functional

Category	Tokens	%
Lexical	56,579	46.4
Functional	65,418	53.6
Total:	121,997	100.0

terms which form part of a ritual (for example, "bye-bye"). Finally, indeterminate terms have ambiguous or multiple usage.

These four categories are all lexical. Gentner's (1982) study was of patterns in early vocabularies, and, as such, data were collected from children as young as 1;2. Only one child was older than 2;0 (2;5), and the sample of words used by this child was fifteen. It is well known that function words such as pronouns, auxiliaries and determiners are extremely rare in the first stages of lexical development (Caselli et al. 1995, 180), constituting less than 5 per cent of all words used in the first and second years of life. Thus, as one would expect, no pronouns or auxiliaries were included in Gentner's data.

Functional categories form a large part of the speech of the CLAR three-year-olds, however, and must therefore be included in any discussion of the composition of the lexicon. This is illustrated in table 3.5, where we see that functional items constitute more than half of the total token count of the children. To arrive at these numbers, nouns, verbs, adjectives and adverbs were included as lexical categories; pronouns, auxiliaries, copulas, modals, gerunds, conjunctions, determiners, prepositions, verbal particles, quantifiers, relative pronouns, negators, infinitives and complementizers were included as functional categories.

Gentner's category *indeterminate* would also be problematic for the CLAR data. As is typical of Creole languages, there are numerous forms which would fall into a category comprising multifunctional elements. These would include *a*, for instance, which functions in at least the following ways in adult JC, and which has been used grammatically with all those functions by the CLAR children:

(7)   **focus marker**

OSS: *a   yuu   mash op im   kyaar.*
        FOC 2S.SUBJ mash up 3S.POSS car
        'You're the one who destroyed his car.'   [V3-MOB:1 1004-3;4.15]

(8)   **lexical verb**

    BRI: *mi   no   a   waata in de.*
             1s.SUBJ NEG have water in there
             'I don't have any water in there.'   [V1-AN2:l 505-3;7.29]

(9)   **copula**

    OSS: *mi   a   dangki*
             1s.SUBJ COP donkey
             'I'm a donkey.'   [V6-MOB:l 422-3;8.12]

(10)   **aspect marker** – progressive (also habitual, iterative (see section 5.2.1))

    KHA: *bikaaz im   a   laaf.*
             because 3s.SUBJ PROG laugh
             'Because he's laughing.'   [V3-SMR:l 514-3;6.14]

(11)   **preposition** – translated into JE as 'of', 'at', 'in', 'on', 'to'

    GAB: *mek   mi   kuk sohn [/] sohn tin a   suup.*
             make 1s.SUBJ cook some   some tin **OF** soup
             'Let me cook some tins of soup.'   [V2-SER:l 194-3;7.4]

    ODA: *shi   de   a   yaad.*
             3s.SUBJ COP **AT** yard
             'She's at home.'   [V2-KN1:l 49-3;3.27]

    KHA: *di   man we   de a big klaas.*
             DEF man REL COP **IN** big class
             'The man who is in the big class.'   [V6-SMR:l 468-3;10.6]

    SEB: *... kaa   i   jrap a   grong.*
             ... because 3s.SUBJ drop **ON** ground
             '... because it fell on the ground.'   [V2-AN1:l 387-3;3.22]

    BRI: *im   a   gu we   a Uochi.*
             3s.SUBJ PROG go away **TO** Ocho Rios
             'He's going away to Ocho Rios.'   [V2-AN2:l 510-3;9.17]

This is not an unusual phenomenon in JC. Note also, for instance, another multifunctional element such as *fi* used as infinitive particle, preposition 'for', possessive, modal verb and complementizer.

Another example of what Gentner terms Indeterminate would be the use of English 'pee' as either a nominal ('a pee') or as a predicate term ('to pee'). This is the result of conversion, the word-formation process which changes the word class of existing words, but not their form (Valera 2006, 172). Conversion differs from affixation, another common means of deriving a new word. As suggested by the name, affixation involves the addition of a morpheme. So, for example, the noun 'driver' in JE is derived from the verb 'drive' by the addition of the agentive suffix -er.[17] In contrast, in conversion, a word is derived by changing the syntactic class, but without the use of an added affix. For this reason, it is also known as zero derivation. This word formation strategy is widespread in English, and is one of the early strategies used by children. Clark (1993, 145) explains this early use as being in keeping with the principles of transparency and simplicity, which she claims guide child word formation: transparency will lead children to form new words from known elements, and guided by simplicity, they will make the fewest changes possible when creating words.

Conversion is said to be one of the most widely employed strategies for new word formation in Pidgins and Creoles (see, for example, Plag 2006, 306), enriching the lexicon by using apparently semantically and syntactically underspecified forms in different syntactic environments (Plag 2009, 355). Plag (ibid., 355n16) indicates that in Valdman's (1981) Haitian dictionary, for instance, more than three hundred forms are identified as belonging to more than one syntactic category.

The CLAR children used just under one hundred different forms as both nouns and verbs. They include those used regularly in adult JC, as well as novel[18] word creations such as *kyuuteks*, an eponym formed from the brand Cutex, to refer both to the polish and to the activity of polishing nails.

Well-known also in Creoles, and commonly occurring in the CLAR data, is both the adjectival and verbal use of forms which, in JE, represent only adjectives. In (12) below, for example, ODA indicates that her ears are 'soring' her. In (13), the teacher clarifies for the investigator that when the child JES answered *beks* 'upset' (verbal) to the question *we dem a du?* 'What are they doing?', she really meant that they were upset.

(12) ODA: *mi   iez   a   suor mi.*
      1S.POSS ears PROG sore 1S.OBJ
      'My ears are sore.'   [V6-KN1:l 572-3;8.14]

(13) INV: *we   dem   a   du?*
      what 3PL.SUBJ PROG do
      'What are they doing?'

JES: _beks_.
       'Upset.'

INV: dem   a   du wa,   beks?
       3PL.SUBJ PROG do what, upset
       'They are doing what? Upset?'

JES: ye.
       yes

TEA: shi   se dem   veks.
       3S.SUBJ say 3S.SUBJ upset
       'She said they're upset.'   [V3-ADR:l 246-3;3.13]

That such forms, used only adjectivally in JE, are verbal in JC is underlined by the use of the verb 'do' by the investigator in her question:

(14) INV: so if i   no   kliin _wa   i   du_?
             so if 3s.SUBJ NEG clean what 3s.SUBJ do
             'So, if it's not clean, what is it [lit. what does it do]?'

KAM: _dorti_.
       'Dirty.'   [V6J-CLA:ll 402ff.-4;1.9]

Such usage is prevalent in adult JC, and suggests, therefore, that the children have internalized morphological rules of new word formation. For this reason, it is considered that the words so used by the CLAR children ought to be included in their respective contextually determined lexical categories and not relegated to an "indeterminate" category.

    I now investigate the system of classification used by Dhillon (2010). He follows Caselli et al. (1995) in counting noun and verb categories in the way they are counted in adult language. This is not to say that it is assumed that the categories exist in the mind of the child, necessarily. Instead, they are simply used as a short-hand way of referring to semantic, grammatical and/or phonological differences in the input to which the child is exposed (Caselli et al. 1995, 192).

    Dhillon (2010) examined the noun bias among English-, Spanish- and Mandarin-speaking children at three age levels.[19] He established three categories of word types: nouns, verbs and "other" (p. 55). For him, the noun bias is taken to mean that nouns form the majority of children's early vocabularies (p. 51), and the aim of the study was to determine whether there was a noun or a verb bias evident in the children's vocabulary. As a result, the category "other" included adjectives, adverbs, conjunctions (such as 'and' and 'or'), prepositions, determiners "and the like" (p. 55), that is, presumably all word categories other than nouns and verbs. He excluded onomatopoeic words, and other portions of speech which were difficult to categorize. In his count of nouns, in addition to common and proper nouns, he included pronouns, and for verbs, in addition to lexical verbs, he included auxiliary verbs and gerunds.[20] Applying Dhillon's (2010) categorization to the CLAR data to determine bias yields the results shown in table 3.6.

The measure used for determining bias is the noun-verb ratio, computed using proportions, as shown in columns 3 and 5 of the table. The proportion of nouns, for instance, is the number of tokens or types divided by the total. The noun-verb ratio is calculated as the proportion of nouns divided by the sum of the proportion of nouns and the proportion of verbs (0.46/(0.25+0.30)), or 0.65. A noun bias is indicated when the result of this calculation is greater than 0.50 and a verb bias when it is less than 0.50.[21] The result of 0.65 for the CLAR children indicates a strong noun bias relative to verb tokens; when calculated relative to verb type, the result is an even stronger bias of 0.80.[22]

De Lisser (2015) adopts Radford's (1990) classification of lexical categories as comprising nouns, verbs, prepositions and adverbs (including the subclass adjective), but adds pronouns within this domain. She includes determiners, inflections (taken to be tense and aspect markers, for instance) and complementizers as functional categories. The data (tokens only) that she provided for the most advanced of her children are as follows: 20,871 nouns (including pronouns), 10,742 verbs (lexical verbs only), and 14,832 other (prepositions, adjectives, determiners, complementizers and inflections). The noun bias

Table 3.6. Tokens and types: Dhillon (2010) applied to the CLAR data

Category	Tokens	Proportion	Types	Proportion
Noun	55,734	0.46	1,752	0.71
Verb	30,109	0.25	431	0.17
Other	36,154	0.30	285	0.12
Total	121,997		2,468	

for this group of children would be 0.55, or just under the 0.60 of the CLAR children.[23]

There is a caution that the bias may be cultural. A strong noun bias seems to be consistently evident in the acquisition of English (see Bornstein et al. 2004, 1116–20, for a review); however, children acquiring Japanese and Mandarin have been found to show less of a noun bias than children acquiring English. In a study focusing on object play and involving Japanese and American mothers playing with their children at home, Fernald and Morikawa (1993, 649–50) found that American mothers label objects more frequently and consistently, and tend to emphasize the names of the objects. In contrast, Japanese mothers were found to use objects to engage infants in rituals of social exchange and to emphasize verbal politeness routines.

Importantly, Tardif, Gelman and Xu (1999) show that the bias depends on a variety of factors, including the methods used to sample the vocabularies as well as the contexts in which the observations occur – regardless of the language spoken, vocabularies were dominated by nouns when children were engaged in book reading, but not when they were playing with toys.

Data results which would allow for a conclusion regarding the influence of the nature of interactions with children on noun bias are not available for either the CLAR data or for De Lisser (2015), the two studies on Jamaican child language syntax currently available. Two comments, however, with regard to the ways in which the CLAR data were elicited would seem to suggest lack of methodological influence in this regard. First, the children were involved both in book reading, and in playing with toys (see section 1.2.2 for details). Second, investigators asked just over 1,763 questions using the question word *wa?* 'what'. Of these, 757 or 42.9 per cent would most likely result in the production of nouns; they included *a wa ...?* ('What is it?'), *dat a/dis a wa?* ('What's this/that?'), and those eliciting an object such as *waahn wa?* ('Want what?'). This suggests a balance in object and non-object elicitation.

Tables 3.7–3.9 show the breakdowns of the CLAR data for each of the three main categories represented in table 3.6 (viz. nouns [table 3.7], verbs [table 3.8], other [3.9]), with an indication in each case of the percentages of total category which their subcategories represent. Categorization is based on Dhillon (2010).

I note that lexical nouns (total tokens 27,442) include common nouns (23,048), proper nouns (1,966), compounds (1,167), *pluralia tantum* nouns[24] (1,194) and letters of the alphabet (67). Note also that pronouns are considered to be nominal by Dhillon, as they can be used to replace nouns, but they are classified as non-lexical nouns, and that the count for possessive pronouns

Table 3.7. The make-up of the nominal domain (tokens)

Nouns	Tokens	% Total	% Pronouns
Lexical	27,442	49.2	
Pronouns:			
Personal	18,339	32.9	64.8
Demonstrative	2,872	5.2	10.2
Locative	714	1.3	2.5
Possessive	3,153	5.7	11.1
wh-	1,435	2.6	5.1
Indefinite	1,664	3.0	5.9
Reflexive	115	0.2	0.4
Total:	55,734	100.0	100.0

Table 3.8. The make-up of the verbal domain (tokens)

Verbs	Tokens	% Total
Lexical	21,975	73.0
Auxiliaries	5,222	17.3
Copula	1,717	5.7
Modals	1,181	3.9
Gerunds	14	0.0
Total:	30,109	100.0

actually includes both possessive adjectives and possessive pronouns occurring in the data (see section 4.4 for discussion).

Following Dhillon, gerunds were included not as nouns, but as verbs. As we might expect, there were very few gerunds in the CLAR data – a total of only fourteen across all files.[25]

Dhillon (2010), includes pronouns in the lexical noun count, and auxiliaries in the lexical verb count. The classification of pronouns as lexical is questionable, and Dhillon does not provide theoretical justification for it. Pronouns have been treated by many as D constituents, and therefore functional, since Postal (1966) and Abney (1987). Radford (1997, 42–43) considers that because they lack descriptive content, they are "clearly" functional categories. The same

Table 3.9. The make-up of the category Other (tokens)

"Other"	Tokens	% Total
Determiners	10,096	27.9
Prepositions	7,482	20.7
Adverbs	4,436	12.3
Conjunctions	3,045	8.4
Adjectives	2,726	7.5
Focus marker *a*	2,517	7.0
Verbal particles	2,230	6.2
Negators	2,165	6.0
Quantifiers	669	1.9
Infinitive	618	1.7
Complementizers	170	0.5
Total:	36,154	100.0

would apply for auxiliaries, which traditionally have been considered to be functional. If so, this would mean that functional categories are included within lexical ones.

Nonetheless, that lexical nouns and pronouns ought to be categorized together may be justified since they serve the same functions in the utterance, and that lexical verbs and auxiliaries ought also to be categorized together since auxiliaries are commonly thought to form a verbal subcategory. This would allow for discussion of the "nominal" and the "verbal" domains, crossing a strict lexical–functional divide. In recognition of the basic categorical lexical–functional distinction, the breakdown of categories in tables 3.5 and 3.6 includes non-lexical nouns and verbs, but subtotals "lexical" elements separately.

The category "other" includes adverbs. In JC, these play an important role in establishing tense as well as aspect.[26] As shown in table 3.9, our children produced a total of 4,436 adverb tokens.

The type count of different adverbs used was ninety-two, and included interrogative wh- (such as *we* 'where'), temporal (*yeside* 'yesterday') and locative (*de* 'there') adverbs.[27]

Table 3.9 includes a second lexical category in addition to adverbs – adjectives. Adjectives are a small category for our children, with relatively few occurrences when compared to other lexical categories. The use of adjectives by the children is discussed in section 3.3.[28]

3.3 Adjectival Modification

It is common in discussions of structure to distinguish between attributive and predicative adjectives. Attributive adjectives form a constituent with the noun, and immediately precede it in JC and JE. An example is _likl_ _baks_ 'little box'. Predicative adjectives form part of the predicate in JE, in the form subject + copula + adjective. A JE example would be 'The box is little'. In this section, I discuss the use of attributive adjectives in the CLAR data.

We saw in section 3.2 that the CLAR children exhibit a noun bias, as is reported in first language acquisition for some cultures. Even though there is this relatively fast and seemingly errorless acquisition of object names, it is reported in the literature that children are slow to acquire adjectives modifying those nouns (Sandhofer and Smith 2007, 234). Fenson et al. (1994, 95) report that by thirty months, 9.8 per cent of the production of 620 words by the American children in that study are adjectives. Only 3.3 per cent of the vocabulary of the CLAR children are adjectives, though the youngest is three months older than the oldest children in the Fenson et al. study.

Difficulties children face when acquiring adjectives may be due to the fact that the semantic content denoted by them is diverse (Klibanoff and Waxman 1998, 443). This diversity is captured by the Dixon and Aikhenvald (2004, 3–4) categorization of four core types of semantic content (dimension, age, value, colour) and three peripheral types (physical property, human propensity, speed) as follows:

(15)   Dimension: 'big' 'small' 'long' 'tall' 'short' 'wide' 'deep'

   Age: 'new' 'young' 'old'

   Value: 'good' 'bad' 'lovely' 'atrocious' 'perfect' 'proper/real'

   'odd' 'strange' 'curious' 'necessary' 'important' 'lucky'

   Colour: 'black' 'white' 'red'

Physical Property:

   'hard' 'soft' 'heavy' 'wet' 'rough' 'strong' 'clean' 'hot' 'sour'

   'well' 'sick' 'tired' 'dead' 'absent' (corporeal properties)

Human Propensity:

'jealous' 'happy' 'kind' 'clever' 'generous' 'cruel' 'proud'

Speed: 'fast' 'quick' 'slow'

What this suggests is that there is no one principle guiding children to interpret an adjective with regard to the type of property they can expect it to describe. This is unlike the noun, which children appear as a general rule to interpret as a name for a basic-level object category (Klibanoff and Waxman 1998, 443, and references there).

Another problem raised by Klibanoff and Waxman (ibid.) is the notion of relative adjectives. An example is 'big', which does not refer to a particular size. For example, there is a great difference in size between a big elephant and a big ant. In these cases, then, the child will need to realize that there is no absolute application of the meaning. Instead, the meaning will vary according to the object to which it is applied.

Klibanoff and Waxman (2000, 650) show that many adjectives used by children refer to properties of objects that are readily evident from simple perceptual observation, adjectives such as 'wet' and 'hot', for instance. The corresponding semantic types for Dixon and Aikhenvald (2004) which represent such properties would be primarily dimension, age, colour and physical property.

Table 3.10 applies these categories to the CLAR data, and ranks the top twenty adjectives in terms of frequency of use. It is important to note that the category chosen relates in each case to the assumed canonical (adult) meaning of the adjective. There was a range of meanings covered by some of them, however, such that categorization elsewhere as well would be appropriate.[29] For example, big 'big', the adjective most commonly used by the children, did not only identify objects in relation to their size. It was used, in addition, to modify sista 'sister' with the meaning of "older", ruop 'rope' (meaning "long" or perhaps "thick"), klaas 'class' and skuul 'school' ("more advanced"), moni 'money' ("a bill of a high denomination"), sii 'sea' ("open"), naiz 'noise' ("loud"), ier 'hair' and ed 'head'[30] ("thick" or perhaps "fluffy") and as an antonym of maaga 'skinny'.

The table shows that all but six of the top twenty most frequently used adjectives[31] fall into the perceptual categories of dimension, colour and physical property. The only two adjectives in the semantic class Dimension are those describing objects as being big or little; these top the ranking. Seven of the twenty adjectives represent colours.[32] Physical properties relate to being dirty, dead, painful, sick and hungry. Adjectives falling in age, the other perceptual category, were *nyuu* 'new', *uol* 'old'. They do not appear in the table, since they ranked below 20, but they did appear in the top fifty; *yong* 'young' ranked below that.

Two of the adjectives categorized as values might arguably fall instead under physical property; these are 'pretty' and 'ugly', and so the only categories which could not be considered to be evident from simple perceptual observation are *nais* 'nice', *frieda* 'afraid of', *gud* 'good' and *redi* 'ready'.

That the children in the Fenson et al. (1994) study, who are younger than the youngest CLAR child, use far more adjectives than do the CLAR children, suggests a seemingly restricted expressive vocabulary among the latter. In addition,

Table 3.10. Top twenty adjectives used by the CLAR children (frequency-based)

Adjective		Rank	Semantic Type
JC	JE		
big	big	1	Dimension
likl, luku, litl	little	2	Dimension
priti	pretty	3	Value
bluu	blue	4	Colour
dorti, doti	dirty	5	Physical property
ogli	ugly	6	Value
red	red	7	Colour
ded	dead	8	Physical property
nais	nice	9	Value
griin	green	10	Colour
pingk	pink	11	Colour
blak	black	12	Colour
at	painful (< hot)	13	Physical property
sik	sick	14	Physical property
frieda	afraid (of)	15	Human propensity
yelo	yellow	16	Colour
gud	good	17	Value
redi	ready	18	Speed (?)
onggri	hungry	19	Physical property
wait	white	20	Colour

Note: The JC *likl* ranked third on its own. Since this is a ranking of semantic types (that is, based on meaning and not form), the variants *luku*, a child form, and *litl*, a JES, were included. These variants both appeared also in the top twenty; their inclusion brought the type "little" to second place.

the wide range of meanings ascribed to a single adjective, as discussed for *big*, is reminiscent of the so-called neutral adjective 'nice': its use is traditionally discouraged by teachers of writing who promote the use instead of words which express the desired quality more precisely. This is an area of potential concern, given that expressive writing has its roots in expressive speech (Britton 1982, 97).

3.4 Word Formation Strategies

Smith, Jones and Landau (1996, 144) indicate that children typically learn object names by having parents point to an object in view and label it. This is one of the miracles of the acquisition of language – that even after hearing a single object named only once, and accompanied by no explanation or training, very young children are able to master word learning.

Children must also master the processes which the language they are acquiring uses to derive new words from existing words. In section 3.2, I discussed conversion and the extent to which it is used in Creole languages and by the CLAR children. In the following sections, I look at derivation (3.4.1) and at how the children fill lexical gaps (3.4.2).[33]

3.4.1 Derivational Affixation

Derivation is the word formation process which creates a new word with a related but new meaning from an existing word, usually by attaching an affix. As we shall see, sparse use is made of derivational morphology by the CLAR children. This ought not to be surprising, since it is not widely used in adult JC, and so would not have formed a significant part of the input. Plag (2009, 354) generalizing over a number of Creole languages, indicates that a Creole language has much less derivational affixation than the richest (in terms of affixation) of its input languages. In keeping with his Interlanguage Hypothesis,[34] he shows that findings concerning the development of derivational morphology in second language acquisition can help to explain these Creole patterns: suffixation is far less common in interlanguages than compounding, the most frequently used word formation process. Reasons include the general avoidance in acquisition of the use of morphologically complex words, as simplex words are often sufficient in communication (ibid., 341).

In JE, derivational affixes can be either attached to the beginning of the word (prefix) or to the end of the word (suffix), and commonly result in a change in the syntactic category of the original word. An example of derivation resulting in a change in category in JE is 'boy-ish', an adjective formed by attaching the suffix '-ish' to the stem 'boy'. The derived meaning would be something like "behaving in a manner characteristic of that of a boy".

There are patterns in languages in the way derivation operates, as we might expect: particular affixes attach consistently to words of certain classes, for instance. So, the '-ish' suffix in the example above attaches only to nouns, resulting in the formation of an adjective having the same kind of relation with the root: paralleling 'boyish', the suffix '-ish' in the adjective 'childish', for example, attaches to the noun 'child' meaning "like a child". However, when '-ish' attaches to an adjective such as 'red', it behaves differently: it does not result in a change of word class ('reddish' is still an adjective), and it means "sort of red".

In English interlanguage, the agentive morpheme '-er' is the most common derivational suffix (Plag 2009, 344). It attaches to a verbal stem and indicates the name of the person or object (a noun) which causes the action expressed by the verb. The JC counterpart is the suffix *-a*. Forms containing the agentive suffix were elicited using pictures and questions such as *What would you call a man who ___?*.

All told, whether in elicitation or spontaneously, sparse use was made of the derivational affix with JC words by the CLAR children: the most frequently used were *laita* 'lighter' (thirteen occurrences); *jraiva* and its variant *jraivor* 'driver' (twelve); *schriena* 'strainer' (ten) and variants *chreena* and *streena*; *swinga* 'monkey bars' (one) and *jroma* 'drummer' and *raitor* 'writer', one occurrence each.

With regard to novel words created using the morpheme *-a*, there were four as follows: *bluoa* 'blow-dryer' (lit. blower) as in (16) below; *ruola* 'rolling pin' (lit. roller) in (17); *wipa* 'whisk' (lit. whipper) in (18); and *flaiya* 'pilot' (lit. flyer) in (19).

(16) INV: *yu   a   du wa?*
            2s.SUBJ PROG do what
            'You're doing what?'

      SEB: *bluo out ier.*
            blow out hair
            'Blow-drying hair.'

INV: *so wa   dis   niem   den?* [pointing to the blow-dryer]
       so what DEM name then
       'So what's this called, then?'

SEB: **_bluo- a_**.
       blow-AGT
       'Blow-dryer.'   [V4-AN1:l 729-3;5.24]

(17) INV: *tel im   a   wa,   Donique!*
             tell 3s.IND OBJ FOC what Donique
             'Tell him what it is, Donique!'

      DON: **_ruol-a_**.
             roll- AGT
             'Rolling pin.'

      SHA: *luk ou   it   a   ruol!*
             look how 3s.SUBJ PROG roll
             'Look how it's rolling!'

      SHA: *wach de!*
             watch LOC
             'Look there!'   [V3-KN1:ll 851ff.-DON-3;7.20 SHA-3;6.8]

(18) INV: *we   yu   a   du?*
             what 2s.SUBJ PROG do
             'What are you doing?'

      BRA: *mi   a   spin di sopn.*
             1s.SUBJ PROG spin DEF thing
             'I'm spinning the thing.'

      INV: *we   di   sopn niem?*
             what DEF thing name
             'What's the thing called?'

BRA: **wip- a**.
      whip-AGT
      'Whipper.'

LEA: *a   no   wip- a.*
      FOC NEG whip-AGT
      'It's not a whipper.'

LEA: *a   somting   fi   spin.*
      FOC something INF spin
      'It's something to be spun.'
                    [V1-SMR:ll 1105ff.-BRA-3;10.5-LEA-3;10.5]

(19) ALL: *a   **flaiy-a**   a   flai di plien.*
            INDEF fly- AGT PROG fly DEF plane
            'A pilot is flying the plane.'   [V6-SMT:l 620-3;10.5]

In each case, it was clear that the object or person was associated with the activity in which they were involved. Note that LEA in (18) denies that the function of the instrument is to whip; it is simply used to spin, and would therefore be a toy. The instrument was identified by many of the children in this way.[35]

Agentivity was expressed by combining a noun or a verb root with a head noun like *man*, more often than it was by attaching the suffix to the relevant verb. This strategy is said to be typical of the Hebrew and English-speaking three-year-olds studied by Clark and Berman (1984, 547), even while they make some use of the agentive *-er*. An example is *kyaar+man* 'car man' for *jraiva* 'driver' [V6-AN1-CAL:l. 170-3;09.06]. A mango seller was named *manggo+man* [V6-AN1-SEB:l.268-3;7.19].[36] This same child had no suggestion for a label for a man who drives a car:

(20) INV: *we   yu   kaal wahn man we   jraiv kyaar?*
            what 2s.SUBJ call INDEF man REL drive car
            'What do you call a man who drives cars?'

      SEB: *mi   no   nuo.*
            1s.SUBJ NEG know
            'I don't know.'

SEB: *di   man we   jraiv i.*
         DEF man REL drive 3s.OBJ
         'The man who drives it.'   [V6-AN1:l 295-3;7.19]

SEB is aware of the use of the agentive morpheme. Two visits earlier, at age 3;5.24, she was the child who had created the noun *bluoa* for 'blow-dryer' (lit. blower) in the interaction in (16) above.

A combination of both these word-formation processes is used in *jraiva+man* to produce 'driver-man' [V3-SMR-TAS:l 830-3;5.6].

Instead of using an agentive such as *jroma* 'drummer', another child created the reduplicative form *jrom jrom* 'drum drum' [V6-MOB-DAN: l. 504-3;4.16], very likely focusing on the activity rather than on the individual.[37] Finally, yet another child used the association of drummers with church services to produce *choch+man* 'church man' [V6-ADT-DAE l.514 4;1.13].

In general, however, the children tended to identify people not in terms of their occupations or the activities in which they were involved, but simply in terms of their gender. A lady who sells mangos was *grama* 'grandma' [V6-CLA:l 214 Bia 3;6.9] and *mami* 'mummy' [l.210]. When asked what you call ladies who clean windows, the child repeated the input 'ladies', perhaps because window-cleaning is not identified as an occupation by the children. A lady in front of a class of children, was identified simply as a *uman* 'woman' [V1-SMT-ROC l.927 3;07.07], even though *tiich* 'teach' and *tiicha* 'teacher' are known and used regularly. It is as if the act of teaching is not necessarily associated with the word *tiicha* 'teacher'. Instead, *tiicha* is used as a proper noun, as shown in (21) below.

(21) GAB: *mi   a   go gi tiicha som.*
            1s.SUBJ PROG go give teacher some
            'I'm going to give Teacher some.'   [V3-SER:l 96-3;7.17]

Prefixes in JE derivation do not change the word class. An example is 'redo' meaning "to do again". Only one derivational prefix was used by the CLAR children, in *anchuut* 'untruth', a regular JC word, and perhaps not analysed by speakers as involving a prefix, but taken to be an unanalysed word.

Finally, the only derived verb which was attested is *shaapn* 'sharpen', where the suffix '-(e)n' is added to the adjective 'sharp' to form the verb meaning "to make sharp". This was used three times by two children, and is deemed to be a regular word in JC.

We see, then, that little use is made of derivational morphology by the children. Because these are isolated instances, it may be that some, such as *schriena* 'strainer', have been learned by the children as unanalysed chunks, but the use of novel forms *flaiya* and *bluoa,* at least, do point to the productive use of a word-formation strategy.

The only derivational morpheme specifically elicited in data collection sessions was the agentive *-a* '-er'. Those used spontaneously by the children are nominalizations: *aisnin* 'icing', *baalin* 'bawling' and *fiidn* 'feeding'; and *atenshan* 'attention', *divooshen* 'devotion', *gradieeshan* 'graduation' and *televizhon* 'television'. These nouns are all used regularly in JC, but there is no way to verify from existing data that the children understand how they function in the language, since there are no uses of the stems *aisn, baal, fiid, aten, divuot, gradiet* or *televaiz* without the suffixes. Those which would have been borrowed into JC from JE, such as *atenshan, divooshen, gradieeshan* and *televizhon*, may have been acquired as single units, rather than having been produced using a word-formation strategy; the roots of others such as *baal* and *fiid* would be expected to be known and used by the children, and would indicate, therefore, the productive use of nominalization in addition to the agentive *-a*.

3.4.2 Filling Lexical Gaps

Using a question such as *wa dat?* 'What's that?', children were asked to identify objects presumed unknown to them. We see below how they sought to fill these lexical gaps.

In contrast to the sparse use of derivational morphology for word formation, paraphrasing was widely used when an apparent lexical gap was confronted. This is not uncommon universally: Clark and Berman (1987, 555) found in an experimental study on the production of compounds in Hebrew, that the three-year-olds in their sample produced compounds only occasionally, and that paraphrases constituted 81 per cent of their non-compound productions.

When paraphrasing, extensive use was made of *sopn* 'something' or its variants. These forms were called on, in the place of an actual vocabulary item, 908 times, as follows: JC variants *sopn / sopm* (664 occurrences), *sitn* (178), *sinting* (3), *sutn* (1) and JESs *somting* (58), *something* (4). For 135 of the total, the children sought to explain further by using the infinitival *fi*, indicating function, known or imagined. Explanations were often accompanied by a demonstration. The oven mitt, for example, was identified variously, as seen in the examples below, with function being specified even when the name of the object was requested:

(22) INV: *wa   dat   niem?*
            what DEM name
            'What's that called?'

      SHA: *sitn   fi kuk.*
            something INF cook
            'Something for cooking.'   [V3-SER:l 471-3;10.2]

(23) INV: *wat dis   niem?*
            what DEM name
            'What's this called?'

      JAY: *sopn   fi put pahn han.*
            something INF put on   hand
            'Something to put on your hand.'   [V2-MOB:l 27-3;4.3]

(24) INV: *wa   dis?*
            what DEM
            'What's this?'

      DAV: *sopn   fi put an   in dier.*
            something INF put hand in there
            'Something to put your hand in.'

      INV: *hmm?*

      DAV: *put an   in de.*
            put hand in there
            'Put your hand in there.'

      INV: *put an in de?*

      DAV: *an kil i   guot.*[38]
            and kill DEF goat
            'And kill the goat.'   [V1-AN2:ll 241ff.-2;09.22]

(25) INV: *wa   dat?*
             what DEM
             'What's that?'

     RAM: *sopn   fi   paint.*
             something INF point
             'Something to point.'   [V3-SER:1 409-3;2.16]

A rotary hand mixer was also identified in terms of function, even when the children were questioned about its appearance:

(26) RAM: *wa   dis?*
             what DEM
             'What is this?'

     RAM: *a   wa   dis?*
             FOC what DEM
             'What is this?'

     INV: *mi   no   nuo.*
             1S.SUBJ NEG know
             'I don't know.'

     INV: *we   it   luk   laik?*
             what 3S.SUBJ look like
             'What does it look like?'

     RAM: *sopn   fi   spin roun.*
             something INF   spin round
             'Something that you spin.'   [V1-SER:ll 312ff.-3;1.13]

In addition to paraphrasing, children choose labels known to them for objects perceptually related to the one to be named. So, for instance, a watermelon was identified variously as *sopn fi iit* 'something to eat', as a similar-looking food item such as *pongkin* 'pumpkin', *bred+fruut* 'breadfruit', or even as a non-food item such as *baal* 'ball'.

In the case of the expression of events, the CLAR children use paraphrasing to explain what is being done. For a picture of an egg being poured into a bowl, a child identified the hand and offered the following in answer to what the hand was doing:

(27) TAS: *uol   dish ... ahn put it   ina di   kop.*
           hold dish ... and put 3s.OBJ in   DEF cup
           'holding the dish ... and putting it in the cup.'
                                              [V1-ADT:ll 197,200-3;6.0]

In (28), skipping is identified as falling over the rope, and in (29), watering plants as throwing water on the leaves:

(28) MOY: *im   iz   jrap oova di   ting-z.*
           3s.SUBJ PROG drop over DEF thing-PL
           'He is falling over the things.'   [V1-ADT:l 293-3;4.24]

(29) BRA: *shi   a   chuo waata pan i   liif.*
           3s.SUBJ PROG throw water on   DEF leaf
           'She's throwing water on the leaf.'   [V1-SMR:l 97-3;10.5]

For the naming of events, much like for the naming of objects, rather than coining words or creating compounds, words were chosen based on association, in this case, association with an activity. The act of watering plants with a watering can was variously described in the following ways:

(30) KIM: *put i   wata in de # mek   i   flosh.*
           put DEF water in there make 3s.SUBJ flush
           'Put the water in there and made it flush.' [V1-CLA:l 199-3;0.27]

(31) TAM: *shi   a   sprie pan i   kukumba.*
           3s.SUBJ PROG spray on   DEF cucumber
           'She is spraying on the cucumbers.'   [V1-SMT:l 142-3;04.11]

(32) JAY: *shi   a   wash i   flouwaz dem.*
           3s.SUBJ PROG wash DEF flowers INCL
           'She's washing the flowers.'   [V6-SMT:l 143-3;5.22]

In summary, then, paraphrasing was commonly used to fill lexical gaps, with the children making extensive use of descriptions of function primarily, but also of appearance. Perceptually related nouns, when chosen, tended to fall within the same category as the object being named. For example, if the object was a food item, another food item would be called on. Related words were also chosen on the basis of general appearance.

These patterns reveal the organizing tendencies to which children adhere. In section 6.4, I consider how these trends can be instructive to the language and literacy teacher, suggesting that the relations already known to children be exploited by reinforcing and building on them through morphological awareness.

4 | What the Children Do with Nouns

SEB: *a <u>mai siit</u> ova yaso ahn <u>fi im siit</u> ova deso.*[1]

[V1-AN1:l.420-3;2.3]

The noun is the most frequently used of the lexical categories by the CLAR children. We looked at nouns in chapter 3, as part of a discussion of lexical acquisition, and saw that this predominance of nouns, called the noun bias, is, arguably, universally evident in language acquisition. The noun bias calculation, following Dhillon (2010), included pronouns as well as all subcategories of lexical nouns such as proper nouns and compounds. The concern of this chapter is specifically common nouns and how they are used in constructions.[2]

In section 4.1, we see that (common) nouns operate quite differently in JC than they do in JE, and that these differences have consequences for the JC-speaker's understanding of how the count–mass distinction in nouns is treated by JE grammar. Other issues concerning the nominal domain are: pluralization (section 4.2); (in)definiteness as expressed both in the absence and presence of the articles *di* 'the', *wahn* 'a' and their variants (section 4.3); and possession (section 4.4). For each of these structures, I look at how they are formed in JC and in JE, how features from the languages are woven in the speech of the children, both in terms of structural and superficial weaves, as well as how that speech compares with what has been reported in the literature for other children acquiring English as an L2 and as an L1, as relevant.

4.1 Count and Non-Count Nouns

A common semantic distinction applied to nouns is the count–mass distinction. A count noun may be said to have "discrete reference" (Gentner and Boroditsky 2003, 223). A "chair", for example, is considered to be an object which is solid, bounded, which moves as a single unit and is cohesive (Bloom 2002, 96–97). As a result, it can be identified as a separate item and is said therefore to be individuable; it can be individuated.

In contrast, a mass noun may be considered to be a substance having the semantic feature [+Homogeneous]. "Water" is an example of a [+Homogeneous] noun. It is cumulative, in that if we add some more water to water in a glass, we still refer to it as "water". It is also dissective, to an extent, in that after we have drunk some of the water in the glass, the glass will still contain water. A mass noun such as this is said to have "scattered" reference, referring to "stuff" of a certain material. It is not able to be divided into discrete entities; we may say that it is unable to be individuated, or that it is not individuable. Other examples might be "gold" or "flour".

Languages vary as to the extent to which the grammar provides support for this distinction. In JC, a bare noun, that is, an undetermined noun (appearing without a determiner), may receive either an individuated or a non-individuated interpretation. As indicated in the range of possible translations of THO's response in (1) below, JC *manggo* can be interpreted as a singular (in JE 'a mango') but also as a plural count noun without any plural marking (in JE 'some mangoes'). It can also receive a non-count part-of interpretation, without any further modification ('a piece of mango'). Finally, the same form may be used in JC as a mass noun. This mass interpretation would be quite odd in JE, as signalled by the "??" preceding the translation.

(1)   INV: *so wa   di   uman   a   du ierso?*
            so what DEF woman PROG do here
            'So, what is the woman doing here?'

       THO: *iit <u>manggo</u>.*
            eat mango
            'Eating a mango/some mangoes/a piece of a mango.'
            ?? 'Eating mango.'   [V6-STT:1 295-3;3.26]

There are two important differences between JC and JE, which together may be said to provide the basis for an explanation of these observations. First, in JE, a count interpretation needs to be signalled in the syntax ('She's eating a̲ cake/ two̲ cakes̲/some̲ cakes̲'). No such signalling is necessary in JC (*im a iit kiek/tuu kiek, som kiek*).

In JE, there is a grammatical distinction – a distinction in the syntax – between count and mass nouns: they are determined differently ('a̲ chair' versus 'some̲ flour' but not *'a̲ flour') and are pluralized differently as follows:

(a)   two chairs̲ – a count noun pluralized with the plural inflectional -s
(b)   *two flours̲ – direct pluralization of a mass noun is not grammatical
(c)   two cups̲ of flour – with a unitizer ('cup'), the interpretation of units is forced, then the unitizer may be pluralized

So in JE, count nouns are pluralized directly, since they are viewed as being cohesive units; the expression 'two chairs' denotes two separate (individuated) chairs. Mass nouns must first be measured, then the units so defined may be counted.

Second, JE and JC differ in the use of the count–mass distinction. In JE, there are count nouns which may also be used as mass nouns. An example is 'cake': we may say, 'She's eating two cakes' (count use), but we may also use 'cake' as a mass noun ('She's eating cake'). However, the mass use of a count noun is not the norm in JE. It may only be used if it can be subject to a process known as *grinding* (Murphy 2010, 164). Grinding allows for the interpretation of the (primarily count) noun as a kind of substance, resulting in an extension of the meaning. This "count to mass" pattern is not uniform, but applies most productively to only a subset of count nouns, those to do with certain countable kinds of food. Goddard (2009, 159) suggests that in order to be used as a mass noun in English, the object must be edible ("something of one kind that people can eat"), and it must be such that its present state is not its natural state, but is due to it having undergone some processing. This holds also in JE: we may speak of eating "cake", "chicken" or "egg", but not of "eating mango", since mango would not be perceived to be in some derived state, as a result of some culinary activity.

Importantly, as Gathercole (1997, 833) points out, in English the count–mass distinction obligatorily applies to every noun, and determines the distributional opportunities for that noun, that is, which determiner may accompany it, if any, and whether or not it can occur in the singular or plural. The distinction also determines the way in which the referent of the noun is viewed by the speaker or the hearer, that is, whether as a discrete, individuable object or not.

JC operates quite differently, as we have seen. The result is that there is not always a one-to-one correspondence between JE nouns that are considered countable, and their formally similar JC counterparts that are not. It may be that determiners, presumably including null determiners, are unspecified for the count–mass distinction in JC, and so can combine with both mass and count nouns. In such a case, pragmatic inferencing based on contextual information must be used to infer the precise interpretation of a bare NP in JC.[3]

Alternatively, this may be explained by Rijkhoff's (2004, 38)[4] claim that in languages like JC, where plural marking is not required for a plural interpretation, nouns are different from those in languages like JE. He refers to the JC-type noun as a set noun. Set nouns are distinguished neither in terms of being necessarily solid and bounded (see the definition of count nouns above), nor of being necessarily homogeneous, as are mass nouns. They do, however, have shape, and so it is possible to identify them without a determiner both as discrete entities, hence with a count interpretation, and as unbounded "stuff", with a mass interpretation.

If both count and mass interpretations are available for the undetermined noun in JC, it would follow that nouns which may be considered mass in other languages should be able to be measured without the help of unitizers. This explains why there is no need to indicate "a piece of" in (1) above. This is also apparent in the examples below. In (2), DEV, having identified that the tongs are used for taking up food, indicates that they are used for taking up *wahn rais* (INDEF rice). This construction is not possible in JE, since "rice" is a mass noun. Here, the implication is that some understood amount of rice can be taken up with the implement.

(2)   INV: *wa   kain a   fuud   yu   yuuz it   fi   tek   op?*
                what kind of food   2s.SUBJ use   it INF take PTL
                'What kind of food do you use it to take up?'

      DEV: *wahn   rais*.
                INDEF rice
                *'A rice.' ('a specified amount of rice')   [V1-SMR:1 716-3;9.14]

Similarly, in JE, "hair" would be considered to be a non-count noun, though we may speak of individual strands of hair as being "hairs". This works differently in JC. In (3), KIM uses *wahn hier* (INDEF hair) to refer, not to a strand of hair, but to a hair extension.

(3) KIM: *mi   mada se im   a   go bai <u>wahn hier</u> fi   mi*
           fi   put aan.
           1s.POSS mother say 3s.SUBJ PROG go buy INDEF hair COMP 1s.SUBJ
           INF put PTL
           'My mother says she's going to buy a hair extension for me to put
           on.'
                                                    [V5-CLA:l 628-3;5.14]

Consider also (4): *tii* 'tea' is a substance which in JE cannot be modified by the
indefinite 'a'; instead it must be modified by a unitizer ('a cup of tea'). This is not
the case in JC.

(4) ASH: *im   a   jringk <u>wahn tii</u>.*
           3s.SUBJ PROG drink INDEF tea
           'It [the horse] is drinking a (serving of) tea.'
                                                    [V4-KN2:l 581-3;10.28]

With regard to the count–mass distinction, then, whereas in JE, in the case of
a noun considered to be mass, a measure or unitizer phrase[5] must be used to
allow for it to be individuated, in JC, the unit by which it may be measured is
assumed, and the noun is counted directly.

4.2 Number Marking in JC versus JE

The term number refers to the singular–plural distinction. In JC, plural number
is grammatically marked only for [+definite] count nouns. This is achieved by
the addition of the particle *dem*. As a result, an unmarked (bare) noun can be
interpreted as plural. In (5) below, for example, the bare noun *bwai* 'boy' is used
as a generic (in JE 'boy<u>s</u>'); in (6), it is used with the numeral *tuu* 'two'.

(5) KIA: *a <u>bwai</u> fi   go fi waata.*
           FOC boy MOD go for water
           'Boys are the ones who should go for water.'
                                                    [V6-ADT:l 428-3;4.1]

(6) SAS: *mi   breda   an   mi   <u>tuu sista</u>.*
           1s.POSS brother and 1s.POSS two sister
           'My brother and my two sisters.'   [V5-STR:l 780-4;0.12]

The JC plural has traditionally been thought to consist of the definite article *di* (or its variant *i*) preceding the noun, as well as the form *dem* following it, for example, <u>*di*</u> *chier* <u>*dem*</u> 'the chairs'. This will be referred to as *di*+N+*dem*. *Dem* is homophonous with the third-person plural pronoun meaning 'they' or 'them' in JE; both *di* and *dem* are independent morphemes.

This traditional analysis of *di*+N+*dem* as plural marking has been re-conceptualized as *dem* being a marker of inclusiveness (Stewart 2007; Kennedy 2012). Inclusiveness is a feature of definiteness, as defined by Lyons (1999, 10), so its co-occurrence with the definite in JC is not surprising. Lyons provides the following example of inclusiveness being expressed through the definite in English, resulting in reference to a group, to all '<u>the</u> anaesthetists':

(7)   [Nurse about to enter operating theatre]
       I wonder who <u>the anaesthetists</u> are.   [Lyons 1999, 10, ex. 29a]

We see this group reference at work in JC in the sentence below. Notice that *di*... *dem* in this sentence is not required to indicate plurality; this is already achieved using the numeral *chrii*. Instead, it indicates that the three boys acted as a group to kill their (one) father:

(8)   *Di   chrii bwai dem kil dem   faada.*
       DEF three boy INCL kill 3PL.POSS father
       'The three boys (together) killed their father.'   [Stewart 2011, 379, ex. 30]

Much in the same way, *dem* in a phrase such as *Mieri dem* is used to identify a group of people in relation to Mary, for example, 'Mary and her friends' or 'Mary's family'.[6]

A phrase in which *dem* is used as a marker of inclusiveness can be interpreted as being plural. This has to do with the fact that when used, the marker has group reference, and by definition, a group must consist of more than one individual. We may say, then, that plurality arises through the expression of inclusiveness. For details of this analysis, see Stewart (2007, 384–88; 2011, 367–70) and, for discussion, Durrleman-Tame (2008, 154–59) and Bobyleva (2013, 185–91).

An interesting alternative analysis is suggested by Radford (pers. comm.). It is that *dem* may be a nominal element (perhaps a suffix) carrying uninterpret-able number and definiteness features which need to be checked and deleted by agreement with higher functional heads carrying interpretable number and definiteness features (see section 2.5 for a discussion of [un]interpretable features in minimalism). This would explain the requirement that *di* occur with *dem*, and also its ability to occur with a proper noun.

CLAR children of all ages used JC *di+N+dem* a total of 189 times. De Lisser (2015, 265), who studied six children in the age range 1;6–3;4, reports that one child used the form at 2;2, that three others used it at 2;3, and that it was used a total of seventy-two times by all children, but not at all by one child up to age 3;1, her age at the end of the study. She concludes that from the beginning, children acquiring JC demonstrate target-like knowledge of plural forms (p. 267).

There are cases in the CLAR data where the inclusive construction is used, but plurality would not be made explicit in JE. In (9), for example, the possessive pronoun 'mine' seems to be followed by a null N pluralized by *dem*. This null N may correspond to JE 'thing'.[7] Such a construction would not exist in JE.[8]

(9)   CHR: *aahn mi   put main   dem*[9] *ina pat aahn iit dem   aaf.*
               and   1s.SUBJ put 1s.POSS INCL in pot and eat 3PL.OBJ off
               'And I put mine in a pot and ate them off.'
                                                              [V3-SMT:l 102-3;2.30]

In (10), *di . . . dem* appears with *fuud* 'food', rendering a translation in JE of 'all the food'. The sense here is that *fuud* is not being used as a mass noun as it is in JE, but that what is being spoken about is the collection of different food items, providing further evidence of the JC set noun allowing for a count interpretation of a noun which would be considered to be mass in JE.

(10)   ANN: *we   i   fuud   dem de?*
               where DEF food   INCL LOC
               'Where is (all) the food?'   [V4-KN2:l 775-3;3.7]

This brings us to a discussion of collective nouns. An example is *paliis* 'police' or its JES[10] counterpart *poliis*. It would seem that it ought not to be assigned to the special subclass *collective*, since it behaves much in the same way as any other set noun in JC. Thus, much like the set noun *daag* 'dog', *paliis* 'police' may be interpreted in the plural (see [11–12]) and, in the same form, may be directly modified by a numeral as in (13) and (14).

(11)   JER: *poliis a   mai   fren.*
               police COP 1s.POSS friend
               'The police are my friends.'   [V5-AN2:ll 906,885-3;8.13]

(12)   KAM: *mi   av   <u>daag</u>.*
                 1s.SUBJ have dog
                 'I have dogs.'

       INV: *ou   moch <u>daag</u> yu   av?*
                 how much dog 2s.SUBJ have
                 'How many dogs do you have ?'

       KAM: *fuor.*
                 'four.'   [V4-CLA:ll 126ff.-3.11.10]

(13)   CHA: *a   <u>tuu poliis</u> roun   de.*
                 FOC two police around there
                 'There are two policemen around there.'
                 ≠ 'There are two police around there.'   [V2-SER:l 356-3;4.26]

(14)   SHA: *<u>tuu daag</u> an   di   foul.*
                 two dog   and DEF foul
                 'two dogs and the fowl.'   [V5-KN1:l 153-3;9.8]

Group reference is achieved using *di*+N+*dem*, as we see in (15):

(15)   JER: *an   luk   fi   <u>di   poliis dem</u> an   <u>di   poliis dem</u>   gaan.*
                 and look for DEF police INCL and DEF police INCL gone
                 'And look for the policemen and the policemen are gone.'
                                      [V5-AN2; l 902-3;8.13]

This works differently in JE. A group interpretation in JE may be expressed using collective nouns, so, for example, a group of students at school may be referred to as a 'class'. In JE, 'police' may be used either collectively to refer to a group of policemen or to more than one individual policeman, and the difference may be signalled by the form of the verb which follows – 'the police is/are …'.

Other nouns such as *piipl* 'people', which function as plural in English, refer also in JC to more than one, as in (16), but may nonetheless be used with *di . . . dem* when a collective interpretation is intended (17).

(16) INV: What kind of people go to the doctor?

      DAE: *piipl   we   sik.*
             people COMP sick
             'People who are sick.'   [V6-ADT (JE):1 688-4;1.13]

(17) ORR: *main yu   mash op di piipl dem sitn, ino.*
            mind 2s.SUBJ mash up DEF people INCL thing, you.know
            'Be careful not to destroy the people's things, you know.'
                                      [V2-ADT:1 429-3;9.4]

In sum, plurality can be expressed in JC using the bare noun. The inclusiveness construction *di*+N+*dem* is used for group reference in JC, and nouns such as *piipl* 'people' or *paliis* 'police' whose JE counterparts are considered to be collective nouns, behave much like any other set noun in JC and quite differently than they do in JE.

4.2.1 Weaving in Plural DPs

As we have seen, there is no inflectional morpheme to express plurality in JC. In JE, the plural is signalled using the inflectional -s ('boy<u>s</u>'), a bound morpheme attached to the noun as a suffix. Forms of the morpheme are dependent on the phonological environment in which they appear. There are three variants of the regular plural: /s/ as in 'cat<u>s</u>', /z/ as in 'dog<u>s</u>' and /iz/ as in 'church<u>es</u>'. Note that in the data presented here, plurality is indicated using '(i)z', regardless of pronunciation.

For children acquiring English as their first language, the plural inflection is among the earlier inflections to be acquired, preceded only by the progressive -ing (Brown 1973). Acquisition with 90 per cent accuracy[11] was achieved by all three L1 American English children in Brown's study between the ages of 1;11 and 2;10.

The JE plural morpheme was used by the CLAR children, but sparingly. Among the two-year-olds in the sample, it was used only five times by four of eleven children participating in fifteen interviews. The youngest of these was 2;9. Across all ages, it was used an average of once every two half-hour interviews. In the numeral+N construction, only 5.5 per cent of the total used by the children appeared with the plural morpheme -s, even though 17.9 per cent of the nouns in the constructions were JES forms.

Importantly, it is not the case that the JE plural inflection is reserved only for JES forms: the majority of the nouns carrying the morpheme are JESs (46 per cent) and SHared nouns (24 per cent), but the remaining 30 per cent are JC, indicating that the JE pluralization strategy has been internalized and applied also to JC speech, and pointing yet again to superficial weaving and blurred boundaries between the two languages.

The only example in the CLAR data of an overgeneralized plural form was *manz* (instead of 'men'); it was used by a child at age 3;5. This contrasts with overgeneralization rates of use in plural NPs in English L1 acquisition. Maslen et al. (2004, 1323), for instance, report the overall rate by the child in their study (age range 2;0.12–3;11.06) to be 7.2 per cent, occurring at least once with ten of the nineteen irregular plural nouns he used; it was attested from as early as 2;02.00 when the rate was 5.9 per cent.

Interestingly, there are six instances of the use of both the JE inflectional morpheme and the inclusiveness marker (see section 4.2 for the introduction of this term): *di taiz dem* (JC stem-x2) 'toy'; *di toiz dem* (JE stem) 'toy'; *di animalz dem* (x2) and *di dishiz dem* (SHared stems). These forms are considered to be examples of structural weaving, since they combine different (pluralization) strategies from the two languages for the formation of syntactic constructions.

(18) GAB: *mi   no waahn dem   bisaid <u>mi   toiz   dem.</u>*
              1S.SUBJ NEG want   3PL.SUBJ beside 1S.POSS toy-PL INCL

       we   mi   a   go kuk.
       COMP 1S.SUBJ PROG go cook
       'I don't want them beside the toys that I'm going to cook.'
                                                    [V3-SER:l 485-3;7.17]

They were used both with and without the inclusiveness marker in the same discourse, as shown in (19):

(19) MOY: *mi   waant <u>i   dishiz.</u>*
              1S.SUBJ want   DEF dishes
              'I want the dishes.'

              ...

       wash op <u>di   dishiz dem</u>!
       wash up DEF dishes INCL
       'Wash up the dishes!'   [V2-ADT:ll 115,179-3;5.22]

This is an example of what has been called a double-plural in second-language acquisition, that is, the use in one noun phrase of the pluralization strategies of both the first and the second languages. Doubling also takes place with other grammatical constructions such as with the past tense, but the plural morpheme is the one which is doubled most often in interlanguages (Myers-Scotton and Jake 2001, 94). In the CLAR data, the contexts in which doubling is used suggest strongly that group reference is intended. Given the very common tendency to incorporate the plural into the stem so as to form what I call *plural fossils*, it is likely that the nouns in these constructions constitute unanalysed plurals. That is, the children are using the forms with the plural marker, seemingly without recognizing that its function in the L2 is to indicate plurality. We shall see more such cases in the following section.

The use of the so-called double-plural by the CLAR children is unsurprising. There has been mention of its use also in adult speech by Patrick (2009).[12] It may be that over time, the marker will become increasingly used, to the point where it will be incorporated into JC's own grammatical system, following the stages of adoption of bound inflectional morphology from other languages outlined by Grant (2012, 118–19).

4.2.2 The Use of *Plural Fossils*

There is widespread use among the CLAR children of nouns carrying what appears to be the JE plural inflectional morpheme,[13] and directly modified, nonetheless, by the singular indefinite *wahn*. Examples are seen in (20) and (21):

(20) INV: *wa   dis?*
               what this
               'What's this?'

      ERN: <u>*wahn panz*</u>.
               INDEF pants
               '(a pair of) pants.'   [V4-STR:ll 653ff.-3;9.30]

(21) ODA: *mi   put aan <u>a   shaatz</u>*.
               1s.SUBJ put on   INDEF shorts
               'I put on a (pair of) shorts.'   [V6-KN1:l 392-3;8.14]

In JE, nouns such as 'pants' and 'shorts' must be modified by what are known as unitizers such as 'a pair of'. These nouns do not have a singular form (*a pant; *a short). As Acquaviva (2008, 16) points out, they cannot be further suffixed (*pantses; *shortses): to speak about more than one pair, it is the unitizer which must be pluralized ('two pairs of pants/shorts'). In many cases, the single unit comprises more than one defining part, and bears the plural morpheme – a pair of pants has two legs. Such nouns are called *pluralia tantum* nouns. This contrasts with the canonical use of the plural, that is, to express 'more than one' of the object denoted by the noun (boy–boy<u>s</u>).

CLAR children from all areas, and of all ages, used thirty different nouns with the JE plural morpheme in this way, just over eleven hundred times; only six of the thirty nouns could be considered to be *pluralia tantum* nouns in JE. A list of such nouns used by the children is presented as appendix 7. They are all accepted by my native speaker consultants as forming part of regular adult Creole usage. Some do refer to nouns where the unit is presumed to consist of a pair, but they are not *pluralia tantum* nouns in JE. Examples are *globz* 'gloves' and *iez* 'ears'. Others are nouns which would be most frequently used in JE in the plural – *antz* 'ants' and *chipz* 'chips', for instance – and so the children would most likely have had the plural forms in the input as a model.[14]

Since the plural form is used in both singular and plural contexts for these words, it would appear that the plural ending has been misanalysed as a part of the stem of the noun. We may say that the plural morpheme has been incorporated, that is, it seems to have lost its plural function. Instead it is a morphologically simple word used as a singular noun and, as such, is pluralized in the same way that any other JC noun is. I coin the phrase *plural fossils* to refer to these nouns.

DAN (V6-MOB:1 254-3;4.16) speaks of a single plant as *dis flouwaz* 'this plant', of two plants as *tuu flouwaz*, and of the plants a lady is watering as *flouwaz*. JAY, as seen in (22), uses the plural (*d*)*i flouwaz dem*, referring again to the plural plants, but in using the definite *di . . . dem*, acknowledges that these are the (group of) plants which have been the topic of conversation.

(22) JAY: shi   a   wash i   flouwaz dem.
              3s.SUBJ PROG wash DEF flowers INCL
              'She's washing the plants.'   [V6-SMT:1 163-3;5.22]

When unitizers are used with plural fossils, they operate differently in JC. *Shuuz* 'shoes' is a plural fossil, and as we would expect, one shoe, as well as one pair of shoes, are ambiguously referred to by *wahn shuuz* 'a shoe' or 'a pair of shoes'. In (23), SEB has asked for the other shoe. To underline that reference is being made to one shoe only, and to prevent it from being interpreted as a pair of shoes, she follows up the question using the unitizer *fut*.

(23) SEB: we   i   neks <u>*shuuz*</u> de?
               where DEF next shoe COP
               'Where is the other shoe?'

      SEB: we   di   neks <u>*fut a shuuz*</u> de?
               where DEF next foot of shoe COP
               'Where is the other shoe?'   [V5-AN1:l 555-3;6.21]

In (24), CHA indicates that she will wear the new sandals her mother just bought when the other pair gets destroyed; in this case, that it is a pair of sandals is presumed, with no need for the unitizer.

(24) CHA: wen   <u>*di neks slipaz*</u> pap op mi   wier   i.
              when DEF next slippers pop up 1s.SUBJ wear 3s
              'When the other (pair of) sandals break I'll wear it.'
                                              [V5-SER:l 299-3;8.8]

It is commonly reported in the literature that the plural morpheme in English is one of the first to be acquired by L2 learners of English (Andersen 1978, for example), and that children learning English begin by using the bare noun for both singular and plural meaning. It has been argued that its early acquisition cross-linguistically for L2 learners of English is due to [number] being interpreted not as a grammatical feature, but as an inherent and formal property of the noun associated with the feature [count] (Müller 1994, 68–71, 76). In minimalist terms, we would say that the plural morpheme encodes an interpretable, not an uninterpretable, feature (see Meisel 2011, 71 for discussion). It would be expected that being interpretable, number would be acquired early, before uninterpretable features (see section 2.5 for a discussion of features).

It may be that the sparse use of the JE plural in the CLAR data is due to the lack of inflectional morphology in JC, the children's L1. Dressler (2010, 116) indicates that children become aware of the role of inflectional morphemes and become more "tuned" to morphology in the L1, if the language is rich in morphology. Studying the acquisition of the English plural morpheme by ten native speakers of Mandarin Chinese, a language without inflectional morphology, Jia (2003, 1307) found that three of the ten participants had not attained mastery of the plural after five years of L2 immersion, even though typically developing L1 acquirers of English achieve that level by three years of age.

It may be the case, then, that it is to be expected that JC-speaking children would detect JE morphology later than children whose L1 is morphologically rich.

4.3 The Expression of (In)Definiteness

In what follows, the determiner phrase, or DP, is taken to consist of the functional category housing the determiner D and a complement noun phrase or NP. Articles are examples of D. The definite articles are *di* or *i*, 'the', as in (25) and (26), and the indefinite, *wahn* or *wan*, 'a' in (27) and (28).

(25) GAB: *mi   a   go kuk i   pan di   pat.*
              1s.SUBJ PROG go   cook 3s.OBJ on   DEF pot
              'I'm going to cook it on the pot.'   [V4-SER:l 40-3;9.27]

(26) GAB: *si   i   ambrela ier.*
              see DEF umbrella here
              'See the umbrella here.'   [V4-SER:l 171-3;9.27]

(27) SHE: *mi   a   go bai wahn kuom.*
              1s.SUBJ PROG go   buy INDEF comb
              'I'm going to buy a comb.'   [V1-CLA:l 631-3;1.3]

(28) JAY: *dadi   jraiv   wan   van laik dis.*
              Daddy   drive   INDEF van like DEM
              'Daddy drives a van like this.'   [V3-MOB:l 18-3;4.25]

Determiners are considered to be functional. We say that D *determines* the NP. The resulting structure of the DP is $[_{DP}$ D+NP].[15]

One would think that if a child is learning JE, she would need to know that the JE form corresponding to the JC *di* is 'the', and that we would translate the JC *wahn* as 'a' in JE. We shall see that the task the child faces is far more complex than this. The discussion begins with a (semantic) consideration of how definiteness might be characterized.

The definite article has what might be called a *referential function* (Epstein 2002, 334), that is, it serves to indicate that the noun phrase it determines is to be distinguished in some way. Lyons (1999) has characterized definiteness in terms of the identifiability condition, which states that for an expression to be definite, the speaker must be in a position to assume that the hearer is able in some way to select the referent.[16] It may be that the hearer is able to identify the referent as having been previously mentioned in the discourse or, alternatively, it may form a part of knowledge which the speaker and the hearer share. In (29), NICL refers to the open book which they have been reading; here, identifiability results from its presence in the immediate environment.

(29) NICL: *mek   mi   lak   i   buk!*
             make 1s.OBJ lock DEF book
             'Let me close the book!'   [V3-CLA:l 354-3;7.23]

A second condition, the condition of familiarity states that the referent must be familiar to both the speaker and hearer. Familiarity is subsumed under identifiability – when identifiability pertains, it is familiarity which allows the hearer to identify the referent.[17]

The following shows that DOM has a clear understanding of the use of the definite, since having introduced *wahn man* 'a man' into the conversation, he is then able to refer to him as *i man* 'the man', when saying what he did:

(30) DOM: *wahn man de pan i   ruod an i   man ... shat op ina i   ier.*
             INDEF man COP on   DEF road and DEF man ... shoot up into DEF air
             'A man was in the road and the man ... shot up in the air.'
                                                          [V4-CLA:l 420-3;1.20]

According to this characterization, what differentiates a definite from an indefinite NP is only the ability or inability of the hearer to identify the intended referent by some means. Returning to the examples above, then, we see that GAB in (25) and (26) fully expects that the investigator is able to identify the pot and the umbrella among the items in the room, but SHE in (27) and JAY in (28) are introducing reference to a comb and a van for the first time, with no expectation that the referent will be able to be identified.

Note that informally, it has been said that we use "the" when we are referring to a *specific* thing. Specificity is distinct from definiteness, however. A noun phrase is *specific* if the speaker has the actual referent "in mind" and intends to refer to it (Slabakova 2009, 316n2). We would refer to the van in (28), but not the comb in (27), as being specific. When JAY in (28) says that his father drives *wan van* 'a van' like this, he has a particular van in mind – the one his father drives. This indefinite DP is specific. In contrast, when SHE says in (27) that she is going to buy *wahn kuom* 'a comb', she is not referring to any particular comb; this is an example of a non-specific DP. Thus the children generate both specific and non-specific indefinite DPs.

Traditionally, only indefinites were characterized in terms of non-specificity, since all definite noun phrases were considered to be specific. Ihsane and Puskas (2001, 40) show that it is possible for a definite expression to allow a hearer to refer to a class of possible referents, but not any particular object within that class. An example might be "I need to go to the gas station", where the speaker may not be referring to any specific gas station, but instead is establishing the need to get gas for the car. Such expressions are considered to be non-specific definites. MOY is speaking about an imaginary person named Rastalo, and indicates that he has gone to the bathroom. Note that after being questioned about the person's name, she repeats the location, without using the definite, confirming that no specific bathroom was being referenced.

(31) MOY: *Rastalo gaan <u>ina i   baachuum</u>.*
             Rastalo gone in   DEF bathroom
             'Rastalo has gone into the bathroom.'

   INV: *wa   im   niem?*
           what 3s.SUBJ name
           'What's his name?'

   MOY: *Rastalo.*

   INV: *Rastalo?*

   MOY: *iihn   gaan <u>ina baachuum</u>.*
           3s.SUBJ gone in   bathroom
           'He's gone into the bathroom.'   [V3-ADT:ll 444ff.-3;6.13]

Semantically, both definiteness and indefiniteness are attested universally. As we have seen, these features, as well as (non-)specificity, are available both in JC and JE. It has been suggested that their (semantic) characterization and functions in JC parallel those which we find in JE.[18] There are, however, differences between how the phenomena are expressed in the two languages. In the next section, I look at the acquisition of the articles, and pay some attention to these differences; we shall see clearly that the task of the child in acquiring JE as a second language involves much more than simply acquiring the JE equivalents of the JC articles.

4.3.1 The Emergence of Articles

Stewart (2010a) reports on three Kingston children ranging in age from 2;1.5 to 2;9 and forming part of the pilot of the CLAR project. She indicates that the definite article *di* is not used until 2;6, except in restricted contexts for the most part – in prepositional phrases headed by (*p*)*an* 'on', *ina* 'in' and *outa* 'out of', followed by DP complements such as *di ruod* 'the road', suggesting routines. In this period, definiteness is expressed overtly in object DPs using the variant *i*.

There has long been recognition that children omit articles altogether in the earliest stages of acquisition. Brown (1973) in his seminal study of the L1 English acquisition of three children, Adam, Eve and Sarah, found that the English article system was acquired between the ages of 2;8 and 3;5. Recall, however, that Brown's benchmark was 90 per cent use in obligatory contexts. In other studies, using different benchmarks, early acquisition of articles is reported. Radford (1990, 276–91), for instance, speaks of children entering a functional stage of development before age 2;2, and that once the principles determining functional aspects of grammar have come "online", a range of functional structures is acquired in parallel (p. 284).

Brown (1973, 351) indicates that both the English definite and indefinite articles are acquired as a system, suggesting their simultaneous acquisition. This is not borne out for JC in the CLAR data, where six of eleven two-year-olds in a total of fifteen interviews did not use the indefinite *wa*(*h*)*n* at all; the remaining five children made use of it only eight times. In contrast, the definite *di ~ i* was used by all CLAR two-year-olds in the same interviews more than 180 times. Overall, across all ages, the JC definite accounted for 89.4 per cent of JC articles used, leaving a production of only 10.6 per cent indefinites. I note that De Lisser

(2015, 284) reports a similar trend: the indefinite was "minimally attested" though not impossible among the children in her study.

Clark (2003, 339), citing research from as far back as the 1970s, shows that by age three, children acquiring English as a first language are able to contrast the definite and indefinite articles, but they erroneously use the definite in contexts requiring the indefinite, through to age nine. Similar results obtain even for children acquiring L1 French, a language where articles are rarely omitted.

Recall that the definite is used in cases where the speaker expects that the hearer will be able to identify the referent, since it is familiar either because of shared knowledge or because it has already been introduced in the discourse. Clark (ibid.) suggests that the overuse of the definite by children may be because they are mis-assessing what their hearers might actually know, or that they may be going by what they themselves know, on the presumption that the hearer knows as much. Schaeffer (1997, quoted in Schaeffer and Matthewson 2005, 69) refers to this tendency on the part of young children as a result of lacking the concept of non-shared assumptions. This is a pragmatic concept which holds that speaker and hearer assumptions are always independent. Without it, it is predicted that there will be situations in which speakers attribute their own assumptions to the hearer. When applied to the acquisition of article systems, if the child believes that knowledge is shared by the hearer, the article chosen will tend to be definite 'the'.

The CLAR children of all ages do consistently use the definite when referring to the participants in activities depicted in pictures, even at first mention. This does suggest a presumption that investigators are privy to the same information they are, and therefore would not need to have the referent introduced. We see below a wide range of other interactions where this is the case. In all the examples, the definite predominates, as if the investigators were themselves present, or at least know what is being spoken about.

In (32), KAR asks where *i bag* is, presuming shared knowledge since the investigators had brought the bag to the previous interview.

(32) KAR: *we   i   bag?*
             where DEF bag
             'Where's the bag?'

      INV: *wich bag?*
             which bag
             'Which bag?'

INV: *a   wich   bag yu   a   luk   fa?*
FOC which bag 2s.SUBJ PROG look for
'Which bag are you looking for?'

KAR: *i   bag we   i   plie+plie+sopn   ina.*
DEF bag COMP DEF play+play+something in
'The bag in which the toys are.'   V3-CLA:l 595-3;9.27]

In (33), the story of Michael Jackson's music video is being related: characters are all referred to using the definite.

(33) ROS: *an dem   don si   i [/] i   likl gorl ron go ina i   ous.*
and 3PL.SUBJ PERF see DEF   little girl run go in   DEF house
'And they saw the little girl run into the house.'

ASH: *an di dopi in de   tu.*
and DEF ghost in there too
'And the ghost was in there too.'

ROS: *ahn wen   Michael Jackson tek   aar   out a i   bed ...*
and when Michael Jackson take 3s.OBJ out of DEF bed ...
'And when Michael Jackson took her out of the bed ...'

ROS: *im   torn roun   wid aar   an im   se   haa haa haa haa haa.*
3s.SUBJ turn around with 3s.OBJ and 3s.SUBJ say haa haa haa haa haa
'He turned around with her and he said haa haa haa haa haa.'
                                    [V3-KN2:ll 330ff.;Ros-3;4.23-Ash-3;9.2]

An imaginary scenario is being created in (34). Here, no stone, food or boy had previously been mentioned in the discourse by ODA, yet they are all modified by the definite.

(34) ODA: *im   bring di   rak   stuon an baks di   fuud ... di bwoi jrap dong.*
3s.SUBJ bring DEF rock stone and box DEF food ... DEF boy   drop down
'he brought the rock and boxed the food ... the boy fell.'
                                    [V3-KN1:l 148-3;4.25]

Finally, in (35) DAV is explaining what an oven mitt might be used for. Instead of abstracting away from a particular instance, and formulating her response in general terms by indicating that it can be used in the killing of a(ny) goat, she uses the definite *i guot*, under the presumption that for the mitt to be used, there would first need to be a goat.

(35) DAV: *sopm   fi   put an   in dier ...   an kil i   guot.*
              something INF put hand in there ... and kill DEF goat
              'Something to put your hand in and kill the goat.'
                                                    [V1-AN2:ll 251ff.-2;9.22]

A different explanation is suggested by Clark (2003, 339), who notes that it has been reported (O'Neill 1996) that children as young as two have, in fact, been able to take good account of what an addressee knows, and so it may not be feasible to imagine that they overuse the definite as a result of mis-assessing their addressee's knowledge. As a result, she suggests that it may be more likely that children lack the skill to use articles to mark information as given (using the definite) versus new (using the indefinite). This is of interest to us, for two reasons. The first is that using the indefinite to signal new information may not be a dominant strategy in JC, and so its absence cannot be construed as evidence that it has not been acquired. An alternative strategy to introduce information in widespread use in adult JC, and heavily used by the CLAR children, is to focus the constituent. This is achieved by fronting it, either with (as in [36]) or without ([37–38]) the focus marker *a*.

(36) ASH: *a   bachri in de.*
              FOC battery in LOC
              'It's a battery that's in there.'   [V4-KN2:l 208-3;10.28]

(37) INV: *a   we   yu   a   kola?*
              FOC what 2S.SUBJ PROG colour
              'What are you colouring?'

      GAB: *chrii mi   a   kola.*
              tree 1S.SUBJ PROG colour
              'It's a tree that I'm colouring'   [V5-SER:ll 49ff.-3;10.16]

(38)   MAU: _kyaar mi_   _waahn plie wid._
        car   1s.SUBJ want   play with
        'It's a car that I want to play with.'   [V5-KN1:l 635-3;8.30]

In (39), ANN fronts the object _lonch+pan_ and in addition uses the indefinite, though its use is optional as we saw in (37) and (38).

(39)   ANN: _wahn lonch+pan_ _mii_   _av._
        INDEF lunch+pan 1s.SUBJ have
        'It's a lunch-pan that I have.'   [V4-KN2:l 721-3;2.27]

A second possible acquisition-independent reason for a far greater use of the definite article than of the indefinite is that it is a common storytelling strategy among Creole speakers, and indeed universally, to re-enact scenes, almost as if live commentary were being provided. A pragmatic explanation for this is presented in Schiffrin (1998, 208–9). It is that background information can be contextually provided by a situation, allowing us to make assumptions with regard to what might be expected in such a situation. In this case, the definite may be used for the first mention of things which may be typically relevant to the setting.[19] In storytelling, for instance, once the scene is set, such assumptions are possible.

The trends in the CLAR children's use of the definite, then, may not be attributable to an inability to distinguish new from old information, but to the use of other syntactic means available in the language for expressing the distinction, or perhaps to strategies available in discourse.

As we have seen, until the articles are fully acquired, children universally use the bare noun where the target requires an article; the CLAR children are no different. However, there are also environments in adult JC where the bare noun is grammatically correct. In these instances, the bare noun can be grammatically accounted for. This is another case of trends in first language acquisition not needing to be called upon to explain the data. In (40), for example, since the river forms part of the children's daily life, this shared knowledge allows for the identification of the river – definiteness is expressed without the use of the definite article.

(40)   ORR: _a_ [/] _a_   _riva wi_   _a_   _go._
        FOC[20]   river 1PL.SUBJ PROG go
        'It's <u>the</u> river that we're going to.'   [V3-ADT:l 876-3;9.26]

Similarly, the indefinite can be expressed in the absence of an article as in (41):

(41)   OSS: *mi*   *waahn* <u>*kreyan*</u> *fi   rait   wid.*
               1s.SUBJ want   crayon INF write with
               'I want <u>a</u> crayon to write with.'   [V6-MOB:1 858-3;8.12]

Since the meaning is expressed, but there is no (overt) article, it must still be accommodated in the syntax. It is housed in D, and is known as the null determiner Ø. The bare noun in these instances, then, is the noun with a null determiner. Table 4.1 lists environments where the article may be omitted, that is, where the bare noun may be used quite grammatically in adult JC speech. Such sequences are ungrammatical in JE, requiring an article, as seen in the English translations of (40) and (41) above and in the table.[21]

Note that in these contexts, the undetermined noun can be modified by an adjective (42), or can take the form of a complex noun (43), and that these structures are also grammatical in adult JC.

(42)   GAB: *uhm mi*   *a*   <u>*big gorl*</u>.
               uhm 1s.SUBJ COP big girl
               'Hmm, I'm a big girl.'   [V6-SER:1 646-4;0.0]

(43)   SHA: *mi*   *av*   <u>*api   bortdie   kiek*</u>.
               1s.SUBJ have happy birthday cake
               'I have a birthday cake.'   [V6-KN1:1 279-3;10.0]

There are clear differences, then, between how (in)definiteness is expressed in JC and in JE, differences which involve far more than learning the translation equivalents of the articles and which must be understood, therefore, for proficiency in JE.

4.3.2 The L2 Acquisition of JE Articles

We have seen that the JC definite article is used far more often than the JC indefinite. Occurrences were 6,048 definite and 719 indefinite. This is in sharp contrast to the use of the JE counterparts: definite 'the' – 47 occurrences – as opposed to 688 instances of the indefinite 'a'. The differential in the use of the indefinite and of the definite could point to difficulty being experienced by the CLAR children, in the acquisition of the JE definite.

Table 4.1. JC vs. JE sequences Det+N in adult speech

	Environment	JC	JC Example	JE	JE Example
1.	Naming, in answer, e.g., to *Wa dat?* 'What's that?'	(D) N	*Wa dat?* 'What's that?' *guot* 'goat' <u>*wahn*</u> *guot* 'a goat'	D N * Ø N	What's that? <u>a</u> goat. * goat.
2.	Object of a Prep(osition)	Prep (D) N	*pahn <u>bed</u>* 'on the bed' *pan <u>i</u> bed*	Prep D N * Prep N	on <u>the</u> bed * on bed
3.	Singular Noun in Subject position	(D) N V	<u>*rat*</u> *bait i* 'a rat bit it' <u>*wahn*</u> *rat bait i* 'a rat bit it' *popi naa bait yu, ino* 'the puppy won't bite you, you know' <u>*di*</u> *daag bait it op* 'the dog destroyed it'	D N V * N V	<u>a</u> rat bit it * rat bit it <u>the</u> dog destroyed it * dog destroyed it
4.	Object of a Verb	V (D) N	*fi opin <u>duor</u>* 'to open the door' *fi opm <u>di</u> jiel* 'to open the jail' *im av <u>ambrela</u>* 'he has an umbrella' *mi av <u>wahn</u> van* 'I have a van'	V D N * V N	to open <u>the</u> door * to open door he has <u>an</u> umbrella * he has umbrella
5.	Coordination	(D) N *an* (D) N	*bwai an <u>gorl</u>* 'boy and girl' <u>*wahn*</u> *man an <u>wahn</u> bwai* 'a man and a boy'	D N 'and' D N * N and N	<u>a</u> boy and <u>a</u> girl * boy and girl

(Table 4.1 continues)

Table 4.1. JC vs. JE sequences Det+N in adult speech (*continued*)

	Environment	JC	JC Example	JE	JE Example
6.	In a Foc(us) Construction	Foc (D) N	*a gon dis, ino* 'This is a gun, you know' *a wahn fan dis* 'This is a fan'	Foc D N * Foc N	It's a gun * It's gun
7.	After a Neg(ative) V	Neg V Neg N	*mi naa no fuon* 'I don't have a phone'	Neg V D N	I don't have a phone * I don't have no phone
8.	After the Comparative *laik* 'like'	*laik* N	*tiel laik fish* 'tail like a fish'	'like' D N	like a fish * like fish
9.	In a Nominal Predicate	Cop N	*dat a foul* 'that's a fowl'	Cop D N	that's a fowl * that's fowl

This goes against what has been found for the L2 acquisition of English articles by children who are learning an additional, standardized second language, generally recognized as being quite separate from their first language.[22] Findings from these studies suggest that regardless of L1, there is a sequence of L2 acquisition for English articles, where the definite precedes the indefinite, and that, further, children whose L1 has an article system (as JC also does), have an advantage over speakers of article-less languages. Two studies examining child L2 learners with L1s that have articles are Zdorenko and Paradis (2008) and Morales (2011). Zdorenko and Paradis (2008) studied seventeen children between the ages of 4;02 and 6;09 for two years. Children whose L1s had articles showed an average of 25 per cent overuse of "the". Morales (2011) studied thirty L1 Spanish learners of English, ranging in age from eight to ten years. She found also that indefinites were more problematic for learners than definites, and (p. 88) calls on a suggestion by Lardière (2004) that the semantic characteristics of indefinites are complex and therefore more difficult to learn.

With regard to the use of JE forms by the CLAR children, the preference for the use of indefinite 'a' over definite 'the' might not be surprising, notwithstanding the marked preference for the use of the definite in the L1. This is because 'a' is a very common form in JC grammar, a multifunctional element (see section 3.2 for a discussion). This contrasts with the JE definite 'the' which contains the sound [ð], absent from the JC inventory of sounds. In fact, the JE definite, though appropriately used, appears either in utterances which consist only of the DP in which it appears, or else, in utterances where the majority of other words are JESs. In all cases, speech becomes halting and deliberate (see section 6.2 for further discussion).

I look now more closely at the internal make-up of the DPs used by the children and discuss in more detail possible causes for the dispreferred status of the JE definite.

4.3.3 Superficial Weaving in Article+Noun Sequences

The JE definite 'the' was not used with JC nouns; all JE definite articles selected JES or SHared nouns only.

It may be that article-noun sequences are fixed in the speech of the children. Eisenbeiß (2000, 31) speaks of such units as being unanalysed parts of formulaic utterances in first language acquisition. This phenomenon is also well known in second language acquisition, and the unit is commonly referred to as an *unanalysed chunk*, an utterance which represents an imitation, though not always accurate, of a sequence heard, and which the child may use in appropriate contexts without understanding the meaning of its parts. Prime examples are the rote learning of greetings. In (44), the child seems to have heard 'are you', is reminded of the exchange involved with 'How are you?' and launches into the relevant response.

(44)   INV: where are you?

      CAL: I am fine tangk yuu.

      CAL: an ou are yuu?   [V6-AN1:ll 532ff.-3;9.6]

That the children would hear article-noun chunks modelled by their teachers would be expected. First, 'the' is considered to be a target for teaching. Lacoste (2012, 31), in a study of children learning the sound system of JE in Jamaican schools, observes that although other speech patterns are taught in the Jamaican classroom, "systematic, corrective pressure on the pronunciation of S[tandard]JE is on the whole absent", but for the pronunciation of the voiced interdental fricative, the initial consonant of the definite article. She suggests that the tendency of Jamaicans to produce the dental stop /d/ in place of the fricative is a universally recognized linguistic mark of JC speech, and so teachers would feel some pressure to correct this in the children's speech. Second, the way teachers are said to go about the teaching of the pronunciation of words would promote the learning of chunks, that is, by methods involving the imitation of modelled patterns by children, resulting in the learning of "whole-word forms" (p. 58).

Evidence of this is the relatively small number of different nouns used with the article: twenty-two types and forty-seven tokens, a ratio of .47, suggesting that it is not used productively. In addition, material, such as an adjective, only intervenes between it and the noun once, in *the fat dog*. Even this one occurrence may be considered to be an imitation, since it was first modelled by the investigator. Notice that the child follows the pattern used in the investigator's question: 'what dog is this? – the fat dog is this'). Note further, however, that the resulting string of JESs does not form an acceptable JE utterance.

(45)   INV: what dog is this?

      INV: okay show me the fat dog.

> DAE: *the fat dog iz   this.*
>   DEF fat dog COP this
>   'This is the fat dog.'   [V1-STT:ll 379ff.-2;10.12]

Patterns in the use of the JE indefinite article 'a' were very different. Recall that it was used just under seven hundred times, or more than fourteen times as often as the JE definite. In eleven instances, it was followed by a noun beginning with a vowel. In JE, this would call for the use of the variant 'an' (for example, 'an elephant'); there were no uses of this variant by the CLAR children.

A quarter of the indefinite DPs follow a form of the JE copula 'to be', all but six of which take the form of the invariant *iz* 'is' or *dats* 'that's'.[23] It would seem that, again, the children have been exposed to drills which identify objects or people. One of the children repeatedly recited paradigms such as the one in (46); here we see that after changing the verb form to *iz* in line 462, he was unable to maintain the pattern:

(46)   460 ORR: I am a boi.

        461 ORR: I am a boi.

        462 ORR: MOY iz a gorl.

        463 ORR: mii iz a boi.   [V1-ADT:ll 460ff.-3 ;8.7]

This construction is known as a nominal predicate. In JE, it consists of the copula and a noun modified by the indefinite: BE+indefinite+N. In a JC nominal predicate, there is no indefinite. Instead, the invariant copula *a* is followed by the bare noun. This is illustrated in (47):

(47) OSS: *mi   mada   tel mi   se   mi   a   dangki.*
             1s.POSS mother tell 1s.IND OBJ COMP 1s.SUBJ COP donkey
             'My mother told me that I'm a donkey.'   [V6-MOB:l 422-3;8.12]

Other DPs using the JE indefinite appeared as objects of the verb or the preposition, as subjects, or simply as stand-alone utterances.

The JE indefinite introduced over twenty compound nouns as well as a JE possessive construction (a baby's jacket), and thirty-nine of the nouns used were modified by adjectives of colour, size or characteristics such as *dorti* 'dirty' or *priti* 'pretty'.

All this indicates productive use: the JE indefinite appears to form part of the JC grammatical system.

In addition, the JE indefinite is able to be (superficially) woven into the children's language. Unlike the JE definite where no DP contained a JC noun, in a third (33.9 per cent) of the DPs containing the JE indefinite, a JC noun was used. Often, these constructions were introduced with the pronoun *dis* (*dis iz a kyanggl* 'this is a candle' [V3-STR:l 179-3;7.28]), or else the JC noun is woven into otherwise JE constructions. In (48) below, for example, the child uses JC third-person subject pronouns *iihn*, then *im*, each time correcting himself,[24] to decide finally on the JE *hiiz* 'he's', followed by the JE indefinite 'a' and the JC noun *dakta*.

(48) NAT: &*iihn*   &*im*   *hi-*   *iz*   *a*   *dakta.*
              3S.SUBJ 3S.SUBJ 3S.SUBJ-COP INDEF doctor
              'He's a doctor.'   [V4-MOB:l 713-3;8.23]

Table 4.2 shows the internal make-up of definite and indefinite DPs where the determiner was immediately followed by the noun, indicating the percentages of totals when total includes SHared forms. Interestingly, of 1,420 indefinite articles used, 726 or 51.1 per cent were JC and 694 or 48.9 per cent were JE. The language of nouns following the JE indefinite was also fairly evenly distributed.

Table 4.2. The internal make-up of Def and Indef DPs (article+N)

JC Definite	Tokens	%	JC Indefinite	Tokens	%
$Def_{JC} + N_{JC}$	3,574	58.6	$Indef_{JC} + N_{JC}$	374	51.5
$Def_{JC} + N_{JES}$	722	11.8	$Indef_{JC} + N_{JES}$	87	12.0
$Def_{JC} + N_{SH}$	1,808	29.6	$Indef_{JC} + N_{SH}$	265	36.5
Total:	6,104	100.0	TOT:	726	100.0
JE Definite	**Tokens**	**%**	**JE Indefinite**	**Tokens**	**%**
$Def_{JE} + N_{JES}$	37	78.7	$Indef_{JE} + N_{JES}$	206	29.7
$Def_{JE} + N_{JC}$	0	0.0	$Indef_{JE} + N_{JC}$	235	33.9
$Def_{JE} + N_{SH}$	10	21.3	$Indef_{JE} + N_{SH}$	253	36.4
Total:	47	100.0	TOT:	694	100.0

This may also suggest that the JE indefinite is being incorporated into the speech of the children.

As indicated above, there was no mixing of codes in DPs headed by the JE definite. Table 4.2 shows that approximately 66 per cent of the nouns used with the JE indefinite were JES or SHared forms. The majority of DPs headed by a JE article, then, did not contain JC nouns.

With JC articles, the converse is true, but to an even greater degree: almost 90 per cent (88.2) of DPs headed by JC articles did not contain a JES noun.

Though not a majority (14.9 per cent), mixed DPs – DPs with a mix of components from the first and the second languages – were evident. Mixed constituents have been the topic of much discussion in the literature (see section 2.4), in particular those which, like the DP, contain a functional element and a lexical item (see section 6.3.2 for details). Petersen (1988) is a study of a Danish-English bilingual three-year-old who had never been exposed to a code-switching bilingual community. Her findings are presented in table 4.3 and merged with the CLAR data from table 4.2. Here, SH words are factored out on the basis that they are of ambiguous affiliation. Note that the dominant language for the CLAR children is JC, the non-dominant, then, being JE.[25]

Patterns of mixing within indefinite and definite DPs differ in the CLAR data, as we have seen. Nonetheless, when combined, my findings are similar in a general way to Petersen's: the greatest percentage of combinations of article+noun are from JC and the smallest, though by a far smaller margin for Petersen, combine the JE article with the JC noun.

Fundamental to the generative approach which is followed in this work is the notion of the selection of lexical items being determined by features associated with functional categories. Spradlin, Liceras and Fernández Fuertes (2003,

Table 4.3. Grammatical+lexical mixings from Petersen (1988, 46) applied to the CLAR data

Percentage Petersen	Combinations G(rammatical)+L(exical) dom(inant)/nondom(inant)	Percentage CLAR	Combinations
50.4	G-dom + L-dom	75.4	$Det_{JC} + N_{JC}$
28.5	G-dom + L-nondom	15.5	$Det_{JC} + N_{JE}$
20.6	G-nondom + L-nondom	4.6	$Det_{JE} + N_{JE}$
0.5	G-nondom + L-dom	4.5	$Det_{JE} + N_{JC}$

Table 4.4. Features Associated with JC and JE Articles

Language	Definite Article	Indefinite Article
JE	[definiteness]	[number]
JC	[definiteness]	[number]

301), for instance, predict that the bilingual child will favour the functional morpheme which has a more explicit realization of uninterpretable features. So, for the English-Spanish bilingual child, there will be a clear preference for the sequence Spanish D+English N since, setting definiteness aside, the Spanish determiner has two uninterpretable features (number and gender), while English only has number (p. 305). Such considerations would not apply to the Jamaican child learning English, since (as shown in table 4.4) there are an equal number of features associated with JE and JC articles.

An interesting alternative suggested by Radford (pers. comm.) would be one linking phonological and sociological or perhaps pragmatic trends. This is considered in sections 6.3.2 and 6.3.3.

What is taken here to be significant, and what we see developing as a recurrent pattern across the nominal and verbal domains in the discussions, is that a functional morpheme which there is reason to believe stands out in the children's minds as being associated with JE, will tend to occur in constructions with other JE items. It is along these lines that a clear picture of the nature of code-mixing in this (Jamaican) Creole environment will emerge.

4.4 Possessive Noun Phrases

To begin, I look at how possession is expressed in JC, using examples from the CLAR children's speech, followed by an indication of JE possession and how it differs from JC. In section 4.4.1, I consider findings on the L1 and L2 acquisition of English possession. The remaining sections explore the CLAR children's use of these forms: the JE Saxon genitive (section 4.4.2); possessive adjectives (4.4.3); possessive pronouns (4.4.4); the JC possessive *fi* construction (4.4.5); and finally, the JC possessive *uon* construction (4.4.6). Section 4.4.7 serves as a summary of the use of possessive noun phrases in the children's speech.

In JC, the possessive relation is commonly expressed using the sequence [possessor+possessed]. There were over eight hundred instances of this construction in the CLAR data; (49) is an example.

(49)   [possessor + possessed]

CHA: *mi   a   put aahn* [*di   biebi frak*].
        1s.SUBJ PROG put on   DEF baby dress
        'I'm putting on the baby's dress.'   [V5-SER:1 864-3;8.8]

Such a sequence may also be preceded by the possessive preposition *fi*, originally borrowed, perhaps, from English 'for':

(50)   prep *fi* + [possessor + possessed]

GAB: *a   fi   [i   dali   hier*].
        FOC PREP.POSS DEF dolly hair
        'It's the dolly's hair.'   [V6-SER.1 29-4.0.0]

The language makes use also of possessive pronouns. The distinction adopted
here is as follows: when the pronoun performs the function of possessor, it is an
adjective (*yu buk* 'your book'); otherwise, it is a pronoun (*fi yu* 'yours').

    JC possessive adjectives are homophonous with subject pronouns, and may
be constructed minimally as in (51), followed by the possessed. They may modify the possessor in the sequence [possessor+possessed] (52), and may also be
optionally preceded by the prepositional *fi* (53).

(51)   [poss adj + possessed]

SAS: *mi   a   go kaal* [*mi   mada*].
        1s.SUBJ PROG go call   1s.POSS mother
        'I'm going to call my mother.'   [V5-STR:1 733-4;0.12]

(52)   [poss adj + possessor] + possessed

OSS: *an* [*mi   mada*] *fut wehn sik   rait   yaso.*
        and 1s.POSS mother foot PAST sick right here
        'And my mother's foot was hurt right here.'
                                                    [V5-MOB:1 230-3;7.14]

(53)   (prep *fi*) + [poss adj + possessor] + possessed

KHA: *im   go op a   fi   [im   mada]   skuul.*
        3s.SUBJ go up to PREP.POSS 3s.POSS mother school
        'And he went up to his mother's school.'   [V3-SMR:1 703-3;6.14]

In addition, there is an adjective of possession *uon(a)* 'own'[26] which may follow a DP to result in the order *fi* +DP +*uon*, as in (54).

(54)   [prep *fi* + DP] + *uon*

      GAB: *a   [fi_____i____biebi] uon.*
               FOC PREP.POSS DEF baby own
               'It's the baby's.'   [V4-SER:l 549-3;9.27]

More rarely (only three instances), the sequence [possessive adjective + *uona*] appeared followed by a noun, as in (55). In these cases *fi* was omitted by the children, but is possible in adult JC, where *fi* can always introduce the possessor.

(55)   [poss adj + *uona*] + possessed

      ANN: *nau shi[/]shi naav   [aar___uona] kyaar yet.*
               no 3S.SUBJ NEG.have 3S.POSS own   car   yet
               'No, she doesn't have her own car yet.'   [V3-KN2:l 702-3;1.1]

Possessive pronouns preceded by *fi* typically occur in focus constructions (56), and may also be followed by *uon* (57). These pronouns are homophonous with possessive adjectives (see table 4.5), but are grammatically distinct since they replace the noun (Patrick 1999, 145).

(56)   [prep *fi* + poss pronoun] + (*uon*)

      BIA: *a   [fi_____mi].*
               FOC PREP.POSS 1S.POSS
               'It's mine.'   [V1-CLA:l 516-3;0.20]

(57)   BIA: *a   [fi_____mi]____uon.*
               FOC PREP.POSS 1S.POSS own
               'It's mine.'   [V1-CLA:l 526-3;0.20]

The JE possessive construction differs from that of JC. The relation is typically expressed in JE using the constructions in (58a–d).

(58a)   the Saxon genitive -s [pre-nominal possession]

      Mary   's   book
      possessor 's   possessed

(58b) <u>the of-genitive construction</u> [post-nominal possession]

the book of   Mary
possessed of   possessor

(58c) <u>possessive adjective</u> +N [the weak genitive form]

her   book
poss adj   possessed

(58d) <u>possessive pronoun</u> [the strong genitive form]

hers [no noun included]

To report on general trends in contemporary adult English, Anschutz (1997) draws on written and spoken data comprising five hundred noun phrases. Setting aside the possessive pronoun/adjective distinction, she finds that 66 per cent of the possessive constructions involving a human possessor consisted of the Saxon genitive -s form and the remaining 34 per cent, of the 'of'-genitive (p. 13).

Table 4.5 lists the forms of possessive adjectives and pronouns in the two languages. Recall that we say the form is an adjective if it is followed by a noun, but a pronoun, if not. Note also the following: unlike JE, the JC adjectives and pronouns have the same form; in both cases, JC distinguishes the second singular and second plural forms, and in the third-person singular there is no obligatory gender distinction, so that *im* (and variants *i, ii, ihn* and *iihn*) can have either male or female reference.

Table 4.5. Possessive systems: JC and JE

Person-Number	ADJECTIVES		PRONOUNS	
	JC	JE	JC	JE
1st singular	*(fi) mi*	my	*fi mi*	mine
2nd singular	*(fi) yu*	your	*fi yu*	yours
3rd singular	*(fi) im*	his or her	*fi im*	his or hers
1st plural	*(fi) wi*	our	*fi wi*	ours
2nd plural	*(fi) unu*	your	*fi unu*	yours
3rd plural	*(fi) dem*	their	*fi dem*	theirs

4.4.1 L1 and L2 Acquisition of English Possession

With regard to the L1 acquisition of the construction, Brown (1973) reported that the three monolingual L1 English children he studied produced the sequence possessor+possessed without possessive -s from age 2;0. The age at which the morpheme appeared 90 per cent or more of the time in obligatory contexts varied between 2;2 and 3;2 (p. 271).[27] It was the sixth functional morpheme to be acquired of the fourteen studied by Brown.

Radford and Galasso (1998) also report a prolonged period of absence of the possessive morpheme -s. They trace the L1 acquisition of English possessives in a monolingual child named Nicholas between the ages of 2;3 and 3;6, using transcripts of weekly recordings in the period. Nicholas did not use the possessive -s at all prior to age 3;2, in 118 obligatory contexts, using instead the juxtaposed possessor+possessed construction, as in 'Daddy car'. After that time, from 3;2-3;6, he used the possessive -s morpheme in only fourteen (23 per cent) of sixty obligatory contexts (p. 1).

Vásquez-Carranza (2010) discusses the L1 acquisition of English possessives, using data from CHILDES of children ages 2;0–5;0, to determine the relative frequency of the occurrence of pre- and post-nominal possessive constructions. She found that possesssive constructions were only used in 0.63 per cent of overall utterances (134 of 21,227 total), and that of those occurrences, only four were the post-nominal of-possessives. She reports that in the cases of pre-nominal possessives, the Saxon genitive -s marker was "often" omitted (p. 155).

For possessive adjectives and pronouns, Radford and Galasso (1998) indicate that singular forms only were used by Nicholas up to 3;6, his age at the end of recordings. The only pronominal forms used were the first-person 'mine' and the third-person 'his', but they were used ungrammatically as adjectives, that is, with a noun following (for example, 'mine book'). The first person was earliest to be acquired, and the most frequently used. There were different trends for the emergence of first, second and third persons; these are detailed below.

- The first-person adjective was used 231 times, accounting for 71.5 per cent of total use for the period 3;1–3;6. The predominant form used as the first-person possessor between 2;6 and 2;8 was the object pronoun form 'me'. The weak genitive 'my' and strong 'mine' were initially confused occasionally, and used relatively infrequently, but they gained ground until they predominated by age 3;0 (93 per cent). By 3;6, they were used correctly in 97 per cent of obligatory contexts (p. 6).

- The second-person possessor only appeared from 3;2 onwards. During the period (3;2–3;6), 79, or 24.5 per cent, of total possessors used were second person. Initially it is the form 'you' which occurred predominantly (88 per cent of total second-person forms). By age 3;5 the possessive form 'your' predominated with 79 per cent usage, and by 3;6 with 93 per cent (pp. 8–9).
- The third-person possessive forms used were 'him' and 'his', first appearing later, at 3;6, but again following the pattern of the objective form 'him' predominating initially at 77 per cent (p. 10). I note that the base for the third person was far smaller than that of first or second persons: only 13 occurrences, or 4.0 per cent of total use in that month.

L2 acquisition studies show differences in patterns of acquisition from the L1 acquisition of possessives; the possessive /s/ morpheme is acquired far later for the L2. Zobl and Liceras (1994, 169) cite a number of studies of the orders of the L2 acquisition of morphemes (Bailey, Madden and Krashen 1974; Krashen 1977; Larsen-Freeman 1975; Andersen 1978), all of which rank the possessive -s near the bottom, clustering with the third-person singular present tense inflection and the regular past tense.

4.4.2 The CLAR Children's Use of the JE Saxon and of-genitive

Both JC and JE express the possessive relation as possessor + possessed. To master JE possession, the JC child must only discover that the possessive relation is signalled in JE with '-s' attached to the possessor. Nonetheless, the data show sparse use of the construction by the CLAR children. While the task may seem simple enough, the difficulty may lie in the learning required of the speaker of a language lacking inflectional morphology, and in the lack of salience of the possessive -s, which does not stand out in the phonetic string.

There were only two instances of the use of the Saxon genitive by the CLAR children. The first was by a 3;4-year-old child from St Thomas, in the JE section of the last visit, in answer to a question in JE. The very next possessive construction used by the child omitted the possessive morpheme.

(59) INV: is there a jacket?

　　 DAE: <u>a   beebi-z   jakit</u>.
　　　　　　 INDEF baby-POSS jacket
　　　　　　 'A baby's jacket.'

　　 INV: your baby's jacket.

　　 INV: okay.

　　 DAE: *kyahn tek   aaf <u>i   beebi jakit</u>?*
　　　　　　 can   take off DEF baby jacket
　　　　　　 'May I take off the baby's jacket?'   [V6-STT:ll 488ff.-3;4.0]

The second use of the Saxon genitive was by a child from St Ann at age 3;6.21:

(60) INV: *a   wa   dis   mi   a   put pan har?*
　　　　　　 FOC what DEM 1S.SUBJ PROG put on   3S.OBJ
　　　　　　 'What's this that I'm putting on her?'

　　 SEB: *kluoz.*
　　　　　　 Clothes.

　　 INV: *we   di   kluoz   niem?*
　　　　　　 what DEF clothes name
　　　　　　 'What kind of clothes?'

　　 SEB: <u>beebi- z   kluoaz</u> [: kluoz].
　　　　　　 baby-POSS clothes
　　　　　　 'Baby's clothes.'   [V5-AN2:ll 200ff.-3;6.21]

Like DAE, SEB also used the JES *beebi* as the possessor. I note that she said the phrase deliberately and haltingly, even mispronouncing JC *kluoz* and that although she used JC *biebi* eight times and JC *kluoz* fifteen times otherwise in the course of this session, this was her only use of the JES *beebi* in the session, and of the form *kluoaz* in any session. This would seem to suggest a certain lack of ease on her part with the production of the construction. Such lack of ease may not be surprising given Patrick's (2007, 145) report that he found no examples of the possessor -s in his (adult) data, indicating to him that its usage powerfully marks a speaker as using JE.

The N+'of'+N construction was used in three different situations, none of which could be said to be expressing possession. Instead, they provided a measure of some kind: (a) *a piis a fish* 'a piece of fish', *wahn piis a ruop* 'a piece of rope' used with the JE indefinite 'a' and the JC *wahn* respectively; (b) containers *tin a soup* 'tin of soup' and *kop a waata* 'cup of water' and (c) *fut a* +N 'foot of+N' indicating a single unit of a pair of socks or shoes. A fourth case is shown in (61). Here, the 'of' construction could be said to be used to express possession, but even so, this was not in the sense of ownership. Instead, the *kova* 'cover' is a part of the *pat* 'pot'. These are all acceptable JC constructions.

(61) CHA: *mi   waant i   kova a di pat*.
            1S.SUBJ want DEF cover of DEF pot
            'I want the cover of the pot.'   [V4-SER:1 859-3;7.19]

We see, then, that the JC possessive construction is dominant in the children's speech. This is unsurprising, given that JC is deemed to be the L1.

4.4.3 The Use of Possessive Adjectives

I first look at the relative distribution of the possessive adjectives across persons, and then consider aspects of how the JES forms were woven into utterances produced by the children.

Plural forms accounted for a mere 1.1 per cent of all possessive adjectives used. Recall that Radford and Galasso (1998) found no plural forms up to the end of data collection when the child was 3;6. Though the CLAR data reveal sparse use, they first appeared at age 3;0.20. The third person accounted for 67 per cent of all plural forms.

As was reported by Radford and Galasso (1998) for the L1 acquisition of English, the first-person singular was the most frequently used of all possessive adjectives by the CLAR children, with some two thousand occurrences. Just under one quarter (23.8 per cent) of these possessive adjectives were JESs (*mai* and *ma*); the balance (76.2 per cent or just over fifteen hundred) were JC *mi*.

Though reduced, it would seem that *ma* is not a proto form,[28] since it was used by children ranging in age from 3;0.1 to 3;9.27. Further, informal discussions with native speakers have indicated that it is used in adult speech, and is considered to be a mesolectal form. It is reported in neither Patrick (2007) nor in Bailey (1966), however.

Far fewer second-person singular possessive adjectives (just under four hundred tokens) were used. JC *yu* accounted for 89.2 per cent of occurrences; the remaining 10.8 per cent were the JE *yor* 'your'. JE *yorz* 'yours' was used pronominally twenty-four times.

Finally, the third-person singular was used 1,080 times; 93.8 per cent were the JC forms *im* and its variants *ihm*, *ihn*, *ii* and *iihn*. The third-person singular adjective is of particular interest because of the range of JESs used, and the mixing found in these DPs. This is discussed next.

There was consistent JC dominance in superficial weaving within DPs using the possessive adjective. As seen in table 4.6, both JC and JES possessive adjective forms are followed predominantly by JC forms.

Two trends seem worthy of note: first, JE second-person *yor* is followed by a larger number of JES nouns than any other possessive. This would seem to point to the second-person *yor* being distinctively JE in the minds of the children, by virtue of the vowel+rhotic sequence, neither of which would be expected in JC. Such a distinctive association would provide the context for the activation of the JE lexicon (see section 6.3.2 for discussion). In contrast, JC *mi* and *yu* are followed by the least number of JES nouns, presumably, therefore, far less associated with JE.

Second, though overall 25.4 per cent of JES third-person possessive adjectives are followed by JES nouns, a more fine-grained analysis reveals variation in percentages for certain forms. The JES third-person possessive adjectives take many forms – *hor*, *har*, *shi*, *ar*, *aar* ('her') and *hiz*, *him* ('his'). As seen in table 4.7, the occurrences of the form which might be considered to show the greatest JE influence (*hor*) are very few (four only); they are followed only by JES, but not by

Table 4.6. Mixing in singular possessive adjective + N constructions

Possessive Adjective		# Tokens	+ JC Noun	+ JES Noun	+ SHared Noun
JC	*mi*	1,547	81.7%	6.1%	12.2%
	yu	348	56.9%	6.6%	36.5%
	im (3rd person)	1,013	67.1%	11.1%	21.8%
JES	*ma, mai*	483	65.8%	12.7%	21.5%
	yor	42	47.6%	26.2%	26.2%
	3rd person	67	50.7%	25.4%	23.9%

Note: Third-person forms used by the children are listed in table 4.7.

Table 4.7. Third-person possessive adjectives+JES nouns

FORM	Language	Meaning	Tokens	+ JC Noun	+ JES Noun	+ SH Noun
hor	JE	**her**	4	–	100.0 %	–
har	JES	her	24	58.4%	20.8 %	20.8%
shi	JES	her	25	64.0%	12.0%	24.0%
ar	JES	her	88	59.1%	17.1 %	22.8%
aar	JES	**her**	175	66.3%	7.4 %	26.3%
hiz	JE	his	9	55.6%	44.4 %	–
him	JE	his	4	100%	–	–

SHared or JC nouns. In contrast, the "most Creole" JES variants (*ar* and *aar*) have the greatest number of occurrences, and are followed by relatively few JES nouns. They do not appear to have strong JE associations in the minds of the children.

It would be expected that the "most JE" possessive form *hor* would present challenges in pronunciation for the children, since it has both an initial /h/, not used in that position in JC, as well as a vowel /ɔ/ which does not occur before /r/ in JC (see section 3.1 for discussion). I note, however, that children from Westmoreland where /h/ is said to be regularly pronounced word-initially, accounted for all occurrences of *hor* and *hiz*. For these children, then, the pronunciation difficulties would only involve the vowel+r sequences in *hor*.

In addition, the JE object pronoun 'him' was used as a possessive adjective four times, only in the context of brushing teeth, followed by a JC form (*tiit* 'teeth'), by children in Kingston, Clarendon and Montego Bay. This is perhaps surprising, given the "same language" trends outlined previously.

Plural forms, as indicated above, were not extensively used by the children. There is a total of a mere four uses of the JC first-person plural possessive adjective *wi*, by two children in one conversation. They were discussing the location of items belonging to them (for example, *wi bag dong de* 'our bag is down there').

Unu, the JC second-person plural form is said (Patrick 2007, 146) to be the most stigmatized of JC pronominal forms. It was used five times as a possessive adjective with JC nouns by children from St Elizabeth, Kingston and St Andrew (town),[29] and once with JE *ai* 'eye' (see [62]). Note that in this utterance, perhaps surprisingly, JC *unu* is flanked by JESs: it modifies the JES *ai* and is the object of *kooz* containing the JES 'oo'.[30]

(62) MOY: *dohn luk; <u>kooz</u>* [: *klooz*] *unu*   <u>*ai!*</u>
            don't look close   2PL.POSS eye
            'Don't look; close your eyes!'   [V3-MOY:l 719-3;6.13]

No JE third-person plural possessive ('their') was used; but JC counterparts occurred sixty-one times as adjectives as follows: *dem* (fifty-seven) *dehn* (seven) and *deng* (one), almost always followed by a JC noun: the only form followed by a JES noun was *dem* and that, nine times.

4.4.4 The Use of Possessive Pronouns

In JE, the possessive adjective and the pronoun have different forms (see table 4.5). Table 4.8 shows the JE pronoun forms used by the children.

     JES first-person singular *main* 'mine' appears both in utterances which are predominantly JE, as in (63a), and predominantly JC, as in (63b), where it is used quite naturally alongside the JC *fi yu*.

(63a) AMO: *iz   nat <u>yorn</u>   iz   <u>main</u>.*
            COP NEG 2S.POSS COP 1S.POSS
            'It's not yours, it's mine.'   [V3-STT:l 424-2;11.28]

(63b) DOM: *a   no   <u>fi</u>   <u>yu</u>   biebi a   <u>main</u>.*
            FOC NEG PREP.POSS 2S.POSS baby FOC 1S.POSS
            'It's not your baby, it's mine.'   [V3-CLA:l 519-3;0.11]

The second singular *yorn* was used twelve times by children from St Ann, Yallahs, Kingston and Clarendon, while *yorz* accounted for twenty-four uses. Pronominal *yorz, yorn* 'yours' never occurred with a noun following.

Table 4.8. JES possessive pronouns used by the children

Person/Number	Meaning	JES	Occurrences
1st singular	mine	*main*	187
2nd singular	yours	*yorz, yorn*	36
3rd singular	his, hers	–	0
1st plural	ours	–	0
2nd plural	yours	–	0
3rd plural	theirs	–	0

No other JES possessive pronoun forms were used by the children. The third-person singular JE 'her' seems to be explicitly avoided in the following dialogue, while the JE forms for first and second persons are used.

(64) INV: *a   uufa   panz dis?*
      FOC WH.POSS pants this
      'Whose pants are these?'

      DAM: *main.*
            1S.POSS
            'Mine.'

      INV: *a   uufa   panz dis?*
            FOC WH.POSS pants this
            'Whose pants are these?'

      DAM: *yorz.*
            2S.POSS
            'Yours.'

      INV: *a   uufa   blouz dis?*
            FOC WH.POSS blouse this
            'Whose blouse is this?'

      DAM: *fi   aar.*
            PREP.POSS 3S.POSS
            'Hers.'   [V1-KN2:ll 193ff.-3;10.13]

There was evidence of sensitivity to the adjective–pronoun distinction (*mai* 'my'+noun versus *main* 'mine' not followed by a noun). This was generally adhered to. An example is provided in (65).

(65) JER: *mami   kuk di   chikin   mek mi   iit it.*
            mummy cook DEF chicken make 1S.SUBJ eat 3S.OBJ
            'Mummy cooks chicken for me to eat.'

      DAV: *mai   mami   kuk miit.*
            1S.POSS mummy cook meat
            'My mummy cooks meat.'

JER: _main_   *kuk miit*   *fi mi.*
1s.POSS cook meat for 1s
'Mine cooks meat for me.'

[V1-AN2:ll 160ff.-JER 3;3.26-DAV 2;9.22]

The JE pronominal form of the possessive, then, is used in the first-person singular, with less use of the second-person singular. We see in sections 4.4.5 and 4.4.6 that the constructions of choice for expressing the pronominal function of the possessive were JC *fi* and *uon* constructions.

4.4.5 The Use of Possessive *fi* Constructions

Recall that the word class of JC possessive *fi* is taken to be a preposition, and that it can be used to (1) (optionally) introduce a possessive DP; (2) (optionally) introduce a possessive adjective + N; and (3) (obligatorily) introduce a possessive pronoun. There were five hundred constructions using the JC possessive preposition *fi* not followed by *uon*. Of these, 198 or 39.6 per cent were followed by possessive adjectives, 265 or 53.0 per cent by pronouns, and the remainder (7.4 per cent) by either a full DP headed by a JC determiner, or a proper noun.

Only four *fi*+possessive adjective+N sequences contained a JES possessive adjective; two were instances of *yor* and two of *har*. The nouns in these constructions were JC (*shuuz* 'shoes' x2, *ambrela* 'umbrella') or SHared (*bag*).

All other possessive adjectives following *fi* were JC, that is, 194 or 98.0 per cent. Of these, 64.4 per cent of the nouns they in turn modified were JC, 28.4 per cent were SHared (totalling 92.8 per cent);[31] only 7.2 per cent of nouns were JESs.

There was a strong tendency, therefore, for constituents in *fi* constructions to be JC.

Of the 265 possessive pronouns following *fi*, only seventeen or 6.4 per cent are JESs; the remaining 93.6 per cent were JC.[32] The highly stigmatized JC *unu* was used only once (*fi unu* 'yours (pl.)').

There is no JE counterpart to the JC possessive preposition *fi*, but the object forms of the pronoun which would normally follow a preposition in JE are: 'me', 'you', 'her', 'him', 'us' or 'them'. The seventeen uses of JES pronouns following *fi* revealed a mix of subject, object and possessive pronoun forms. The distribution is shown in table 4.9. Again, the overwhelming majority of elements following *fi* are JC forms.

Perhaps surprisingly, there are 50.8 per cent more occurrences of the JE *main* 'mine' (without *fi*) than there are of the JC pronominal *fi mi* 'mine'. This

Table 4.9. Forms of JES pronouns following JC *fi*

Function	Form Used	Meaning	# Tokens
Subject	*shii*	'her'	3
	wii	'us'	1
Object	*mii*	'me'	4
Subject/object	*yuu*	'you'	2
Possessive	*main*	'mine'	1
	yorn	'your'	1
Object/possessive	*har*	'her'	5

may be because it is a target for teachers since it is an obvious JC form, so that children would have learned to replace the form which is closer to JC with the JE *main* 'mine'. Alternatively, it may be that, like third-person *ar* and *aar*, the form is becoming more commonly used, and is being taken as JC. There are cases, for instance, where it is embedded in otherwise JC structures. An example is provided in (67).

(67) DAE: *non   mi   n-   aa   gi   non   a   <u>main</u>.*
     none 1s.SUBJ NEG-FUT give none of 1s.POSS
     'None; I'm not giving any of mine.'   [V3-ADT:1 351-3;9.15]

4.4.6 The Use of Possessive *uon* Constructions

The possessive *uon* 'own' may be used to emphasize possession, and may appear with *fi* in adult speech for contrast (Patrick 2007, 145). The children also use the JES variant *oon* very minimally (six instances total, by two children). Only 10.9 per cent of all *fi* constructions also contained *uon*, and 61 (or 31.4 per cent) of the 194 total *uon* constructions also appeared with *fi*.

There were fifty instances of the sequence *fi*+(possessive adjective or pronoun)+*uon* in the children's speech and eleven 'other' sequences such as *fi*+ DP+*uon* or *fi*+proper noun+*uon*. Recall that in the previous section, it had been determined that sequences introduced by *fi* tended to contain JC constituents. A JES pronoun occurred in only 4 *fi . . . uon* constructions: *mai* 'my' x2, *yor* 'your' and *har* 'her'. All other pronouns were JC. When the JE *mai* 'my' modified *uon*, *fi* did not appear, but all instances of *mi uon* were introduced by *fi*, further evidence of the trend of *fi* selecting JC constituents.

There were only three occurrences of *uona*; all were followed by a noun; an example is presented in (68) below. Like in adult JC, *uona* did not appear with the possessive *fi*.

(68)   KAM: *mi   a   go get mi   uona ruum.*
           1S.SUBJ PROG go get 1S.POSS POSS room
           'I'm going to get my own room.'   [V5-CLA:l 132-4;0.27]

4.4.7 Possession in Summary

There is no evidence that either JE possessive -s or 'of' genitives is being acquired by the children. Instead, the possessive constructions used are predominantly JC. It would appear that there is a strong tendency to use JConly constituents when the JC *fi* expresses the possessive relation. The relatively frequent use of the forms *main* and *a(a)r*, as well as their incorporation into JC structures, suggests that they may be gaining a foothold in the speech of JC-speaking children, and may therefore not be strongly associated with JE.

It would appear also, based on the use of subject and object pronominal forms to express possession, that the notion that different functions may be signalled by different forms, as is the case in the JE pronominal system, has not been acquired. In minimalist terms, it is the uninterpretable features of JE case and gender which have not been acquired. This is to be expected, since there are no case or gender distinctions in JC.

It is important to note that JC and JE forms are used interchangeably throughout. One child, ASH from Kingston, in six half-hour interviews used ten different third singular possessive adjectives/pronouns 265 times. The ten pronoun types were: *ar, aar, har* (variants of JE 'her'); *him, shi, shii* (JE) and *ihn, ii, iihn, im* (JC). Another striking case was a heated exchange between two children from St Mary, revealing a range of forms used in a battle of ownership of a pot cover, then a car, each ending with one child, JAY, relenting and handing over the object:

(69)   CHR: *a   main.*
           FOC 1S.POSS
           'It's mine.'

     JAY: *a   mai.*
           FOC 1S.POSS
           'It's mine.'

JAY: *<a   mai>* [>] *<u>uon</u> dis.*
FOC 1S.POSS   OWN DEM
'This is mine.'

CHR: *<a   <u>main</u>>* [<].
FOC 1S.POSS
'It's mine.'

JAY: *a   <u>mai   kova</u> dis.*
FOC 1S.POSS cover DEM
'This is my cover.'

CHR: *a   <u>main</u>   dis.*
FOC 1S.POSS DEM
'This is mine.'

JAY: *<tek <u>fi_____mi</u>>* [>]*!*
take PREP.POSS 1S.POSS
'Take mine!'

CHR: *<si <u>fi_____yu</u>   de>* [<]*!*
see PREP.POSS 2S.POSS there
'See yours there!'

JAY: *a   <u>fi_____mi</u>   dis.*
FOC PREP.POSS 1S.POSS DEM
'This one is mine.'

CHR: *a <u>fi mi</u>   dis.*

JAY: *a <u>fi mi</u>   dis.*

CHR: *a   <u>main</u>   dis.*
FOC 1S.POSS DEM
'This one is mine.'

JAY: *a   <u>mai</u>   dis.*
FOC 1S.POSS DEM
'This one is mine.'

CHR: *a   mai   kaar dis   we   fi   shraiv* [: *jraiv*] *go op deso.*
FOC 1s.POSS car   DEM COMP INF drive   go up there
'This is my car for driving up there.'

JAY: *si   it   de.*
see 3s.OBJ there
'See it there.'   [V3-SMT:ll 1099ff.-CHR 3;2.30,JAY 3;2.2]

4.5 Concluding Remarks

I have reviewed aspects of the nominal domain, namely, the count–mass distinction, pluralization, the use of the definite and indefinite determiner and the possessive construction, and have indicated how these structures work in JC and in JE, showing the differences between the two, and highlighting how the CLAR children chose to weave them in their speech, both structurally at the level of the syntax and superficially at the level of phonology. For each aspect of the language, I compared forms used by the children with those of other learners of English as an L2 as reported in the literature, with the full recognition that the language situation in Jamaica is far more complex than that of the L2 learners reported on in the literature.

Projecting a bit into the discussions of chapter 6, it is assumed that a knowledge of what the children bring linguistically to the literacy and language education classroom, that is, how they use the linguistic resources available to them from the input, will allow for informed decisions by teachers on the areas of language structure which could benefit from attention. In addition, having a grasp of how language works, and an ability to speak about the grammars of the languages involved will allow teachers to pass on to students the means by which to "unblur" the boundaries between the two systems. In other words, sharpening the metalinguistic skills of teachers will allow them in turn to sharpen the metalinguistic skills of their students.

I now look at aspects of the verbal domain with a similar approach.

5

What the Children Do with Verbs

KAR: *a wait mi did av.*[1]
[V2-CLA:l.381-3;8.23]

n this chapter, an outline of the basic distinction between the notions of tense and aspect, as presented in the theoretical literature, is provided, before seeking to determine the ways in which the theory may or may not apply to the child language data.[2]

5.1 Tense

Tense comprises categories where time reference is the primary dimension. We may say that it locates an eventuality in time. An eventuality is taken to refer not only to events but also to situations and states. In the following, we will see that JC and JE contrast with regard to tense, both in the form and in the system of tense-marking. In JE, every finite clause must be grammatically marked as to tense, indicating the relation which the eventuality has to the moment of speaking. Such a language is considered to be tense-prominent. As the discussion in this chapter unfolds, we shall see that JC, like other Creole languages, is not tense-prominent, since temporal fixing need not be determined in the syntax by grammatical marking, but that it may be set by other means such as by the inherent meaning of a verb, and by adverbs. Such a language is, instead, aspect-prominent.

Reichenbach (1947) constructed a theory of tense structure which has informed the linguistic study of tense. The components of the theory are the time of utterance or speech (S), the time of the event (E) and the reference point (R). Tense is explained in terms of how these time points are related. This model has been applied to the study of temporal interpretation in Creole languages by Muysken (1981), Lefèbvre (1996) and others; for completeness, I now present a quick overview of the system.

Time points are related in the following way: when E occurs before S, the event has taken place in the past; when E occurs after S, future time is expressed; and when S and RE coincide, the present tense occurs. The diagrams in (1) and (2) below are adaptations of Hornstein's (1990) illustrations of how the notion of R(eference) works. Time points are plotted for 'Mo will have left already by the time Jo gets here' in (1). Here, Jo's (future) arrival is used as the reference point for the event of Mo's (future) leaving – Mo will already have left by that time. Both E and R occur after S.

(1)   S = now   E = Mo leaves   R = Jo arrives

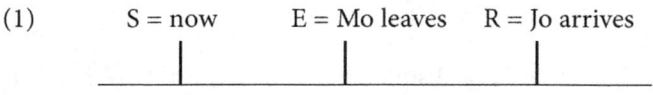

'Mo will have left already by the time Jo gets here'

In (2), R is shown to relate to S and E in the past. The starting point is S, the time of the utterance. 3pm is R, the reference point – this is the anchor in the past. At R, E had already taken place, since John had already left. Thus, E occurs before R, resulting in a past-before-past reading. Of course, both occur before S, since it was in the past that the leaving took place.

(2)   E = John left   R = 3pm   S = now

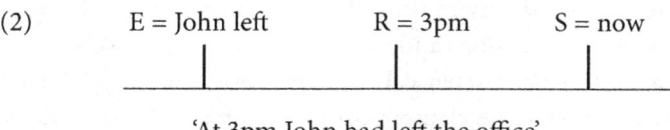

'At 3pm John had left the office'

In the Reichenbach model absolute tense locates E in the past with respect to S. In contrast, tense in Creole languages is said to be relative, that is, E is relative to R, not to S (Winford 2001, 162). One source from which it can take its reference is the discourse, so that the prototypical use of the anterior tense morpheme is to locate some E as occurring prior to the R under focus in the discourse.

In storytelling, for instance, once past time reference has been set, it can be assumed to persist until the speaker notifies otherwise (p. 159). This is said to be an indication that Creole languages are not tense dominant (Bhat 1999, 122).

Further, the location of R is determined in Creole languages by the (semantic) class of the verb. This is the domain of lexical aspect, aspect determined by the verb itself, and it is discussed in section 5.2.6.

The grammatical expression of tense is also different in JE and JC. In both, tense is an interpretable feature. In JE, in addition, there is an uninterpretable tense feature associated with the verb. In the case of the regular past tense, this will be spelled out as /ɪd/ or one of its variants /d/ or /t/, having been valued by interpretable T. The result is an inflected verb form.[3]

Basilectal JC uses independent pre-verbal tense markers *e(h)n* and its geographically determined variants *me(h)n*, *we(h)n*, *mi(h)n* and *be(h)n*. The variants *dii* and *did* have traditionally been considered to be mesolectal, used particularly in urban areas, and presumed to have arisen from JE. The tense marker is housed in T; both the marker and the verb are invariant. In minimalist terms, the lack of inflectional endings on the verb suggests that the verb has no uninterpretable tense feature associated with it that needs to be valued by interpretable tense in T.

We will see in section 5.2.6 that in addition, in the absence of an overt tense marking, there are default tense interpretations in JC for different lexical classes of verb.

Crucially, then, tense operates very differently in JE and in JC, and it is not the case that the child learning JE must learn simply that there are inflectional endings on the verb in that language. Instead, the child must learn that the temporal systems differ in important ways. This will impact the JC native speaker's production and understanding of JE.

5.1.1 The Future Tense

As we see in section 5.2.1 below, the progressive (aspect), for an event in progress, is expressed by the particle *a* or its variants *da* or *de*, followed by the bare verb. Also evidenced in the CLAR data is an immediate future tense expressed using a lengthened *a*, transcribed as *aa*, if obviously lengthened, or as *a(a)*, if lengthening was not detected but the future was apparent contextually.[4] Examples of its use are:

(3) INV: *Bianca yu   afi   go gi im   muor tii!*
             Bianca 2s.SUBJ MOD FUT give 3s.IND OBJ   more tea
             'Bianca, you have to give him more tea!'

      BIA: <u>*mi-a(a) wash*</u> *pliet   fors.*
             1s-FUT wash plate first
             'I'm going to wash the plates first.'   [V3-CLA:l 569-3;1.18]

(4) ORR: *we   ar   shuuz de?*
             where 3s.POSS shoes COP
             'Where are her shoes?'

      DAE: <u>*mi   a(a) si*</u> *if i   de   pahn i   tiebl.*
             1s.SUBJ FUT see if 3s.SUBJ COP on   DEF table
             'I'll see if it's on the table.'
             [Comment: DAE shouts and runs over to the table at the end of
             the room.]
                                     [V3-ADT:ll 341, 343; ORR-3;9.26/DAE-3;9.15]

Durrleman-Tame (2008, 29) considers *wi* to be a future tense, indicating that
it has a similar distribution to the past marker *e(h)n* and its variants, including
did. Children of all areas use this form, as well as its JE counterpart *wil*, but
it appears to be used, not as the future, but as a marker of epistemic modal-
ity, indicating that it would necessarily be the case that the event would take
place. This analysis of *wi(l)* as a modal is also adopted by Patrick (2007, 133). An
example of its use by the children is shown below:

(5) GAB: *poliis kyaahn fait mii   bak.*
             police MOD.NEG fight 1s.OBJ back
             'The police can't fight me.'

      GAB: <u>*mii   wil ded   im*</u>.
             1s.SUBJ MOD dead 3s.OBJ
             'I would surely kill him.'   [V4-SER:l.1014-3;9.27]

Expression of the future using the periphrastic construction equivalent to 'is
going to' in JE is discussed in 5.2.1 below as aspect, rather than tense, following
Durrleman-Tame (2008, 33).

5.2 Aspect

Aspect concerns the temporal structure of the situation, its internal make-up, or as Comrie (1976, 3) puts it, it refers to the different ways of viewing the internal temporal constituency of a situation. Unlike tense, aspect does not locate situations in time. It is not unconnected with time, but it does not relate the time of a situation to any other time-point.

Comrie provides "John was reading" as an example. This illustrates imperfective aspect where "reference is made to an internal portion of John's reading, while there is no explicit reference to the beginning or to the end of this reading" (1976, 4).

The same event could have been viewed differently, as a single complete whole, as in "John read". This illustrates perfective aspect. In this case, the situation is viewed in its totality, as having (successfully) taken place. Note that tense remains constant: in both the imperfective 'was reading' and the perfective 'read', the reading event took place in the past.

Traditionally, the term *grammatical aspect* has been used to refer to the morphological or syntactic means by which aspect may be represented. Imperfective aspect, expressed using the independent morpheme *a* in JC, is taken in what follows, to have as subcategories, the progressive (section 5.2.1), the habitual (5.2.2) and the iterative (5.2.3). Perfective aspect, expressed using the marker *don*, is discussed in section 5.2.4. Each subcategory expresses a different internal structure of the situation.

5.2.1   Progressive (or Continuous) Aspect

Progressive aspect (also referred to as the continuous) expresses duration over some period of time, however short, so that in (6) below, the event (the twisting of the doll's hair) is presented as one taking place (at the present time), an eventuality which would take the form 'You are twisting' in JE.

(6)   TAS: *yu   a   twis i   dali ier.*
             2s.SUBJ PROG twist DEF dolly hair
             'You are twisting the dolly's hair.'   [V1-SMR:1.704-3;3.11]

The bare verb is used to refer to the verb without grammatical marking. Here, for instance, it refers to the verb without the JC progressive marker. The bare verb is used throughout by the CLAR children in subjectless answers to questions using the progressive, as illustrated below.

(7)   INV: *wa   im   a   du?*
                what 3s.SUBJ PROG do
                'What's he doing?'

       ARI: *iit xxx.*
                eat xxx
                'Eating xxx.'   [V1-STT:l 141-2;9.0]

(8)   INV: *we   i   man a   du?*
                what DEF man PROG do
                'What is the man doing?'

       KAR: *jringk out i   waata.*
                drink out DEF water
                'Finishing off the water.'   [V4-CLA:l 854-3;11.15]

The exchange in (9) shows the bare verb being used in this way by the oldest child, at age 4;3.1, in answer to a JE progressive.

(9)   INV: So what is this boy doing now?

       DEV: *brosh ihn   tiit.*
                brush 3s.POSS teeth
                'Brushing his teeth.'   [V6-SMR;l 435-4;3.1]

The absence of the aspectual marker cannot be said, however, to reflect necessarily either a lack of aspect marking as such or incomplete acquisition, since alongside the use of the bare verb, the youngest child in the CLAR study aged 2;9.0 made use of the (adult) JC form *a*+verb.[5] Indeed, the full form was used extensively (over twenty-seven hundred instances) by children of all ages and from all areas in the CLAR study. It may simply illustrate a common conversational strategy used in both adult JC and JE, particularly where it is given as an answer to a question about what someone is doing, as it is in (7–9) above.

In addition to using the progressive aspectual marker to express continuous action, JC uses the combination of progressive *a*+*go* followed by the bare verb, for future meaning. This corresponds to the JE periphrastic construction 'going to'+bare V (Patrick 2007, 130). Durrleman-Tame (2008, 30) treats this as prospective aspect. She cites Frawley (1992, 322) as indicating that prospective meaning marks a point just prior to the beginning of an event.

5.2.2 Habitual Aspect

Habitual aspect describes a situation which holds (or held) for an extended period of time, so extended, in fact, that it is viewed as a characteristic feature of the whole period (Comrie 1976, 27–28). Christie (1986, 185) reports the use in (adult) JC of *a*+V for the habitual, using (10) below as an example:

(10) *wan*   *plies* *we*   *dem*   *a___plie*   *haki*   *mach.*
      INDEF place   COMP they   HAB play   hockey match
      'A place where they play hockey.'

There are few examples of the aspect particle *a* used to express a habitual meaning in the CLAR data; when they do exist, that specific aspectual meaning is often achieved by the combination of the particle and accompanying adverbials, as seen in (11) below:

(11) SHA: *im*   *aalwiez a___mash op mi*   *tingz.*
            3S.SUBJ always PROG mash up 1S.POSS things
            'He is always destroying my things.'   [V5-KN1:l.267-3;9.8]

The child is expressing an event as a process (hence the progressive) which happens on a regular basis (the habitual).

The habitual is said to be more typically represented in adult speech by zero-marked verbs (Patrick 2007, 131). Such occurrences are also found in the data.

(12) INV: *wen unu___go a maakit wa unu___du?*
            when 2PL.SUBJ go to market what 2PL.SUBJ do
            'When you go to market, what do you do?'

      JAY: *sel manggo.*
            sell mango
            'Sell mangoes.'   [V6-SMT:l 110-3;5.22]

(13) ROC: *an   mi   grani gi   mi   medisn   wen   mi   <u>kaaf</u>.*
       and 1s.poss granny give 3s.obj medicine when 1s.subj cough
       'And my granny <u>gives</u> me medicine when I <u>cough</u>.'
                               [V1-SMT:l 1028-3;7.7]

That the habitual is the intended meaning may also be communicated through adverbial modification, as in (14).

(14) ASH: *mai   granma   <u>aalweez</u> <u>sing</u> dem sang de.*
       1s.poss grandma always sing DEM song DEM
       'My grandma always sings those songs.' [V4-KN2:l 841-3;10.28]

Another means of expressing the habitual in JC is *yuustu* 'used to'. It is used rarely by the children – there were only three instances found in the data. All instances indicate the existence of a situation over an extended period of time in the past. (15) is an example.

(15) LEA: ... *big piipu* [: *piipl*] <u>*yuustu av*</u> *an+   bag wid wan   big sitn.*
       ... big   people used to have hand-bag with INDEF big thing
       '... adults used to have hand-bags with a big thing.'
                           [V1-SMR:l.1052-3;10.5]

5.2.3 Iterative Aspect

Iterative aspect describes the repetition of a situation, or the successive occurrence of several instances of the given situation (Comrie 1976, 27). In the JC case in (16), it is the word itself[6] which contributes to the iterative aspect conveyed, since the knocking event involves necessarily the successive occurrence of several instances of "knocking".

(16) GAB: *a   wid di   stik dem   <u>a   nak</u>   i   duor.*
       FOC with DEF stick 3PL.SUBJ ITER knock DEF door
       'It's with the stick that they're knocking on the door.'
                           [V6-SER:l.633-4;0.0]

Much like the habitual, iterative aspect may also be specified using an adverbial. In (17), for example, *evri minit* suggests that the action of frying is repeated:

(17) DAE: *evri   minit* *chikin+ bak* *a   frai*.
             every minute chicken-back ITER fry
             'Chicken-backs are constantly being fried.' [V1-ADT:l.725-3;7.26]

(18) SHN: *evri   taim yu* *a   put yu* *fut   out*.
             every time 2s.SUBJ PROG put 2s.POSS foot out
             'You keep putting out your foot every time.'
                                              [V1-SER:l.792-3;8.29]

Repeated occurrence is often emphasized by using an intensifier, as in (19), or by reduplicating the verb (20).

(19) BRA: *im   a   go juk mi   op*.
             3s.SUBJ PROG go jab 1s.OBJ up
             'He's going to jab me (several times).'   [V3-KN2:l.412-3;2.28]

(20) GAB: *we   im   a   toch toch mi   sopn   [fa] +...*
             what 3s.SUBJ ITER touch touch 1s.POSS something for
             'Why does he keep touching my thing?'   [V3-SER:l.231-3;7.17]

Interestingly, in (21), in expressing frustration over the fact that a classmate kept coming into the "people's room", the child repeats not the verb but its object, indicating repeated action, and expressing iterative aspect.

(21) ORR: *Krais!*
             'Christ!'

      ORR: *yu   jos a   kom ina [piipl   ruum] [piipl   ruum]*.
             2s.SUBJ just ITER come in people room   people room
             'You just keep coming into the room!'   [V3-ADT:l.563-3;9.26]

Here, the use of *a kom* specifically focuses on the fact that the action was initiated close to the time of speaking, but is being repeated.[7] Reduplication of a nominal phrase is unusual, since distributive reduplication, causing multiple events, is normally achieved via reduplication of the verb, as we saw in (20). What might be expected instead would therefore be *yu jos a kom-kom ina piipl ruum* ('... come-come...').[8]

All three subcategories of imperfective aspect, then, may be expressed syntactically by the same means in JC using the aspectual pre-verbal marker *a*.

These constructions may be expressed in the past using the past-tense marker (b)ehn or wehn (22), but the tense marker need not be used if contextual grounding in the past is clear, as seen in (23).

(22) OSS: ... mi   mada   _wehn de_   krai.
               ... 3s.POSS mother PAST PROG cry
               'My mother _was crying_.'   [V5-STJ:l.327-3;7.14]

(23) DON: ye   kaa   mi   si   im   wen   taim im   _a_   _sliip_
              lef   di   biebi.
              yes because 1s.SUBJ see 3s.OBJ when time 3s.SUBJ PROG sleep
              leave DEF baby
              'Yes, because I saw him the time that he _was sleeping_, leaving the baby.'

                                                        [V6-KN1-J:l.493-3;11.12]

5.2.4 Perfective Aspect

The perfective (also _completive_) marker in JC is _don_. As is well-documented, it may appear pre- or post-verbally (Patrick 2007, 132; Alleyne 1980, 91). Perfective aspect conveys the notion of completedness, and is unstressed.[9] Examples of the pre-verbal perfective marker are seen in (24) and (25).

(24)   im   _don nuo_   se   mi   laik im.
        3s.SUBJ PERF know COMP 1s.SUBJ like 3s.OBJ
        'He already knows I like him.'   [Patrick 2007, 132]

(25)   mi   _don fat_.
        1s.SUBJ PERF fat
        'I am (already) fat.'   [Alleyne 1980, 92]

There were no instances of the unstressed pre-verbal aspect marker _don_ in the CLAR data. All occurrences of _don_+V are considered to be lexical, since they are stressed. An example is given in (26). Stressed _don_ is a verb meaning "finish", from which perfective _don_ derives. As illustrated in (27), much like other lexical verbs, stressed _don_ may be modified by the progressive or may appear in the periphrastic future construction.[10]

(26) ASH: *ka   dem   <u>don</u> beed dem-self.*
            because 3PL.SUBJ done bathe 3PL- REFL
            '... because they've finished bathing.'   [V6-KN2:l.570-4;0.22]

(27) BRA: *mi   a   don   iit.*
            1S.SUBJ PROG done eat
            'I'm finishing up eating.'

      INV: *yu   a   don   iit?*
            2S.SUBJ PROG done eat
            'You're finishing up eating?'

      INV: *<Brandon momi> [/-] Brandon se   im   <u>gohn don</u>   iit.* [said
            to another child]
                             Brandon say 3S.SUBJ go   done eat
            'Brandon says he's going to finish eating.'

      BRA: *mi   an   mi   mada   a   go don   iit.*
            1S.SUBJ and 1S.POSS mother PROG go done eat
            'My mother and I are going to finish eating.'
                                                   [V2-KN2:l 302-3;4.23]

Note that *don* as a lexical verb in the sequence V_{don}+V is used by children of all ages, but not extensively, with only twenty-six occurrences.

Post-verbal *don* is considered to be a completive aspectual marker (for example, Durrleman 2008, 34–39), of which there are only three uses; (28) is an example.

(28) INV: *yu   no tel mi   wa yu   a   go kuk.*
            2S.SUBJ NEG tell 1S.IND OBJ what 2S.SUBJ PROG go cook
            'You haven't told me what you're going to cook.'

      JAY: *mi   kuk   don.*
            1S.SUBJ cook PERF
            'I've <u>finished</u> cooking.'   [V2-MOB:l.94-3;4.3]

In another use of post-verbal *don*, there was a juxtaposition of the future and the perfective, as seen in (29). This might have been influenced by the lexical verb *don* in the model provided by the investigator.

(29)   INV: *soo* <*i fuud*> [/] *i___fuud suuhn_don?*
                so   DEF food soon   done
                'So, you'll finish [cooking] soon?'
       [Comment: child nods.]

       KAM: *mi___a___go kuk_don.*
              1S.SUBJ PROG go cook PERF
              'I'll be finished cooking soon.'   [V3-CLA:l.436-3;9.22]

This sparse use of post-verbal *don* is supported by Durrleman-Tame's (2008, 53) claim that younger speakers of JC use post-verbal *don* rarely; that this may be an ongoing trend is suggested by her further claim that it is used more rarely by them than by the older generations.

5.2.5 Other Cases of Aspectual Use

In addition to *a*, the data reveal the use of *de* and *da*, forms known to be rural variants of the JC progressive, and said to be characteristic particularly of western Jamaica (DeCamp 1971b, quoted in Patrick 2007, 130, for example).[11]

These progressive variants were used by the CLAR children a total of fifty-eight times, of which only two were *da*, used once each by two children from rural St Thomas. The two western areas included in the research, St James (Montego Bay) and St Elizabeth, together accounted for forty-four (or 75.9 per cent) of the occurrences of *de*, with St Elizabeth, accounting for only five. The forms *da* and *de* were also attested in the speech of children in St Andrew town and rural (four times), Kingston (four times) and Clarendon (three times). No children from St Mary, St Thomas or St Ann used the form.

There was a small number of occurrences of *de* and *da* outside of the western parishes, then, but the possibility exists that even in the west, the use of these forms is diminishing. All children who used the variants *de* or *da*, used *a* far more frequently (overall, almost fifty-five times more often). As an example, a child JAY from Montego Bay who used *de* eleven times, used *a* 122 times. In addition, neither *de* nor *da* was used by children over age 3;9. A check as to whether this use by the children might be attributable to influence by the speech of investigators, revealed that this seems not to be the case: investigators used *de* eighty-three times in forty-one of 214 interviews, but no more than seven times in any single interview and, with one exception, used it only after the children themselves had introduced it.

There were three cases of interest where *a* represented imperfective/progressive aspect (30), and one (31), where its variant *de* performed the same function; of interest, since they were used with the unambiguously completed event *gaan* 'gone'. The investigator seemed to have thought it strange in (30), and requested, and received confirmation of its use. The use of the progressive seems to reflect the journey in progress after the departure, as indicated by the translation 'on the way to'. Note that in (31), even with *go* as a model, the child uses *gaan*.

(30) BIA: *dem   a   gaan a Mie_Pen.*
          3PL.SUBJ PROG gone to May Pen
          'They are on their way to May Pen.'[12]

      INV: *dem a gaan a Mie_Pen?*

      BIA: *yies.*
          'Yes.'

      INV: *wa   dem   a   gaan   a Mie_Pen go du?*
          what 3PL.SUBJ PROG gone   to May Pen go do
          'What are they on their way to May Pen to do?'

      BIA: *fi   get moni   laik Basil.*
          COMP get money like Basil
          'To get money like Basil does.'   [V1-CLA:l 455-3;0.20]

(31) INV: *wich   paat shi   a   go?*
          which part 3S.SUBJ PROG go
          'Where is she going?'

      OSS: *iihn   de   gaan a werk.*
          3S.SUBJ PROG gone to work
          'She's (left and) on her way to work.'   [V4-MOB-l.614-3;6.16]

Regular use of *gaan* as a verb with perfective meaning in JC is clear from other examples:

(32) DON: *shi   gaan   a har   bed an den piipl [/] piipl biit ar.*
          3S.SUBJ gone   to 3S.POSS bed and then people people beat 3S.OBJ
          'She went to her bed and then people beat her.'
                                         [V5-KIN-l.612-3;10.20]

In addition, the progressive is used in secondary predication which in JE would require a non-finite verb. Consider (33), where the child indicates an activity which she saw a fish engaging in. The construction is known as a small clause, which functions in this case as the complement of the main (perception) verb *si* and which consists of an overt subject *wahn bong fish* and a secondary predicate *a kom frahn out a i sii*. Note that in English, the verb in the secondary predicate would not be finite (instead, 'coming'), yet in JC it consists of what appears to be the full finite *a kom*.

(33) CHR: *mi   si   wahn bong [?] fish a   kom   frahn out a i   sii.*
              1S.SING see INDEF bong   fish PROG come from out of DEF sea
              'I saw a bong fish <u>coming</u> from out of the sea.'
                                                    [V3-SMT:l 185-3;2.30]

Similarly, the secondary predicate *a lorn* in (34) appears to be finite,[13] whereas in JE, the non-finite gerund ('learning') would normally follow a copula+locative construction ('are in school'). Note that the subject *dem* 'they' is shared by both clauses, as it would be in JE.

(34) DON: <u>dem</u>   ina skuul   <u>a   lorn</u>.
              3PL.SUBJ in   school PROG learn
              'They're in school <u>learning</u>.'   [V1-KN1:l 178-3;6.11]

In the causative construction in (35), the child sees a picture of a boy whose upper arm only is shown, and builds a story around this, imagining that soldiers burnt his arm, causing him to be sleeping.

(35) KIM: *an dem   bon im   an an <u>mek im   a   sliip</u>.*
              and 3PL.SUBJ burn 3s.POSS hand and make 3s.SUBJ PROG sleep
              'And they burnt his hand and made him sleep.'
                                                    [V1-CLA:l 577-3;0.27]

Much like examples (11), (17), (18) and even (30) and (31) above, in JC, any event viewed as being in process requires the progressive.

Finally, there were instances of the aspectual marker in V_1+V_2 sequences. Examples are with V_1 *staat* 'start' (36) and *go* 'go' (37). Note the use of both variants *de* and *a* in the same utterance (37), both representing progressive aspect.

(36) ANN: *an im   staat a   tomp   op dadi.*
            and 3s.SUBJ start ITER thump up daddy
            'And he <u>started thumping</u> Daddy.'   [V3-KN2:1 131-3;1.1]

(37) OSS: *iihn   de   go a   bied.*
            3s.SUBJ PROG go PROG bathe
            'She's <u>going bathing</u>.'   [V3-MOB:1.351-3;4.15]

Again, it would seem that in a V_1+V_2 construction, once the action expressed by V_2 is ongoing, the tendency is to use the progressive marker. I note that *ihn de go bied* would also be acceptable.[14] In this case, however, the structure is quite different from that of (37): as before, *de* is a marker of progressive aspect, but here *go* functions as a marker of prospective aspect, indicating that 'He (or she) is going to bathe' (see section 5.2.1 for discussion of this construction).

Importantly, grammatical aspect as discussed above is not the only consideration: it is also true for all languages that verbs differ in what has been called their *aspectual potential* (Dahl 1985, 26). This is the domain of lexical aspect, discussed in the next section.

5.2.6 Lexical Aspect

Lexical aspect, also known as *Aktionsart,* or inherent aspect, refers to cases where aspect is derived from the word itself. As we shall see, in JC this often overrides grammatical aspect as well as tense. Aktionsart distinctions play a prominent role in the verbal system of JC. This is another reason why JC has been considered to be aspect-prominent.[15]

Stativity and non-stativity are dimensions of verbal meaning relevant to the discussion of lexical aspect, to which Bickerton (1975, 72) and others such as Winford (1993) assign the greatest significance in determining the distribution and interpretation of combinations of tense and aspect markers in Creole languages. There have been many and varied terms used as labels for the dimensions of verbal meaning. By way of background, I outline in what follows, the approach adopted by Winford (1993). As will become apparent, two major aspectual classes of verbs, statives and non-statives, have different temporal interpretations when modified by the past-tense marker. In effect, aspect overrides tense, further evidence of JC being an aspect-prominent language.

Stative verbs constitute a relatively small class, including Creole verbs such as *nuo* 'know', *lov* 'love', *waahn* 'want' and *a(v)* 'have', all of which convey (typically continuous) physical or internal states. Following Vendler (1967), using semantic criteria, Andersen (1990, 63) characterizes such verbs as requiring no energy for them to continue once the state has been entered, although entering or leaving a state may be conceived as non-stative, depending on the particular circumstances. I note that the JC stative verbs most used by the children are *waahn* 'want', *nuo* 'know' and *av* 'have', and that they fall within their top eight most frequently used verbs.

Tense interacts with lexical aspect in important ways. The default tense reading for bare or zero-marked (Ø) statives (that is, stative verbs not accompanied by a tense marker) is the present (Winford 1993, 33).[16]

(38) <u>bare stative: present</u>   *im*   Ø   *nuo.*
                             3S.SUBJ TENSE know
                             'He (or she) knows.'

Non-stative verbs such as JC *ron* 'run', *push* 'push', *jrap* 'drop', or *jomp* 'jump' require energy for the action or event to take place and to continue (cf. Andersen 1990, 63, for reference to their English counterparts). For this reason, such verbs have also been termed *dynamic*. The default tense interpretation for bare non-statives is said to be the past.

(39) <u>bare non-stative: past</u>   *di* *man* Ø   *tiif* *i.*
                             DEF man TENSE steal 3s
                             'The man stole it.'

The interpretational consequences of the use of the tense marker, that is, how the marker interacts with stativity, is illustrated in (40). Recall the discussion on relative tense in 5.1: the time of reference (R) may be determined in Creole languages by the (semantic) class of the verb. What happens is that R is established by the verb. It is established as present (S) by statives, and as past (prior to S) by non-statives. The anterior tense marker serves to shift the event (E) to a point prior to R in each case, resulting in past for a stative and past before past for a non-stative, as seen in (40a–40b).

(40a) tense marker + stative: past
    im   *behn nuo.*
    3S.SUBJ PAST know
    'He (or she) knew.'

(40b) tense marker + non-stative: past before past
   [*wen mi   kom*] *di   man behn tiif i.*
   [when 1s.SING come] DEF man PAST steal 3s.OBJ
   '[When I came] the man had stolen it.'

DeGraff (1996, 134) calls on other factors affecting the temporal interpretation of the bare verb. He notes for Haitian Creole that there appears also to be
dependence on the referential properties of the direct object. This has also been
noted for non-Creole languages. If non-specific, as in (41), the direct object
induces a non-past interpretation even for non-statives (whose default tense
is the past). In this case, reference is not to a specific event, and the unmarked
verb has habitual meaning, with the implication that the action referred to takes
place more than once over some extended period of time.

(41) KIM: *gramaa bai parij   fi   jringk an mek   parij ...*
            grandma buy porridge INF drink   and make porridge
            'Grandma buys porridge to drink and makes porridge ...'
                                               [V2-CLA:l 120;3;1.25]

In contrast, if the object is specific or refers to a single object, this points to a
specific event. What becomes significant in (42), for instance, is the fact that the
action specified by the verb *bai* is specific, and a past reading is obtained.[17]

(42) ROD: *fi   mi   faada bai da wan de   gi mi.*
            PREP.POSS 1s.POSS father buy DEM NUM DEM give 1s.IND OBJ
            'My father bought that one for me.'   [V1-SER:l 108;3;3.25]

The examples show that trends found in Haitian Creole apply also to JC.
   The internal structure of some non-stative verbs suggests processes that
involve physical or mental activity, and consist entirely in the process (Smith
1997, 22–25). An example is *plie* 'play'. The activity does terminate, but that
point is arbitrary, since it does not follow from the structure of the event, which
is viewed as ongoing. This class of non-stative verb is termed an activity, and is
semantically compatible with the progressive aspectual marker.
   We would expect children to use activity verbs in order to speak about events
taking place in their immediate environment, since the well-documented tendency in child interactions, universally, is to focus on the here and now. Even
when a stative verb (in this example *ties* 'taste') is used by the investigator in a

direct question, the child changes the construction, thus avoiding its use, and focuses rather on the (non-stative) cooking event:

(43) INV: *so wen   yu   kuk   <u>ou   i   fuud ties?</u>*
             so when 2s.SUBJ cook how DEF food taste
             'So when you cook, how does the food taste?'

      DON: *i   <u>kuk</u>   nais.*
             3s.SUBJ cook nice
             'It's nicely cooked.'   [V1-KN1:l 773-3.6.11]

Notice that the same sort of response is provided in (44) when another child was asked about how he felt (stative) when the dog bit him (non-stative). He answers using the non-stative *bait* 'bite', thereby placing the focus on the event, and avoiding the use of the stative.

(44) INV: *so ou   i   <u>dii   fiil</u> wen   iihm   bait yu?*
             so how it PAST feel when   3s.SUBJ bite 2s.OBJ
             'So, how did it feel when he bit you?'

      ROD: *iihm   <u>bait</u> mi   hat ra.*
             3s.SUBJ bite 1s.OBJ hot EMPH
             'It really hurt when he bit me.'   [V1-SER:l 368-3;3.25]

Statives have different semantic qualities than do activities. As seen in the preceding, a stative verb represents a stable situation (rather than an event). Whatever the length of time for which the situation holds, that period is not viewed as terminating, nor is there any view of an initial endpoint. For that reason, it is not normally compatible with the progressive, which views an event as ongoing.

The children do, however, use the progressive with statives. In (45) the child explains that the foul is laying chickens. He uses *av* 'have', normally a stative verb, with the progressive, and obtains a non-stative reading. In (46), having indicated that another boy was playing dominoes, in answer to the question *we im a du?* 'What's he doing?', the child also uses the progressive with *av*; in (47) it is used with the locative copula *de*, normally inherently stative.

(45) SHY: *di   foul <u>a   av</u> i   chikin   a   lie ...*
             DEF fowl PROG have DEF chicken PROG lay
             'The fowl is giving birth to the chicken.'/*'is having'
                                                            [V3-AN2:l.167-3;1.0]

(46) AMO: *im   a   av plien.*
     3s.SUBJ PROG have plane
     'He has a plane.'/*'is having'   [V3-STT:l.368-2;11.28]

(47) DOM: *i   man a   de pan i   an ii   a   jraiv i.*
     DEF man PROG COP on   3s.OBJ and 3s.SUBJ PROG drive 3s.OBJ
     'The man is on it and is driving it.'/*'is being'
                                             [V3-CLA:l.595-3;0.11]

These verbs seem to be coerced into non-stative status, with the situation being viewed in terms of being an activity. In contrast, in JE, the use of the progressive is avoided with stative verbs, as seen in the ungrammatical translations.

The CLAR data show that stativity can be affected by a particle functioning as an adverb. Modifying the stative *lov* 'love' with the particle *op* 'up', for instance, coerces a non-stative status, resulting in the meaning "hug" or "being involved in some activity which expresses love". This is illustrated in (48) below, where the child is rubbing two paint brushes together, and making a comment as to what they are doing:

(48) GAB: *dem   a   lov op.*
     3PL.SUBJ PROG love up
     'They are loving.'   [V6-SER:l 487-4;0.0]

5.2.7 Summary

To summarize this section on aspect in JC, all three subcategories of imperfective aspect – progressive, habitual, though rarely, and iterative – may be expressed syntactically by the same means in JC using the aspectual pre-verbal marker *a*. They may also be expressed using the unmarked verb, given lexical aspect and the appropriate contextual grounding. There is dependence among JC speakers, then, on semantic characteristics of classes of verbs, and a need to distinguish between statives and non-statives. There is also reliance on the use of other grammatical devices in interaction with the inherent meaning of an unmarked verb: adverbials, for example, *aalwiez* 'always' to express habitual activity, and a verbal particle or a reduplicating verb to express repeated action (iterative aspect).

Such means are not available in JE. Instead, as an example, the progressive is expressed with a form of the auxiliary 'to be' followed by the lexical verb inflected with the participle '-in(g)' as in 'He is playing'. This requires the involvement of uninterpretable features regulating the morphology and resulting in agreement of the subject with the auxiliary, and the inclusion of the progressive inflectional '-ing' on the verb. For habitual meaning, the simple present and the simple past may be used, as well as 'used to' or 'would' for habitual action in the past.

In the case of secondary predication, the second verb remains non-finite in JE, whereas in JC both verbs may be finite (*im staat a tomp op dadi* 'He started thumping Daddy').

It is clear that JC and JE have two distinct grammatical systems with regard to aspect. We look now in further detail at the grammatical category of tense, and see that temporal relations are also expressed differently in the two languages.

5.3 Back to Tense

5.3.1 The Tense Marker in the CLAR Data

We saw in section 5.2.6 that tense is not always marked in JC when reference is being made to an action which took place in the past: the default reading for bare or unmarked non-stative verbs is the past. This section discusses the use of markers.

The CLAR data reveal minimal use of pre-verbal *wehn* (seventeen instances), versus 155 uses of *dii/did*, totalling 172. There were seven cases of the past progressive. A different pattern is reported by De Lisser (2015, 98). She noted seventy-one instances of the past-tense marker by children in the age range 2;5–3;3; of these, thirty-eight, or just over 50 per cent, were used to express the past progressive. Her examples show the use of both *did* and *en*, but there is no indication of the relative extent of their use.[18] These trends may be due to the nature of the speech recorded – the subject matter, for instance.[19]

No variants of the past-tense marker other than *dii/did* and *wehn* were used by the CLAR children; they did not use the JC form *e(h)n*, though they did use its negative counterpart *nehn*, but even so, only twice. I note that *en* was used only four times by investigators, and the negative variants *nehn* or *neehn*, forty times, perhaps influenced by the conversational contexts.

Of the seventeen instances of the JC past-tense marker *wehn*, all but one (by a child from St Ann aged 3;1.0) were used by children from Montego Bay, but not before age 3;4.15. In (49) we see an example; the context has been provided to show clearly that, as might be predicted given the discussion in section 5.2.6, *wehn* accompanying a non-stative is used to give a past-before-past meaning:

(49) INV: *yu   step ina ans?*
           2s.SUBJ step in ants
           '<u>Did</u> you step into an ants' nest?'

     ANG: *yie, i   ans <u>wehn bait</u> mi   op a mi   yaad.*
           yes DEF ants PAST bite 1s.OBJ up at 1s.POSS yard
           'Yes, the ants had bitten me, up at my house.'

     INV: *oo, an it   stil a   krach yu?*
           oh, and 3s.SUBJ still PROG scratch 2s.OBJ
           'Oh, and it's still itching you?'

     ANG: *yie, im   <u>wehn bait</u> mi   an mi   kik i af a   mi*
           han.
           yes, 3s.SUBJ PAST bite 1s.OBJ and 1s.SUBJ kick 3s.OBJ off of 1s.POSS
           hand
           'Yes, it <u>had bitten</u> me and I kicked it off my hand.'
                                   [V3-MOB:672–73;4.22]

It would seem that children from areas other than those from St James may not be familiar with *wehn*. In (50), a child from Clarendon answers inappropriately, indicating perhaps a lack of understanding.

(50) INV: *wich paat i   dali <u>wehn de</u>?*
           which part DEF dolly PAST COP
           'Where was the dolly (at that point)?'

     BIA: *si im   ier.*
           see 3s.OBJ here
           'See her here.'   [V1-CLA:1 785-3;0.2]

Similarly, (51) may be indicative of a lack of understanding of the marker by a child from St Elizabeth, since there is no response, even though the child had been generally very talkative in the session:

(51) INV: *wa   yu   <u>wehn a   du</u> so fa?*
             what 2s.SUBJ PAST   PROG do so for
             'Why were you doing that?'

     ROD: 0.   [V1-SER:1 480-3;3.25]

Finally, in (52) the question is answered by a child from St Mary, but not immediately after the initial model containing *wehn*, suggesting perhaps that the response may have been independent of an understanding of the marker.

(52) INV: *wa   yu   <u>wehn go</u> out de   go du?*
             what 2s.SUBJ PAST go out there go do
             'What had you gone out there to do?'

     DEV: go [/] go.
             'Go.'

     DEV: ii. (a squeal)

     DEV: *go ku [?] aaf i   fens   dem.*
             go cut   off   DEF fence INCL
             'to cut off the fences.'   [V1-ADT:ll 779ff.-3;9.14]

Whether these instances do actually point to unfamiliarity with the form *wehn* is not known. Other plausible explanations may be that the seemingly inappropriate response in (50) is due to the tendency to relate only to the here and now, and so BIA is indicating the whereabouts of the doll at the time of speaking; in (51), the child may simply not have wanted to divulge the reason for his action; and finally the squeal uttered by DEV in (52) may indicate a hesitation on his part to respond to the investigator's question because of the realization that he had done something naughty in "cutting off" the fence.

What may be more significant is the scarcity of the use of *wehn*, and its occurrence predominantly in Montego Bay, contrasting with the use by children of all ages, and from all areas of the variant *did* as a past-tense marker a total of 124 times. This is normally considered to be a mesolectal form, and so its use may be surprising, given the expectation that our children would be speakers of the basilect (see section 1.1.3 for discussion of these *lects*). In addition, the children used the phonologically reduced variant *dii* a total of thirty-one times. Patrick (2007, 129) claims that *did* (and presumably its variant *dii*) is sometimes used among rural speakers, but is more common among urban or educated speakers of JC. Its use is said to be due to exposure to JE. In the CLAR data, however, a full 36.8 per cent of uses of these forms were by children from rural areas, indicating more widespread use than Patrick suggests, and pointing perhaps to a trend of increasing use outside of urban areas. It seems feasible to conclude that its use is not due to urban influence necessarily, but instead may now form part of regular use in Creole-speaking communities.

There are cases of the use of *did* and its variant *dii* conveying a past-before-past reading; (53) is an example. Interestingly, in seeking confirmation on what the child had said, the investigator (originally from Montego Bay) uses *wehn*.

(53) ROD: *Kim <u>dii   bai</u> wahn chriichip fi   mi   aahn rat bait i.*
          Kim PAST buy INDEF CheezTrix for 1s.OBJ and rat bite 3s.OBJ
          'Kim had bought a pack of CheezTrix for me and a rat chewed it.'

      INV: *oo, dehm   <u>wehn bai</u> wahn chriichip fi   yu   aahn rat bait i?*
          oh, 3PL.SUBJ PAST buy INDEF CheezTrix for 2s.OBJ and   rat bite 3s.OBJ
          'Oh, they had bought a pack of CheezTrix for you, and a rat chewed it?'   [V1-SER:l 145-3;3.25]

Note that, like so many other forms, although JC *did* and its variants are similar in form to JE 'did', they function differently in the two languages. In JC, this is an independent past-tense marker (*im did nuo* 'he knew' versus *im did bai* 'he had bought'), functioning like other pre-verbal markers in the language. In JE, however, 'did' functions as an emphatic marker in a declarative sentence ('he <u>did</u> go' meaning "he definitely went"). Differences in stress accompany these functions: in JC it is unstressed, whereas as a marker of emphasis in JE, it is necessarily stressed. Again, therefore, for the JC speaker, learning JE involves learning a new grammatical system, and not simply the translations or pronunciations of words which may not be shared by the two languages.

5.3.2 Time Reference in JC

We saw in sections 5.1 and 5.2.6 that JC, like other Creole languages, is aspect-prominent. A feature of aspect in aspect-prominent languages is that it overrides tense. A non-stative without tense marking, for instance, receives a default past interpretation (54). Yet, with the aspectual marker *a*, this past-tense interpretation is overridden, and the non-stative receives a non-past interpretation (see [55]).

(54) TAS: *shi   bied   ahn gaan a   skuul.*
            3s.SUBJ bathe and gone to school
            'She bathed and went to school.'   [V1-ADT:l.164-3;6.0]

(55) INV: *dem   a   bied   in de?*
            3PL.SUBJ PROG bathe in LOC
            'They're bathing in there?'

      DOM: *ye, an   dem   a   bied dem   an.*
            yes and 3PL.SUBJ PROG bathe 3PL.POSS hand
            'Yes, and they're bathing their hands.'   [V3-CLA:l.299-3;0.11]

In order to have a past progressive reading, a tense marker must normally be used:

(56) ANN: *mai   breda   did   a   bied ina i   shouwa.*
            1s.POSS brother PAST PROG bathe in DEF shower
            'My brother was bathing in the shower.'   [V1-KN2:l.203-2;11.6]

A past-tense marker was used in only seven cases, or 1.1 per cent of all progressive *a* constructions; in all of these, the marker used was *did* or *dii*.

    Time reference may also be indicated by adverbials in JC. We see, for instance, in (57) below, that though *a riid* would normally receive a non-past interpretation, here *wail ago* imposes the past, and the tense marker is not required for a past-tense reading.

(57) ORR: *dis wan   wi   a   riid wail   ago?*
            DEM INDEF 1PL.SUBJ PROG read while ago
            'This one we were reading a while ago?'   [V1-ADT:l 76-3;8.7]

To sum up, we have seen that the temporal interpretation of verbs without contextual modification (that is, the default) is dependent on their stativity status in JC and other Creole languages, because of the inherent perfective/imperfective characteristics of verbal meaning. Specifically, because statives are inherently imperfective, they refer to situations going on in time. As a result, when unmarked they have a present meaning. In contrast, because non-statives are inherently perfective, referring to a situation as one whole entity, they have a past meaning when bare. Grammatical aspect marking overrides this, however, since the progressive *a*, for instance, returns a non-past interpretation even with a non-stative. Finally, time reference may also be determined by adverbials.

5.4 Weaving of JE and JC

There are structures used by the children which reflect features from both JC and JE, but there are detectable patterns in this mixing of the two codes. We call this mixing *weaving* (see section 1.1), and distinguish between superficial weaves at the level of pronunciation, and structural weaves, that is, those that occur in the syntax. In section 5.4.1, I look at the weaves in past-tense constructions and in section 5.4.2 at progressive constructions, including combinations of subject and auxiliary under JE influence.

5.4.1 Weaving in Past-Tense Constructions

Structural weaving, involving the use of JC and JE features alongside each other within a construction, is evident in the expression of the past. Note that, as has been the trend, superficial weaves involving pronunciation differences regularly take place within the structural weave.

Only two verbs inflected with the regular JE past inflectional ending '-d' were attested. In (58), NAT is speaking about going to the beach. He uses the stem *waant* 'want', which must be considered a JES form, since the final 'n+t' cluster represents JE influence – the JC stem *waahn* has a nasalized vowel, with no pronounced nasal consonant and no final [t].

(58) NAT: *an a waant-ed to kach shel.*
       and 1s.subj want- past inf catch shell
       'And I wanted to get shells.'   [V4-STJ:1 443-3;8.23]

The second instance of JE past inflection is a case of overgeneralization. Overgeneralization of the English past-tense marker is well-attested universally in L1 acquisition,[20] and reported to be "perhaps the most notorious error" in language development among English-speaking children (Marcus 1996, 81).

(59) DAN: *di   boi mada   <u>kom- d</u>.*
           DEF boy mother come-PAST
           'The boy's mother <u>came</u>.'   [V6-MOB:l 627-3;4.16]

In this case, the past inflection is attached to a SHared form *kom* 'come', a verb
with irregular past-tense formation in JE. Presumably it was considered by the
child to be usable in JC and JE alike. (58) and (59) were the only occurrences of
a regular JE past-tense form.

The CLAR children used irregular JE past forms, but rarely so: eight different verbs a total of twelve times as follows: *bawt* 'bought' (one instance), *brawt*
'brought' (one), *brook* 'broke' (two), *got* (three), *had* (one), *jangk* 'drank' (one),
keem 'came' (one) and *sed* 'said' (two), all used in past-tense contexts.

I note that irregular past-tense forms are said to be more frequent than the
regular past among L1 English-speaking children as well as in adult speech
(Brown 1973, 260, for instance), some of which occur in the earliest stage,
between 1;6 and 2;3. These include 'broke', 'came', 'fell', 'sat' and 'went'. In the
Trinidad context, Youssef (1991a) studied the son of university graduates in
professional occupations. They exposed their son to both Trinidadian Creole
and English. For the period 2;10–3;11, a total of eighty-eight English past-tense
forms were produced. Of these, 19.3 per cent were accounted for by irregular
'went', 48.9 per cent by other irregular verbs, and the remaining 31.8 per cent by
verbs carrying regular past inflections. The CLAR children's use of JE past tense
was sparse in comparison, as we have seen, likely because of differences in levels
of exposure to English.

Research comparing bilingual and monolingual children's language development indicates that there are no major differences in the acquisition milestones
of the main language in these children, but that bilingual children can sometimes
lag relative to same-age monolingual children (see Nicoladis and Genesee 1997
and Nicoladis, Song, and Marentette 2012 for reviews). With regard to the L2
learning of English by child and adult speakers of Cantonese, a language where,
much like JC, tense is not represented by an affix attached to the verb, Yang and
Huang (2004) report that as proficiency increased, learners did switch gradually
to marking verbs for tense using inflections, relying less on pragmatic and lexical devices for expressing tense, and more on grammatical devices. Perhaps the
same could be expected, then, among Creole speakers; that is, that with increases
in proficiency, the use of inflections for tense marking could also increase.

It is often the case in the speech of the CLAR children, however, that JC and
JE verb forms alternate, and that when used, JE forms may be woven with other

JC ones. In (60), for instance, in the JE section of Visit 6, ANG had indicated in JC, that her mother had bought a Dora mermaid for her (*mi mada bai*). In the ensuing discussion, the investigator makes use twice of the JE irregular form 'bought', after which the child herself uses that form.

(60) INV: I coloured the picture.

     INV: you like it?

     ANG: *mi*   *mada*   *<u>bai</u>*   *dat Dora mormied.*
            1s.POSS mother buy.PAST that Dora mermaid
            'My mother bought that Dora mermaid.'

     INV: you momi bought a Dora mermaid?

     ANG: *mi*   *mada*   *<u>bai</u>*   *i*   *fi mi.*
            1s.POSS mother buy.PAST 3s.OBJ   for1s.OBJ
            'My mother bought it for me.'

     INV: and what you call this?

     INV: you say you Mommy bought it.

     INV: what is this?

     ANG: *mi*   *mada*   *<u>bawt</u>*   *it.*
            1s.POSS mother buy.PAST 3s.OBJ
            'My mother bought it.'   [V6-STJ:ll 598ff.-3;8.19]

In the sequence below, the child becomes increasingly angry at a classmate who will not stop talking. She starts out issuing the command in JC, then in JE. In the third and last command to stop, the sentence is JE and contains the irregular past tense *sed* 'said'. Note that the form *a* for the first-person singular is closer to JE, the JC counterpart being *mi*.

(61) GAB: *stap*   *i!*
            stop.IMPER 3s.OBJ
            'Stop it.'

GAB: *stop   it!*
        stop.IMPER 3S.OBJ

GAB: *a   sed   stop   it!*
        1S.SUBJ say.PAST stop.IMPER 3S.OBJ
        'I said, "Stop it!"'   [V4-SER:1.789-3;9.27]

Example (62) below contains the only use of a JE auxiliary followed by a past participle: "I've done". GAB has just reprimanded the crying doll in JC: *no bada wid i naiz . . . kaa mi naa juok* ('Stop making noise . . . because I'm not joking'). Then she declares:

(62)   GAB: <u>ai-   v   don   koom</u> yor   hier.
                1s.SUBJ-have done comb 2s.POSS hair
                '<u>I've finished combing</u> your hair.'   [V4-SER:1 34-3;9.27]

In this sentence, the English phrase "I've" (*aiv*) is followed by the JC use of the SHared *don* 'done' and the JES *koom* (JC *kuom*), used as it would be in JC, that is, with no inflectional ending. In other words, weaving has taken place. The structural weave is as follows:

aiv: JE subject pronoun cliticized onto JE perfective auxiliary ('I've')
don: bare JC lexical verb homophonous with JE 'done', but used in a V+V construction. More typically in JE this would be followed by a noun phrase, for example, "I've done the work". If followed by a verb, the sequence would more likely be "<u>I'm</u> done comb<u>ing</u>" or "<u>I've</u> finished comb<u>ing</u>" with the second verb bearing the participle -ing in each case (see below). If the child intended for *don* to be used as the JC perfective marker, the JE "I've" would be inappropriate.
koom: bare JES lexical verb (JC *kuom*); expected '-ing' inflection in JE

The construction using the present tense of the verb 'have' functioning as an auxiliary followed by the main verb as a past participle[21] forms the present perfect in JE. An example would be "I've finished combing your hair". The present perfect is used when the event, started at some point in the past, still has some relevance to the time of the utterance – the combing would need to have been finished in the very recent past, for instance. The JC counterpart would have been *mi don*.

In addition to considerations of the verbal elements, the possessive phrase serving as object *yor hier* and consisting of the JE second-person singular possessive *yor* 'your', and the noun *hier* 'hair', involves a superficial weave as follows: initial /h/ as it occurs in the JE counterpart but with a following JC diphthong /ie/, as occurs in the usual JC pronunciation.

In sum, the use of regular inflectional endings to express the past tense is rare, as is also overgeneralization of this. There are eight JE irregular past-tense verbs used twelve times, also considered to be rarely used, then. It is clear that, as has long been reported for Jamaican children as a whole and in descriptions of the Jamaican language situation,[22] the JC grammatical system predominates in the speech of the CLAR children.

5.4.2 Weaving in Progressive Constructions

Data from the CLAR pilot study show that from as early as 2;0.4, the age of the youngest child, the JE sequence question word ('What')+inverted auxiliary ('were')+subject ('you')+V_{ing} is understood (see Stewart 2010b, 191). The child answers here with the bare verb. (In this section, entries in the glosses which are considered to be JE(S) or SH(ared) forms are in bold.)

(63) Investigator: What were you doing to Samantha?

　　　 Child:　　　 *Bait ar.*
　　　　　　　　　 bite **3s**
　　　　　　　　　 '(I) bit her.'　　　　　　　　　　　　　　　　 [2;0.4 FEB1 KAY]

KAY is two years old, and his recorded MLU in the session is 1.3. The use of an uninflected form should not be surprising, then, especially given the primary input which we assume to be JC.

Note that in (63), the bare non-stative would receive a past interpretation in adult JC. Jamaican children acquiring JC in the De Lisser (2015) study also use the bare verb in contexts where their interpretation is present progressive, even though in adult JC, the interpretation would have been the past, given their non-stative status (p. 114). She reports the production of the JC progressive aspectual marker as early as 1;9.5 (p. 106), and its use with five different predicates, indicating consistent use, as early as 1;11.12 (p. 115).

In the early stages of the acquisition of English as an L1, it is also the case that the progressive aspect is not overtly represented. The progressive ending '-ing', the first inflectional morpheme to be acquired, appears in the age range 1;9–2;10 (Brown 1973, 271). Fully formed English progressive constructions with the auxiliary appear in the speech of Brown's subjects in the age range 3;6–4;4. There is a clear developmental path in the acquisition of the progressive, then, from the absence of the auxiliary and the use of the bare verb, to acquisition of the morpheme on the verb, to the fully formed construction.

In Brown's study, the conclusions regarding L1 acquisition refer to children in a recognizable English-speaking environment. Despite this difference, findings re the early acquisition of -ing versus that of the progressive auxiliary among the children in the CLAR pilot compare with his findings – the children began using structures with the morpheme -ing at age 2;5. However, as we now see, no similarly clear developmental path is detected thereafter.

The CLAR children use the JE auxiliary *iz* 'is' followed by an uninflected verb thirty-six times, with just under a half of these (41.7 per cent) by children from rural areas. This use of *iz*+bare V is not associated necessarily with the age of the children. There is one child in his last interview at age 3;5.22 who used JE *iz*+bare V in a progressive construction for the first time, but all others who use the construction make use also of *iz*+V-in(g).[23] This includes the youngest at 3;1.29 and the oldest at 4;2.1. Acquisition is not expected to proceed in discrete stages; here, however, instances of Ø PROG+V-in(g) are used alongside, and twice as often as, JE PROG+V-in(g), even by the oldest children. This variation is extreme and appears to be characteristic of the speech of the children, as indeed it is in the input.

When used, the appropriate structure for representing progressive aspect in English was often said haltingly and deliberately, indicating a certain lack of fluency, if not discomfort with its use.

The only uses of the contracted auxiliary were the first- and third-persons singular as follows: one case of the first person, where 'I'm' was followed by -ing (*aim kuking* 'I'm cooking'), and eight instances of *hiiz* 'he's' and *shiiz* 'she's' followed by the inflected verb. These forms seemed to have been learned as unanalysed chunks, and are not used in otherwise JE utterances. They are used only by children in cities and towns as follows: Montego Bay, Kingston, Clarendon and St Thomas.

In the JE section of Visit 6, one child used the JE *shiiz goin* 'she's going', indicating that she has acquired this form of the JE progressive. After hesitating, as indicated by the symbol # in (64), she used the verb *kalekt*, an example of a word-internal superficial weave: it preserves the JC vowel /a/ in the first syllable but adopts the JE final consonant cluster /kt/ in the second. Importantly, this was uttered slowly and deliberately, with thought and, it seems, uncertainty.

(64) DON *shi-iz   go- in   #   aahn kalekt aar   moni.*
      3S-PROG GO- PROG   and   **collect** 3S.POSS **money**
      'She's going to collect her money.'   [V6-KN1:l.120-3;11.12]

With regard to the uncontracted auxiliary, the only form used other than *iz* was the third plural *are*. A third-person subject *dee* 'they' (see [65] and [66]) was used, involving a word-internal (superficial) weave consisting of an initial JC consonant /d/ followed by the JE /e/. In addition, the stem of the main verb in (65) contains the JC diphthong /ie/, rather than the JE /e/. Structurally, however, the utterances are both JE sentences, these pronunciation differences notwithstanding.

(65) ADR: *dee   are   ries- in.*
            3PL.SUBJ PROG race-**PROG**
            'They are racing.'   [V6-CLA:l.671-3;11.4]

(66) JAY: *dee   are   iit- ing.*
            3PL.SUBJ PROG eat-**PROG**
            'They are eating.'   [V6-MOB:l.594-3;8.22]

The well-formed JE progressive *yu are duin* in (67) appears in JC question form with the (uninverted) sequence subject+auxiliary, a potential structural weave; 'potential', since it may be that it was intended to be a statement, having been introduced by *se* 'say' rather than 'ask'.

(67) JAN: *mumi   di   liedi se* 'wat   *yu   are   du-in?*'.
            mummy **DEF lady** say **what** 2S.SUBJ **PROG** do-**PROG**
            'Mummy the lady says "What are you doing?"'
                                            [V5-SMT:l.466-3;4.25]

In addition, *are* was used with the JES second-person pronoun *yu(u)* 'you', in well-formed questions such as *ou are yuu?* 'how are you?' or *ou uol are yuu nou?* 'how old are you now?'. It is likely that these are unanalysed chunks.

In contrast, the sentence in (68) below is a clear case of a structural weave, indicating that the child has not fully internalised JE progressive formation:

there is the possibility of confusion with the JE third-person plural possessive 'their', followed by the JE auxiliary and the verb, uninflected as it would be in JC.

(68)   ASH: *dier   are   sit doun.*
            3PL.SUBJ PROG sit down
            'They are sitting down.'   [V1-KN2:l.55-3;7.7]

Errors of concord were evident. One quarter of the subjects of the auxiliary *iz* 'is', were not third-person singular, involving, therefore, violations of concord required in JE. These were used with a range of verb forms: bare as in (69), and with the inflection '-in' as in (70) and '-ing' as in (71):

(69)   ERN: *im   iz____waater di   flouwerz.*
            3S.SUBJ PROG water **DEF flowers**
            'She is watering the flowers.'   [V6-STR: l 200-3;11.25]

(70)   MOY: *wai yuu   iz   kaal-in   mii?*
            why 2S.SUBJ   PROG call-**PROG 1S.OBJ**
            'Why are you calling me?'   [V4-ADT: l 759-3;8.14]

(71)   ADR: *dem   iz   go-ing   dis   wee.*
            3PL.SUBJ PROG go-**PROG DEM way**
            'They are going this way.'   [V6-CLA:l 682-3;11.4]

Only five subject pronouns in JE *iz*+verb sequences were first-person singular; they constituted 10.2 per cent of all pronominal subjects. Trends were different in JC progressive constructions: 58.5 per cent of all JC *a*+verb sequences were non-third-person singular, of which 1,520, or 87.2 per cent, were the first-person singular.

Forms such as *yuu iz* would suggest that *iz* is being treated by the children as a JC auxiliary carrying an interpretable tense feature, but no uninterpretable features. This is because for the auxiliary in JE, an uninterpretable agreement feature signals the choice of form ('am', 'is', 'are') based on the person of the subject. Similarly, verbs which do not have the inflection '-in(g)' indicate an absence of the uninterpretable progressive feature. In some cases, however, uninterpretable features are operable in the speech of the children: in (64), (67) and (69), agreement is evident; in (70) and (71), an uninterpretable progressive

feature (but not agreement) appears to exist; and in (65) and (66), both uninterpretable JE features are at work.

Even where the progressive used is a well-formed JE sequence, it is possible for other elements in the sentence to be JC: notice that in (70) above, for
instance, the JE progressive is used in a JC interrogative structure with the
subject-auxiliary remaining un-inverted; in (72), the prepositional phrase
which follows is JC but for the pronunciation of *flor* 'floor' (JC *fluor*); in (73),
the JE inflection is attached to the JC stem *wain*, feasibly originally incorporated
from the English verb 'wind' but now used in JC to mean "dance".

(72) DAN: *OSS iz*   *jraiv-in*   *it*   <u>*dong di*</u> *flor.*
           OSS **PROG** drive-**PROG** 3s.**OBJ** **down DEF** floor
           'OSS is driving it on the floor.'   [V6-MOB:l 692-3;4.16]

(73) DAE: *the gorl iz*   <u>*wain-* ing.</u>
           DEF girl PROG dance-**PROG**
           'The girl is dancing.'   [V1-STT:l 210-2;10.12]

In sum, use of the JE progressive is sparse, and particularly so among children from rural areas. The form of the auxiliary which is most prevalent is the
third-person singular *iz* 'is' but, even so, there are instances where an inappropriate subject is used. The late acquisition of the uninterpretable features
involved is in line with Meisel's conclusion that affixes such as the possessive -s,
the third-person singular and the regular past which involve uninterpretable
feature valuing are the last to be acquired (2011, 70–73).

5.4.3 Other Cases

Patrick (1997, 130) indicates that in adult JC, pre-verbal progressive markers
cannot co-occur with *-in*. This structural weave (the JC progressive aspectual
marker and the JE inflectional ending) was attested five times in the CLAR data,
however. In (74) below, we see an example; the investigator did not understand
what NIO had said, and asked her to repeat; she repeated verbatim. Interestingly, all other constituents are JC, including the stem of the verb.

(74) NIO: *mi   si   wat a   gwaan-in   ova mi   skuul.*
             1s.SUBJ see what PROG go.on- PROG over 1s.POSS school
             'I see what's happening over at my school.'   [V2-CLA:l 84-3;6.9]

There was one occurrence reported in Stewart (2010b, 194) of the JC marker *a*
with JE inflectional '-in'. The marker was taken by Stewart to be the immediate
future, given the context: the people in question were not writing at the time.
This aspectual marker has the same form as the JC progressive, and in JC would
be followed by the bare verb (see 5.1.1 for some discussion).

(75) INV: *wa   dem   gwain do   wi   di   pensl?*
             what 3PL   going do   with DEF   pencil
             'What are they going to do with the pencil?'

     CHL: *dem   a   raitin.*
              3PL   FUT   writing
              'They're about to write.'   [2;7.18 CHL MAR1 l.126]

The construction *duin* ('doing')+V-in was used by one child, twice without an
auxiliary at age 2;10.12 in the first visit (76–77), and once at 3;4.0 with the auxiliary *iz* (78). Note that in (76), the context shows clearly that *gorlz* was intended
to be plural, so the form cannot be interpreted as the contracted auxiliary "the
girl's doing the driving", that is, "the girl is driving".

(76) DAE: *the gorl-z du-in   the   jraiving.*
             DEF girl-PL do-PROG DEF driving
             'The girls are driving.'   [V1-STT:l.68-2;10.12]

(77) DAE: *dem   du-in   taakin.*
             3P.SUBJ do-PROG talking
             'They are talking.'   [V1-STT:l.370-2;10.12]

(78) DAE: *dem   iz   du-in   pleein.*
             3P.SUBJ PROG do-PROG playing
             'They are playing.'   [V6-STT:l.425-3;4.0]

The construction is neither JC nor is it JE,[24] and is reminiscent of the "do" construction, discussed by Myers-Scotton and Jake (1995, 1005–6; 2001, 107) as
being a compromise strategy in CS where "do" bears the L2 inflection and is

followed by a bare L1 content verb.[25] In these cases, however, the second verb bears the L2 inflection, it appears to be nominal and its stem may be a JE form, as in (76) and (78).

5.5 Summary and Conclusion

As has been illustrated, there are fundamental differences between the temporal and aspectual systems of JC and JE. Whereas JC is an aspect-prominent language, JE is tense-prominent.

Where differences in form are concerned, the JC-JE structural weave for the present progressive can potentially involve the variants in table 5.1. The only form which is dependent on (overtly realized) grammatical relations is the JE auxiliary; both participants in the JC progressive are invariant.

The data have shown that when a JE verbal construction is acquired, it is likely that

- the JE construction will be used far less frequently than the JC one;
- the JE construction will be attested among fewer rural children than urban children;
- the JC counterpart of the JE construction will continue to be used alongside the JE; and
- the JE grammatical relation will not be acquired early; in the case of the JE progressive, the grammatical relation is concord.

By way of conclusion, and with an eye to discussions on implications for education, I refer to Craig (2006, 236), who uses contracted verb forms to illustrate that differences between the Creole and the lexifier tend to go unnoticed by young Creole speakers. The English present perfect "He's gone" which is heard,

Table 5.1. The progressive construction in JC and JE

Pre-Verbal			Inflection	
JC Aspect Marker	**JE Auxiliary**	**Lexical Verb**	**JC**	**JE**
a /*de* /*da* (invariant)	am is are (agreement)		No inflection (invariant)	infl -in(g) (invariant)

perceived and received as being identical with "He gone" is an example. This would be predicted when the Creole speaker realizes that the English equivalent of *im* as subject pronoun is 'he', perceives "gone" to be the English counterpart of Creole *gaan*, and, without a knowledge of differences in how tense and aspect work in the languages, believes that all differences between them have been accounted for by producing "He gone". This is not the case: in an English-lexified Creole such as JC, *im gaan* (lit. third-person singular gone) could be translated as 'he left', the simple past (see section 5.2.6). Alternatively, it could be used to mean "him having left, I am able to report that he is not here", that is, with a focus on the result of him having left, rather than on the event itself. An unambiguous focus on the event could be achieved through modification by the adverb *aredi* (*im gaan aredi*, 'He's already left'). The two systems are very different.

Informed by the theory outlined in chapter 2, the final chapter attempts to align the findings on the language acquired by the CLAR children as presented in chapters 3, 4 and 5 with the language situation as discussed in chapter 1, so as to consider how these linguistic insights may contribute to knowledge considered to be foundational for the literacy and language education teacher.

6 | Bringing It All Together

INV:	*wa dat niem?*
%com:	pointing to a big sun.
SHA:	*soni wedor.*
INV:	*soni wedor?*
DON:	*dat tiicha se.*[1]

[V2-KN1:ll.833ff.-SHA 3;5.11/DON 3 ;6.23]

n an attempt to make sense of the CLAR data, the starting point was that JC, a Creole language spoken natively by the vast majority of the Jamaican population, represents a linguistic system which is, in many respects, quite different from that of the official language, English. As an English-lexified language, the bulk of the JC vocabulary arose originally through borrowing from English and incorporation into the JC phonological system. The result is similarities at the lexical and phonological levels, which in turn cause confusion as to which forms "belong" to JE and which to JC, ultimately leading to extreme variation in everyday speech, and a conviction that what is spoken regularly is "bad English". Being unaware of the many structural differences between JE and JC, speakers often assume that they are speaking English when in fact they are not. Another consequence is that there are tendencies to believe that in order to speak JE, what is required is simply to make phonological adjustments.

JC and JE have been taken in this work to be idealized linguistic systems at either end of a continuum. Variation is viewed from a minimalist feature-based perspective, and is informally referred to as the weaving of features from both systems at two levels: superficial weaving of phonological and lexical features and structural weaving of syntactic features. This concluding chapter begins with an outline of the findings with regard to syntactic constructions in the nominal domain (as discussed in chapter 4) and in the verbal domain (chapter 5). In each case, relevant sections in those chapters are indicated so that they may be consulted for details of how the constructions may be explained linguistically. The idea is that with a clear understanding of what constitutes JC versus what constitutes JE in the speech of the children, and with the linguistic tools to be able to speak about these differences, the literacy and language education teacher will have an informed familiarity with the linguistic resources of the students they teach.

In any language situation where there exist two language systems, it is common for one to be acquired somewhat sooner than the other, resulting in it being the "stronger" or more dominant language. The stronger language is expected to develop indistinguishably from that of a monolingual child. The weaker language in such a situation develops more slowly and displays some lexical and structural influence from the stronger (Döpke 1996, 2).

The speech of the CLAR children as revealed in chapters 3, 4 and 5 would lead to a conclusion that JE is the weaker of the two languages. This is as might be expected, given the language situation in Jamaica outlined in section 1.1. I seek ways to formalize this in section 6.2. In section 6.3, the blurred boundaries between JC and JE, a thread throughout the book, are discussed in terms of the languages (6.3.1 and 6.3.2), of social factors (6.3.3) and of cognitive factors (6.3.4). In section 6.4, language awareness is presented as an appropriate pedagogical tool in the language and literacy classroom in such a linguistic environment. Language awareness is viewed in terms of phonological (relevant, given discussions in section 3.1), morphological (sections 3.4, 4.2 and 4.4), syntactic (chapters 4 and 5) and critical language awareness (section 1.1). Concluding remarks follow in section 6.5.

6.1 Specific Issues in the Nominal and Verbal Domains

This section provides a summary of forms chosen by the CLAR children for use in nominal and verbal constructions as discussed in chapters 4 and 5 respectively. Relevant sections in the chapters are referenced for how these constructions might be described linguistically, as well as for details of the differences between JC and JE which they exhibit. Cases where features of JC and JE forms are woven in the speech of the children are taken to signal possible confusion.

6.1.1 Noun-Related Structures

Each finding below indicates its relevance to language education and, where applicable, comments are made on the presumed degree of language association which the phenomenon has in the minds of the children. This leads the way for discussions in section 6.3.2 of the earlier finding that there are patterns to weaving; in this case, influenced by functional categories favouring to varying degrees the selection of complements headed by functional items of a different language.

1.   **Count–mass distinction**: In JE, there are clues in the syntax as to whether a noun is count (individuated) or mass (non-individuated); in JC, the grammar provides no support for this distinction. (See section 4.1.)

This points to the ability of the JC noun, with no corresponding change in grammatical form, to be identified either as a discrete entity, resulting in a count interpretation, or as unbounded "stuff" with a mass interpretation.

Relevance: The (semantic) features which are internalized as children try to make sense of the world may have possible consequences for the learning of vocabulary in a second language, and particularly so if concepts are lexicalized in different ways in the native language. This may have an effect on the properties which our children use to categorize nouns, and therefore on the properties they use as a basis of determining sameness or difference between objects. They may conceive of objects as non-individuated "substances", and may therefore learn new vocabulary by matching objects on the basis of the material of which they are made, rather than on their shape.

This points to the need for lessons to be built around the concepts involved in the count–mass distinction as well as how it is signalled syntactically in JE. One such lesson is presented in section 6.4.1.

2.   JE **pluralization** is signalled using the inflectional morpheme /s/ and its allomorphs. The function of this morpheme is primarily to individuate the noun and to return an interpretation of more than one (plurality). In JC, plurality is expressed as a natural by-product of a group interpretation (inclusiveness) by two independent morphemes *di . . . dem*. Importantly, plurality need not be signalled in this way, but a plural interpretation can be returned with no marking. This is linked to item 1 above, since the noun, as "non-individuated substance" may also take shape, forming an individuated object. (See section 4.2.)

Relevance: The children's concept of how plurality is expressed in JC seems to have affected how they seek to express plurality in JE. It would not seem feasible to suggest that the acquisition of the English /s/ is delayed since it is not perceptually salient. This is because it is among the earliest inflections acquired by children learning English as an L1, acquired with 90 per cent accuracy from as early as 1;11 (Brown 1973). In contrast, only four of the eleven CLAR two-year-olds (2;9.0–2;11.9) used the English plural a total of five times in fifteen interviews, and across all ages, it was used an average of 0.5 times by a child in a half-hour interview.

Patterns of pluralization are linked with the concept of the noun as non-individuated. This indicates the need for attention to JE pluralization *conceptually as well as how it is formed.*

Degree of association with JE: Thirty per cent of the nouns used with the English plural morpheme /s/ are JC. That the children use the JE strategy with JC nouns, points to its internalization, and its *relatively weak association with JE.* (See section 4.2.1.)

This may be due in part to the high frequency of plural fossils. (See section 4.2.2.)

3.   To express **definiteness** in JE, the noun may be accompanied by the definite article 'the' as well as other elements such as demonstratives. Indefiniteness is expressed by the indefinite article 'a'. Like plurality, then, (in)definiteness must be marked syntactically in JE. In contrast, this may be inferred through context in JC.[2] It cannot be the case that the children have not internalized the difference between the two concepts, since they do contrast them correctly in JC, yet, much like the acquisition of English and French, the definite article is overused – the JC definite article accounted for 89.4 per cent of JC articles used, leaving a production of only 10.6 per cent indefinites. (See section 4.3.1.)

Relevance: There is a possibility that (any) children acquiring a language may presume that knowledge which they possess is shared by the adult in the interaction (after all, adults know a lot more than they do). This would cause an overuse of the definite article. However, it is important for the teacher of JE to JC-speaking children to bear in mind at least two differences between the two languages: (a) unlike in JE, in JC (in)definiteness may be expressed at the level of discourse, with no syntactic marking, and (b) there are means other than the use of the indefinite to introduce new information; an example is focus-marking or unmarked fronting of a constituent. (See section 4.3.1.)

Degree of association with JE: There is *a high degree of association* of the JE definite article 'the' with JE. 'The' was seldom used (fewer than fifty occurrences) and was never accompanied by a JC noun.

In contrast, the JE indefinite 'a' was used over four hundred times, and 26.5 per cent of DPs containing it also contained a JC noun.

Comparing frequencies of use of the JC and JE indefinites, JE 'a' was used almost as often (48.9 per cent) as JC *wahn* (51.1 per cent), and with equally spread distributions of JC, JE and SH nominal complements. (See section 4.3.3.)

4.   **The possessive relation** in JC is not expressed using the inflectional morpheme /s/, but simply by juxtaposing the possessor and the possessed. The JE inflectional morpheme was used only once each by two children aged 3;4.0 and 3;6.21. (See section 4.4.2.)

The vast majority of singular possessive adjectives were JC. Plural forms accounted for a mere 1.1 per cent of all possessive adjectives used. (See section 4.4.3.)

The only JE pronouns used were *main* 'mine' and *yorz* or *yorn*. *Main* was used half as much again (50.8 per cent as often) as the JC *fi mi* counterpart. (See section 4.4.5.)

There is a strong tendency to use JC constituents in JC possessive *fi* (section 4.4.5) and *uon* (section 4.4.6) constructions.

There is great variation in the use of JC and JE possessive forms throughout, not only by different children, but in the speech also of individuals. (See section 4.4.7.)

Relevance: The morpheme is learned late in the first language acquisition of English, and later in the acquisition of English as a second language, suggesting that it is to be expected that children will not acquire this morpheme early. Children learning JE will need to learn the following:

- there are only four possessive constructions in JE;
- there are at least twice as many different types of possessive construction in JC than there are in JE;
- when using the sequence possessor + possessed, possession in JE is marked by the inflectional -*s*;
- when followed by a noun, the weak form of the possessive (the adjective) is used;

- this form is different from that used when no noun follows (the pronoun);
- it is possible to express possession using an "of" construction;
- there is a gender distinction for the third-person forms of the JE possessive;
- there is no number distinction for the second person in JE; and
- neither the forms *fi* nor *uon* are used in JE.

Degree of association with JE: There would appear to be *a high association with JE of the possessive morpheme,* since in the two instances of its use, both the possessor and the possessed were JESs. High association with JE has also been reported in the literature (Patrick 2007, 145). (See section 4.4.2.)

With regard to *possessive adjectives, the association is less striking:* both JC and JE possessive adjectives are followed predominantly by JC nouns. The second-person *yor* is followed by a larger number (26.2 per cent) of JES nouns than any other possessive, and JC *mi* and *yu* by the least number of JES nouns (6.1 per cent and 6.6 per cent respectively). This would seem to point to the second-person *yor* being more distinctively JE in the minds of the children, presumably by virtue of the vowel+rhotic sequence, neither of which would be expected in JC. (See section 4.4.3.)

There was an *obvious understanding of the adjective/pronoun distinction,* since pronominal forms were generally not followed by a noun (section 4.4.4). This understanding suggests a readiness for learning about which forms in JE fill these functions.

There is a marked tendency for constructions using the JC possessive preposition *fi* to contain JConly constituents. There is no direct counterpart in JE for this construction (section 4.4.5). It will become important for children to know how this is expressed in JE.

Based on the relatively frequent use of the forms *a(a)r* and *main,* as well as their incorporation into JC structures, these may be gaining a foothold in the speech of Jamaican children, as they seem not to be strongly associated with English. (See sections 4.4.3 and 4.4.5.)

6.1.2 Verb-Related Structures

Chapter 5 shows that the verbal systems in JC and JE differ in fundamental ways, affecting the way in which tense and aspect operate in the languages. Specifically, despite lexical similarities, JC is aspect-prominent, whereas JE is tense-prominent. Clachar (2005, 289) indicates that because of the lexical over-lap, Creole learners' receptive knowledge of oral and written English far exceeds that of other L2 learners of English. Nonetheless, as she points out (p. 294), Cre-ole-speaking students may have specific challenges as they encode the lexical aspectual classes of verbs via Standard English verbal morphology. For example, section 5.2 presents the JC aspectual marker *a* as having many interpretations (the habitual, the progressive as well as the iterative), depending on the aspec-tual class of the verb. In contrast, there is one prototypical meaning associated with the form which the progressive in JE takes.

Similarly, in section 5.3 we saw that tense and aspect interact in JC in ways they do not in JE, such that the semantic features associated with the JC verb influence whether the past-tense marker is used for a past interpretation. Clachar (2005, 323) further points out that there is no Creole marker which is sufficiently isomorphic with the JE past marker, the inflectional '-ed'. This means that the Creole speaker will have difficulty identifying a meaning and function for the JE inflection. Certainly, in JE it is not dependent on the seman-tic features of the verb to which it attaches, as it is in JC.

The form 'did' is of English origin. Although it was originally associated with mesolectal speech, it seems today to be so commonly used as to be associated with JC. However, importantly, this marker in English is used for emphasis: 'he did go' assures the speaker that his leaving actually did take place. In contrast, when used in JC, it functions in the same way as the JC past-tense marker $e(h)n$ and variants.

It becomes clear that being taught only the *forms* of the JE regular and irreg-ular past-tense forms is not sufficient to achieve mastery of the past tense. Sim-ilar considerations apply for aspect, where there are also systemic differences between the two languages.

I look now at how dominant JC really may be in the speech of the CLAR children.

6.2 The Relative Distribution of JE and JC Structures in the Children's Usage

Measures used by researchers to determine the contribution to the children's performance of each of the languages spoken in their environment include a count of the average words in utterances (MLU count) as well as the compara-tive upper bound of words used in an utterance in the languages.[3] This presumes the use of inter-sentential CS[4] from one language to the next. It presumes also that when spoken to in a particular language, though there may be inter- as well as intra-sentential mixing, there are sentences which could be identified as having been said in one language or the other.

It is the case that language use must depend on a variety of factors, not all of which are strictly language-related. They may result, for example, from the subject matter of the conversation, or even the child's mood. It is also the case that in a Creole environment characterized by weaving at both deep and superficial levels, language use may not be as clear-cut as it is in other language situations. Nonetheless, the measures do provide a glimpse of general tendencies of usage.

In what follows, reference to a sequence of JE words does not necessarily imply that the sequence is grammatically well-formed, that is, following the relevant English grammatical rules. Instead, it may diverge along the lines expected of first language acquirers in English-speaking communities, or of second language acquirers of English, or both. For example, it is well-documented that children learning English will have no progressive auxiliary (a form of 'be') as in *shi kukin* 'she is cooking'. Such a sequence is included nonetheless in the two-word English count, consisting as it does of two JES forms. Words are labelled as JC if they are used regularly in JC in the form in which they appear in the child's utterance.

As part of the CLAR project, interviews of twenty-four children at seven schools took place before the end of their first month of Basic School. Their language in these interviews may therefore provide a gauge as to the relative use of JE and JC by children as they enter the formal school system. There were a total of 1,449 utterances of two or more words in these interviews; of these utterances, a mere 91 (or 6.3 per cent) were comprised of only JE, and 1,045 (or 72.1 per cent) of only JC forms. Mixed utterances making use of a combination of both JC and JESs numbered 313, or 21.6 per cent of the total. A breakdown of JE and JConly utterances is shown in table 6.1.

Looking at JE-only utterances, the majority (69/91 or 75.8 per cent) contained only two words (for example, *at werk* 'at work'). Seventeen of the twenty-four children produced these two-word sequences. When taking into account utterances of all lengths, the overall average MLU was 2.6 words. There were twenty-two utterances of more than two JE words; they were all produced by the same five children, with one child from St Thomas responsible for fourteen. There was only one sentence of seven words, the upper limit in the data for JE.

In contrast, 1,045 utterances, or over eleven times as many, contained JC words only, the greatest share of which (32.0 per cent) were three-word

Table 6.1. Children's speech in the first month of school

No. of Words	No. of Utterances	
	JE	JC
2	69	309
3	8	332
4	5	183
5	3	115
6	5	70
7	1	16
8		7
9		7
10		3
11		1
12		2
Total:	91	1,045

utterances. On average, JC sentences of two words or more contained 3.4 words; the longest sentence was twelve words long, of which there were two instances.

The sentences in (1) below are the longest sentences produced by the children in both languages. ERN in (1a) was relating a story in JC about a bullfrog that he had seen at this house, and DAE in (1b) was describing a picture using JE, very haltingly, and swallowing her words to the point of being partially indistinct.[5]

(1a) ERN: *im   go roun di bak roun yaso an mi   luk   pan im.*

[JC 12 words]

3s.SUBJ go round DEF back round here and 1s.SUBJ look on 3s.OBJ

'He went there around the back and I looked at him.'

[V1-STR:l.392-3;6.9]

(1b) DAE: *the boi iz   plee-ing* xxx *in the   skuul* xxx.   [JE 7 words]

DEF boy PROG play-PROG   in DEF school

'The boy is playing in the school.'   [V1-STT:l. 197-2;10.12]

This points to an overwhelming majority of JC utterances of greater length when compared with the JE utterances.

In addition, there are qualitative reasons, such as the way in which they were uttered, supporting JE being the weaker language. These include slow, deliberate and even louder production, compared to the fluency of speech when using JC words only.[6]

With regard to grammaticality, ten of the eighteen JE utterances of two words or more may be said to be grammatically correct. Nonetheless, there are instances of superficial weaves: divergences in pronunciation and at the level of the word, including hypercorrection, such as the final /r/ in 'water'; the use of a variant such as '-in' for the JE progressive '-ing'; or a JC form such as /a/ for the first-person singular 'I'. Other utterances show divergences from the target at a structural level. Presuming, for example, that the target was JE, the indefinite article 'a' and the progressive auxiliary 'is' were omitted in *dee riidin stoori* ('they are reading a story', lit. they reading story), and the bare form of the verb was used to express the past tense (*anti kom tuu* 'Aunty came too', lit. Aunty come too).

The data suggest, then, that JC is the dominant "stronger" language among the CLAR children. However, as we have seen, the language situation is far more complex than this, due in no small part to the mixing of features belonging to (idealizations of) JC and JE, resulting in extreme variation in the input.

Variation in the data has been discussed throughout this work, and interpreted to mean that the boundaries between the two languages are indistinct in the minds of speakers. We saw in section 3.1.1, for instance, that 313, or just under 50 per cent, of the total number of different JC lexical categories (types) used by the children had variants and that 257, or 82.1 per cent, of these types had variants which were attributable to the existence of JE segments.

6.3 Blurred Boundaries and Their "Un-Blurring"

I look now at what I have called SHared forms, traditionally referred to as cognates. They contribute to a lack of separation between the two languages, since they are forms which are used regularly in both JC and JE, and therefore cannot be strongly associated with either language in the minds of speakers. Importantly, I consider how it is that a solution may be found within aspects of the language itself of the CLAR children.

6.3.1 Cognates

In this work, words of the same origin have been referred to as SHared forms.[7] Cognate is the term traditionally used in various contexts, including Linguistics, for such words. In the case here, they are a result of English being the primary lexifier of the Creole. An example is 'man', used regularly in both languages with the same meaning and with similar pronunciations. Gardner-Chloros (1995, 74) speaks of such forms as "belonging" equally to both languages, and Clyne (1987, 744) refers to them as items of ambiguous affiliation, belonging to the speaker's two systems.

More than a third (35.1 per cent or 242) of 690 different nouns[8] used by the children are SH forms with no segment differences between the two languages. In addition, 150 or 21.7 per cent have at least one JE variant. In the case of the variants, there is a difference of one or more segment(s), but the words in the two languages remain recognizably similar. An example is JC *saalt* versus JE *sawlt* 'salt'. Including these words in the cognate count, results in over half, or 56.8 per cent, of all nouns being considered cognates. This underlines the extent of similarity at the lexical level between the two languages.

In his studies of lexical transfer, Ringbom (1987, 2001) found that the more similar the two languages are at the aggregate level, the more likely will be learners' assumptions about similarities among individual pairs of words across the languages. This causes learners to quite readily assume strong formal[9] similarities even where no such similarities exist. We are reminded in this, of Craig's (1980) assessment of the Creole situation as one where lexical and phonological similarities mask differences at the deeper syntactic level.

Despite what may appear to be confusion, however, there is evidence of the existence of clear trends in the data. For instance, in section 3.1.1, table 3.4 lists JES forms which far outnumber their JC counterparts, and may need to now be considered basilectal. These include forms such as *berd* 'bird' (JC *bod*) and *jraiv* 'drive' (JC *jaiv*). We saw also in that section that some lexical items, for example, *gyal* 'girl', despite being traditionally associated with JC, are being outnumbered in the speech of the children by the JE counterpart, with the JC forms reserved only for certain negative contexts.

With regard to the SHared forms, these may be viewed not as a hindrance, contributing to the blurring of boundaries but, instead, as having a possible advantage. This is referred to in the literature as the *cognate advantage*, taken to be the facilitating effect of the overlap in vocabulary between the L1 and the

L2 (see Patterson and Pearson [2004] 2012, 124–26). Psycholinguistic experimental studies have found, for example, that cognates result in an advantage to language processing: when bilinguals are required to name pictures in one language alone, they are faster to name pictures whose names are cognates in the two languages, than those whose names are non-cognate translations (Costa, Caramazza, and Sebastian-Galles 2000). This is the result of both languages remaining activated when a bilingual speaks.

Jarvis and Pavlenko (2007, 203) mention that there will be possibilities for positive transfer, since as learners of the target language gain in proficiency, the presumption is that they will become more aware of the similarities between the two languages, and will acquire the language abilities necessary for taking advantage of them. These include vocabulary knowledge and grammatical competence.

Jiménez, García and Pearson (1996) in a study comparing first and second language reading among successful versus less successful Latino sixth- and seventh-grade readers of English, found that the chief obstacle for both groups was unknown vocabulary, but that the successful readers possessed an enhanced awareness of the relationship between Spanish and English, leading them to successfully search for cognates, and to transfer and translate (p. 106). Such an awareness of similarities may not take place without instruction, however. Malabonga et al. (2008) show that interventions that build cognate awareness, that is, that explicitly teach cognate strategies, result in significant outperformance by students on cognate items over non-intervention subjects. Colorado (2007) indicates that this can be achieved as early as in preschool, because even at this age, children can be taught to use cognates as a tool for understanding an L2.

From a cognitive viewpoint, when language-ambiguous words are encountered within an utterance, both language alternatives are activated in parallel. This simultaneous activation of languages is known as *language non-selectivity*. Kroll, Bogulski and McClain (2012, 6) suggest that activation of both languages is not restricted to the processing of cognates. It is always present, even in proficient bilinguals, and even when words that have an ambiguous language affiliation (such as cognates) appear in the reading of extended text in one language alone.

It has been reported (Costa 2005; Kroll, Bobb and Wodniecka 2006) that language non-selectivity is evident when bilinguals plan speech. Speech planning takes place when a speaker intends to express an idea. Given the nature of the process, it would be expected to be under the speaker's control; in the case of a bilingual, this should include the selection of the intended language.

Nonetheless, alternatives in the language not chosen are activated by the process of selecting even a single word to speak in one language.

It is expected that language mixing will occur in every contact situation. There is a particular likelihood of occurrence in situations such as the one which exists in Jamaica where, as we have seen, lexical similarities so often mask significant grammatical differences between the languages in contact. Making the distinction between the languages is important, given the cognitive consequences (discussed above) of the existence of more than one language system, and perhaps more so given the similarities between the two systems under consideration in this work.

In section 6.3.2, I discuss linguistic evidence that the CLAR children are able to distinguish between the language systems, and I proceed to suggest explanations for this. Social and attitudinal explanations are called on in section 6.3.3, and the possibilities which attention offers in the separation, in 6.3.4.

6.3.2 Language Mixing within Phrases

Table 6.2 summarizes the language selections by functional categories in the CLAR data, thus providing examples of mixing within phrases.

We see clear patterns with regard to tendencies in language selection in the table. The only category which seemingly disallows outright the selection of the "other language" complement is the JE definite determiner 'the'; that is, there are no instances of the JE definite determiner selecting JC nominal complements. Otherwise, there are strong tendencies towards matching: as a general rule, the majority of the complements selected by a functional category match the language of that category. Such patterns support Muysken's (1995, 184) findings that data trends pointed to the formulation of probabilistic statements, rather than clear cases of "all or nothing". This allowed him to establish which kinds of switches are the more frequent ones, while acknowledging that others may be less frequent within the corpus.

A (minimalist) feature-based account such as the Belazi, Rubin and Toribio (1994) functional head constraint (FHC), as outlined in section 2.5[10] is taken to be inadequate as an explanation of how the association of a language form with a particular language might be operational in the grammar of the children. This is precisely because of the existence of trends; if formalized in terms of language features, mixing would predict zero exceptions. For this reason, the *do not switch language* principle cannot be syntactic.[11]

Table 6.2. Select functional categories and the language of their complements

Category	Language		+JC	%	+JE	%	+SH	%	Total	
Definite Determiner	JE	'the'	0	0.0	37	78.7	10	21.3	47	100%
	JC	*di*	3,574	58.6	722	11.8	1,808	29.6	6,104	100%
Indefinite Determiner	JE	'a'	235	33.9	206	29.7	253	36.4	694	100%
	JC	*wahn*	374	51.5	87	12.0	265	36.5	726	100%
Possessive (in D)	JC	*fi*	530	94.5	29	5.2	2	0.3	561	100%
	JE*	'-s'	1	50.0	0	0.0	1	50.0	2	100%
Focus Marker	JE	*iz*	9	17.3	39	75.0	4	7.7	52	100%
	JC	*a*	1,564	69.2	385	17.0	311	13.8	2,260	100%
Infinitive	JE	'to'	29	34.1	14	16.5	42	49.4	85	100%
	JC	*fi*	235	41.8	55	9.8	249	44.3	562	100%

*The two utterances in which the JE possessive '-s' appeared are discussed in section 4.4.2. The possessor in both cases is JE *beebi* 'baby'; one of them is uttered haltingly and deliberately.

This is not to say that feature-based syntactic regulation is ruled out, but only that accounting for code-mixing in terms of the requirements of language features would need to be. The existence, for instance, of a feature of countability associated with the JE indefinite determiner 'a' would require a match of a like feature on the noun in its complement, thus ruling out the SELECTion of a noun from the JC lexicon, where there is reason to believe that no such features would exist (see the discussion of the count–mass distinction in section 4.1).

Looking again at the list of functional categories in table 6.2, mixing (or not) may involve different components of language: there may be phonological differences, causing association with one language versus the other (for example, JE 'the' JC *di*), or there may be lexical differences, such as JE 'a' JC *wahn*. In both those cases, the structure of the construction would be the same, that is, D(eterminer)+NP. In weaving terms, the differences remain relatively superficial, therefore. In the case of the possessive and focus constructions, however, structures are different in the two languages, resulting in "deeper" syntactic differences.[12]

Finally, for both the JE infinitive particle 'to' and its JC counterpart *fi*,[13] the smallest number of forms following are attributable to JE. The learning of the sequence [verb+'to'] as an unanalysed chunk seems to be at work here: just under 70 per cent (69.6) of the occurrences of JE infinitive 'to' appear after variants of 'want' (as in [2]) and of the present participle 'going' (3).[14]

(2) ROS: *kaa   dem   <u>waahn to</u> mek   naiz.*
             because 3PL.SUBJ want   INF make noise
             'Because they want to be noisy.'   [V5-KIN:l 213-3;7.15]

(3) DAN: *tiichor <u>goin to</u> gi   mi   #   tikaz.*
             teacher going INF give 1S.IND OBJ [PAUSE] stickers
             'Teacher is going to give me a sticker.'
                                                [V6 English-STJ:l 279-3;4.16]

There are also differences in the numbers of JE and JC forms chosen by the different functional categories. The JE indefinite determiner 'a' selects a near equal number of JC, JE and SH nouns, indicating that it is not associated necessarily with JE. This may be due to the fact that *a* is a non-distinctive vowel, and that, in addition, that same form exists in JC with many different functions. JC *a* functions, for instance, as a focus marker, a progressive marker, a habitual marker, a copula and a preposition meaning 'at', 'to' or 'of' (see discussion in section 3.2 on multifunctional items).[15] All told, that is, including all functions, the children heard the form *a* more than 19,600 times in the interviews.

One may take this to conclude that the frequency of *a* resulting from its multifunctionality would cause such familiarity with the form that it would not be associated with a particular language. Note, however, that as a focus marker, the same form *a* selects predominantly JC complements, and that a full 75 per cent of the complements of its JE counterpart *iz* are JES forms. Multifunctionality, the resulting frequency of occurrence and the familiarity which would accompany it, cannot be the only factor determining choice of complement, therefore.

All this supports the possible involvement of factors other than formal syntactic features in language choice. This is not unique to the Jamaican context. Giancaspro (2013), while accepting the FHC in principle, notes that a language switch for Spanish-English bilinguals between an auxiliary and its verb phrase complement was allowed more freely for some auxiliaries. He interpreted this to indicate the possibility that bilinguals do not process all functional categories in the same way. Support for this was found in different grammatical judgements for Spanish-English switches than for English-Spanish switches, pointing to a role for language directionality in CS. Processing apart, Giancaspro considers language attitude effects on preferences for switches by the bilinguals (p. 66).

Subjects who showed higher preference for switches in grammatical judgement tests, for instance, thought that switching was "super cool"; those who showed lower tolerance thought that it was an undesirable linguistic pattern, since it reflected a need for more practice or a lack of understanding.

Following Giancaspro (2013), I suggest that there may exist pragmatic or sociolinguistic reasons for a functional category SELECTing a lexical item from the JC or the JE lexicon. We may say that such a feature is *sociolinguistically neutral*.[16] The JE indefinite determiner *a* appears to be such a function word, since there are similar numbers of complements chosen from each language. This may be due to widespread variation in the input: the form *a* is encountered so frequently by the children as an indefinite that, much like cognates, it may not be perceived as belonging necessarily to JE.

Language mixing appears, then, to be a sociolinguistic reality. Possible roles of sociolinguistic factors in the selection of a lexical item from the JC or the JE lexicon are now explored.

6.3.3 Social and Attitudinal Factors

Social context provides a background for illustrating how Jamaican speakers manipulate the language range at their disposal. It is well-known that social and psychological factors such as dominance and group membership play an important motivating role for language choice where languages are in contact (see, for example, Cummins [2009]). Within the Creole context, situational factors such as what I termed the *culture of correction* in section 1.1 are considered to play an important role in this regard. It was illustrated in that discussion that it is the prevailing view, even among native speakers of JC themselves, that JC is nothing but "bad English" or "broken English". In addition, school teachers, parents and grandparents are known to chastise the younger generation when they speak it. It is for reasons such as these that we speak about the existence in Jamaica of a culture of correction.

This tendency to correct is evident among the CLAR children. They correct their classmates, and even the investigators, with variants they believe to be preferred. In (4) below, DAE corrects the investigator, insisting that she use the plural and progressive forms/structures closer to JE:

(4)   DAE: *wat di   boi- z du-in?*
                what DEF boy-PL do-PROG
                'What are the boys doing?'

INV: *yuu   tel mii!*
      2s.SUBJ tell 1s.OBJ
      'You tell me!'

INV: *wa   di   bwai dem a   du?*
      what DEF boy   INCL PROG do
      'What are the boys doing?'

DAE: ... *di   boi- z   du-in.*
           DEF boy-PL do-PROG
      '... the boys doing.'   [V6-STT:ll 418ff.-3 ;4.0]

Interestingly, often the suggested replacement is not really JE. In (4), the JE version of the question used by DAE would involve subject-auxiliary inversion,
rendering 'What **are** the boys doing?', the form of the determiner would be 'the'
rather than *di* and the progressive inflection would end with the velar /ŋ/ 'ng'
rather than the alveolar /n/.

This may not be surprising, given the number of variants which exist in the
input. Forms of "here" were the target of correction by the children. There are
seven variants used both as adverbs and pronouns over twelve hundred times.
The variants with JE segments are taken to be *hierso, hier, ier, ierso*, and the variants *ya, yaso* and *yier* to be closer to JC. Distinctions between the forms may be
viewed in the following terms:

- lexical differences (*hierso* vs *hier*): different words, with *hier* being closer
  to JE;
- phonological differences (*hier* vs *ier* and *hierso* vs *ierso*): different pronunciations of the same word, with the initial segment /h/ associated
  in this environment with JE. Note that the JE pronunciation [heəʳ] was
  not used at all.

The most frequently used of the variants are JE *ier* (505 times) and JC *ya* (475
times). In the examples below, the form *ya* was corrected by a child from St
Elizabeth in the west (5) and also one from St Andrew (town) in the east (6). It
may be, then, that JC *ya* is a stigmatized form.

(5)   GAB: *yu   mos- n   se « si   im   ya »*
             2s.SUBJ must-NEG say   see 3s.OBJ here
             'You mustn't say "See him *ya*".'

GAB: *yu   mos se « si im   hier »*.
2s.SUBJ must say see 3s.OBJ here
'You must say "See him *hier*".'   [V3-SER:1.461-3;7.17]

(6)   DES: *si mi   klak ya!*
see 1s.POSS clock here
'See my clock here!'

ORR: *nat klak ya klak ier.*
NEG clock here clock here
'Not clock "ya", clock "ier".'

[V3-ADT:ll.158-9-DES 3;9.15, ORR 3;9.26]

Whether the corrected form is closest to JE or not, if there are ways of speaking which are strongly associated with "proper" speech, then it would logically follow that there would be an insistence in the society that children *taak prapa* 'speak properly'. Irvine (2005) suggested that the association is based on the phonology and the lexis (see section 1.1 for discussion), both of which are relevant here.

Importantly, this too may be exploited as an advantage. As long ago as thirty years, LePage and Tabouret-Keller (1985, 115) pointed to the importance of motivation and opportunities to adjust speech, for successful second language learning to take place. Children will tend to learn the second language (JE) forms, even without, perhaps, knowing why it is important.

Following Giancaspro (2013), the assumption is that one or another sociolinguistic or pragmatic factor, or perhaps both, are at work here, causing a function word to be associated with a particular lexicon. Factors which would be relevant to the Jamaican situation were outlined in chapter 1. It may be expected, for instance, that the association would be determined based on forms which the children have been socialized to believe to be appropriate for formal or informal situations, or quite simply, via stigma passed on to them through explicit negative input – "Don't say *di*, say 'the'!".

In addition, it was mentioned in section 3.1 and discussed in section 4.3.3 that the fricative [ð] does not exist in the JC inventory of sounds, and that the JC alveolar stop [d] is produced in environments where in JE the fricative is produced. An example is "**th**en". This was said to be a universally recognized linguistic mark of JC speech, and so teachers would feel some pressure to correct it in the children's speech.[17] Such contrasts between individual or group pronunciations on the one hand, and societal norms on the other, though not unusual in any language context, appear to be relatively common in Jamaican speech, a reflection, no doubt, of the differences (and similarities) between JC and JE, as well as pressures exerted on JC speakers in the culture of correction.

This falls in the field of sociophonology, the aspect of sociolinguistics which studies only those differences of pronunciation which are perceived to be socially significant (Honey 1998, 92). Sociophonology makes use also of the continuum of linguistic variation, employing a categorization of linguistic features as being spread along a line showing clustering around the acrolect, mesolect and the basilect, with a speaker's level of education considered to be the most obvious factor associated with a movement along the continuum in the direction of the acrolect (p. 94). The starting point is the principle that different sounds, much like other linguistic features including grammar, encode value systems (p. 97).

In addition, of course, there may be purely linguistic reasons for an association of a word in the mental lexicon with a particular language – in this case, neither the initial consonant that occurs in the pronunciation of JE 'the' nor the vowel following, for instance, exists in the JC inventory of sounds. This would serve to make it perceptually salient in the input.

The claim, therefore, is that language choice may be determined by sociolinguistic or pragmatic as well as by language-internal factors.[18] The level of consciousness of language-appropriateness which this suggests exists in the minds of the CLAR children, would seem to point to their readiness for pedagogies based on language awareness. In the sections which follow, I investigate the components of and the rationale behind such pedagogies.

6.3.4 Attentional Control

Another way to resolve the competition among the alternative candidates made available to children in the input is by calling on a control mechanism, a selective mechanism which will act as a "mental firewall" (Kroll, Bogulski and McClain 2012, 6–7). Costa, Miozzo, and Caramazza (1999), among others, show that control of the language not in use can be effected by an attentional mechanism, serving to inhibit the selection of candidates from the unintended language. Attentional processing is controlled and often results in direct availability to consciousness. It contrasts with automatic processing which cannot be prevented and is not directly available to consciousness (Harley [1995] 2014, 178).

Attentional processing is the basis of Schmidt's (1990, 2001, 2010) Noticing Hypothesis, framed in terms of consciousness as intention, consciousness as attention and consciousness as awareness. For Schmidt, attention is "for all practical purposes . . . necessary for all aspects of L2 learning" (2001, 3). Attention does not refer to a single mechanism, but to a variety of mechanisms or subsystems, including alertness and orientation (p. 17), detection within selective attention (pp. 17–21), facilitation and inhibition (pp. 21–22). These mechanisms have in common the function of controlling information processing and behaviour when existing skills and routines are inadequate (Schmidt 2010, 724).

There are important implications for us in all this, in terms of providing some support for the language issues I have identified. If the boundaries between languages are not clear in the mind of the speaker, as I have suggested is the case in a Creole-speaking environment; if the great number of close cognates which exist mask other differences between the languages; if English is the weaker language among children; and if language non-selectivity exists in the minds of speakers of all levels of proficiency where there are two (or more) languages in contact, this points to a crucial role for language awareness in ensuring that speakers have a (linguistic) basis on which to distinguish the two languages.

What I have called the culture of correction, and the patterns of language selection by functional categories suggest that there is already a certain awareness among the population of differences between the codes spoken in the country, even among children as young as three years old. This awareness is often not evident in actual performance, but its existence does indicate a possible readiness on their part to learn about different ways of speaking. It has been found (see Foursha-Stevenson and Nicoladis [2011] and references they quote) that the very fact that, from a very early age, children exposed to more than one language have extensive experience in choosing the appropriate language for the context, may lead to an enhanced development of attentional control.

Levels of language awareness have been linked to literacy, with distinctions between the contributions of awareness of different linguistic components. Phonological, morphological and syntactic awareness are considered in the next section; critical language awareness is discussed in section 6.4.1.

6.4 Levels of Language Awareness and Literacy

Gee (2015, 57) argues that though literacy must by definition have something to do with the ability to read text, different types of texts such as newspapers, comic books or novels call for "different types of background knowledge, require different skills to be read meaningfully, and are and can be read in different ways". In this sociocultural view, one has to be socialized into, and cannot be viewed as being independent of, social practice. Thus literacy involves not only reading and writing, but also ways of talking, interacting, thinking, valuing and believing (p. 60).

After a broad review of definitions, Lewis (2010, 22) adopts to a large extent Brandt's (2001) view of literacy as an individual development which is connected to literacy as an economic development. This is mediated through sponsors or agents who "enable, support, teach and model, as well as recruit, regulate, suppress, or withhold, literacy – and gain advantage by it in some way" (Brandt 2001, 19). Although the interests of the sponsors and those they sponsor do not need to converge, value is also conferred on the sponsored, in forms such as employability, humanitarian prestige, social status, or mastery of literacy assessments (Lewis 2010, 22). She discusses literacy, then, as being a global good, more specifically, a human right (p. 23), and considers how, in a country like Jamaica that right can be realized at the intersection of literacy with language and policy (pp. 24–27), so as to ensure that the disadvantaged and marginalized are not denied mastery of the language of social access (p. 28).

It is argued in this work that characteristics of the use of language in Jamaica as a largely Creole-speaking environment point to an approach to literacy and language education based on language awareness as a means of ensuring such access.

Phonological awareness has been defined as understanding the various ways in which oral language can be divided into smaller components and manipulated (Chard and Dickson 1999). Snow, Burns and Griffin (1998, 51) distinguish between phonological awareness and phonemic awareness, a finer-grained sensitivity which is "an understanding that words can be divided into a sequence of phonemes". In what follows, I do not distinguish between the two, but use phonological awareness as an umbrella term. Both are intertwined with but different from phonics, which involves the association of letters and sounds, allowing for the sounding-out of written symbols. I do not discuss phonics.

The specific skills which are typical of the phonologically aware concern rhyming (recognition, completion and production of words which rhyme), syllable recognition (blending, segmentation and deletion of syllables), the isolation or deletion of initial and final phonemes as well as phoneme segmentation and substitution (KU, 2015).

Phonological awareness has been shown to be related to progress in learning to read, surviving controls of intelligence, vocabulary and socioeconomic status, and there is evidence that the relationship is causal (Deacon and Kirby 2004, 223, and references quoted there). This is supported by intervention studies conducted by Torgesen et al. (2001). The studies show that children with severe reading disabilities exhibited statistically significant gains in reading ability, following both immediate and long-term training in phonological awareness.

This causal relationship between reading and phonological awareness has furthermore been shown to be bi-directional: certain aspects of awareness play a fundamental role in facilitating early reading acquisition, and acquisition itself readily facilitates the emergence of yet other, more sophisticated aspects of phonological awareness (Riches and Genesee 2006, 73–74). Of significance for us is that results from instructional studies also suggest that phonological awareness in an L2 (in our case, English) can be developed through direct intervention, even if L2 oral development is somewhat limited (p. 74). Though cross-linguistic relationships are complex and interwoven (p. 64), the results suggest that L2 phonological awareness is not dependent on L1 awareness. Instead, phonological awareness has been shown to be a common underlying proficiency which is metalinguistic, therefore, or, "a cognitive substrate to reading acquisition", as Chard and Dickson (1999, 1) put it.

Morphological awareness refers to children's "sensitivity to the morphological structure of words", which allows them to reflect on and manipulate that structure (Carlisle 2004, 323). It follows, therefore, as Carlisle (1995, 194) indicates, that the extent of a child's morphological awareness is limited by her morphological knowledge. There is a substantial existing (and growing) body of literature indicating that morphological awareness contributes to reading competence (Kirby et al. 2012, 392), specifically in reading comprehension, since it supports the interpretation of unknown words. In a study of grades 7 and 8 students in the United States, Nagy and Anderson (1984, 323, table 7) found, for instance, that depending on a child's ability to detect and make use of derived forms, for each word learned, there are between 1.57 and 2.57 other words which involve relatively transparent relationships, with morphemes sufficiently familiar to allow for a reasonable guess about the meaning. There are an additional 1.16–1.90 with regular inflections, comparatives and superlatives, and yet another 0.87–1.42 with minor variations in form. Taken together, this results in a total of between 3.60 and 5.89 other recognizable words for each word known. The authors conclude that "this demonstrates that the ability to utilize morphological relatedness among words puts a student at a distinct advantage in dealing with unfamiliar words" (p. 323).

Competence in word reading is also supported by morphological aware-ness, since it allows for the exclusion of some pronunciations of single mor-pheme words. Knowing that "mishandle" is a morphologically complex word, for instance, will help readers to parse the strings of letters at the right syllable boundary ("mis-handle", not "mi-shandle"), and increase the likelihood of more accurate pronunciation (Kuo and Anderson 2006, 172) and understanding. Additionally, a likely outcome of speedier processing in reading is a contribu-tion to word and text reading speed (Kirby et al. 2012, 394).

Dressler (2012, 3) indicates that it is generally the case that the acquisition of inflectional morphology starts later than lexical, phonological or syntactic acquisition, but earlier than the acquisition of derivation, and suggests that this late emergence might be due to its less essential nature. It would be considered to be less essential, since it is required only by the syntax, and since there are languages, such as Southeast Asian languages, which have few inflections or lack them altogether. Importantly, the degree of morphological richness of a language is a factor pertinent to the speed of the acquisition of morphology: as reported in Laaha and Gillis (2007),[19] morphologically rich languages stimulate children more to acquire morphology than languages which are weakly inflecting.

Sparseness of inflections, particularly, but also of derivations is found in the CLAR data,[20] and is known to be characteristic of Creole languages. This may point to the need for particular attention to be placed on training in morpholog-ical awareness among children from Creole-speaking communities.

Though the concept of attaching (bound) morphemes to roots or stems may not be productive among the CLAR children, we saw in section 3.4 that new word formation is productive, and that the strategies used by the children to fill lexical gaps are systematic and recognizable as following patterns of word for-mation in JC. Increasing vocabulary by capitalizing on strategies already inter-nalized by the children, and by extending their repertoire of strategies will go a far way to enhancing reading competence.

An example of a test for morphological awareness is the word analogy task (Kirby et al. 2012, 397 and appendix), where participants are asked to provide a missing word based on a pattern from a set of words provided, for example, run: ran :: walk: [walked].

Syntactic (or grammatical) *awareness* refers to the ability to manipulate and reflect on the grammatical structure of language. It is a metalinguistic skill, dis-tinct from the comprehension or production of a sentence, because it concerns the conscious ability to consider the structure rather than the meaning of a sen-tence (Cain 2007, 679). Foursha-Stevenson and Nicoladis (2011, 521–22), focus-ing on the ability to judge grammaticality, define it as the ability to think about the well-formedness of syntax, and indicate that this ability starts to emerge as early as age 2;6. Syntactic awareness differs from syntactic knowledge which, as conceptualized by Chomsky, constitutes an unconscious understanding of the rules which govern language (see section 2.1). It may be said that syntactic awareness, a metalinguistic awareness skill, measures the explicit awareness of syntactic knowledge (Brimo and Apel 2011) – a matter of bringing the subconscious into consciousness. It is also the expectation that through explicit noticing, rules will be internalized, thus forming implicit syntactic knowledge.[21]

According to what is known as the simple view of reading, as originally proposed by Gough and Tunmer (1986), and widely adopted since then, reading comprehension comprises two components: word recognition and language comprehension. According to this view, word recognition involves decoding which allows for the "translation" of print into language, and the comprehension component, which makes sense of the linguistic information (Catts, Adlof and Weismer 2006, 278). Syntactic awareness and syntactic knowledge, along with contributions made by vocabulary knowledge, fall within the language comprehension component.

I have spoken about the blurring of boundaries in a Creole language situation, and about the misconception that, because the Creole and the official language sound similar at the level of the word, they are the same at other levels. An important aspect of syntactic awareness in such a situation is that children become aware of the differences between the two languages at the level of the syntax, so that there can be a clear awareness of what constitutes the Creole and how it differs from the standard – "When I say this, it is Creole." and "When I say that, it is English."

Cain (2007, 679) discusses tasks that assess syntactic awareness. They are word-order correction tasks, where the words of a sentence are presented in a jumbled order and have to be rearranged, for example, "strokes the cat Sue" and grammatical correction tasks, where a grammatical or morphological anomaly in a sentence must be repaired, for example, "The girl eat the chocolate."

Areas where it is known that there are differences between JC and JE, such as those outlined in chapters 4 and 5 in this work, would be relevant material for diagnostic testing for syntactic awareness, and could form the basis of lessons.[22] Crucially, there is no need – in fact, there is no place – for guesswork, since languages are systematic, and since language acquisition is systematic (see sections 1.1.1, 2.1, 2.4 and, indeed, throughout this study, for discussions of systematicity). We know how structures between the two language systems differ, we know which features "belong" to JC and which to JE and, as we have seen, we are able to predict, in a general way, how speakers will tend to weave these features in their speech. What becomes important is to ensure that students become aware of these systematic and predictable differences.

Ways in which language awareness has been applied in the language classroom are discussed in the next section.

6.4.1 The Language Awareness Approach to Literacy and Language Education

Tomlinson (2003, 251) points out that language awareness is a mental attribute which develops through paying motivated attention to language in use. This attention enables language learners to gradually gain insights into how languages work. Importantly, it is also a pedagogical approach which aims to help learners gain such insights.

Tomlinson (ibid.) indicates further that a key element of a language awareness approach is that learners "discover language for themselves", and cites E. Hawkins (1984, 4–5), who says that it involves challenging pupils to ask questions about language. The desired outcome is for students to be motivated to learn about language not only within the school environment, but also "to gather their own data from the world outside school". Attention to language will become, then, a means of developing a view of language through a spirit of enquiry.

Much of what has been said about language awareness as attention to how language works, or as explicit instruction about language, does not mean, then, that it is taught by the teacher or by a text. Instead, it is developed, through continuing personal insights by the learners as they are encouraged to discover and articulate patterns of language use.

Language awareness has been distinguished from consciousness-raising (CR). James (1996, 139–40) defines language awareness as "the possession of metacognitions about language in general, some bit of language, or a particular language over which one already has skilled control and a coherent set of intuitions". In contrast, CR is for language learners who are not yet in command of formal knowledge of a language or of consistent intuitions and involves, therefore, activities that develop the ability to locate and identify the discrepancy between one's present state of knowledge and a goal state of knowledge, giving the learner insight into what she does not know and thus needs to learn.

I do not distinguish between language awareness and CR. Guided by the blurred boundaries between the languages as evidenced by the patterns of weaving in the speech of the CLAR children, it seems clear that the focus of language awareness must include the discovery and articulation of how patterns in the Creole and in the official language vary, even while exploiting the similarities between them (see discussion of cognates above). For this, CR activities, such as those outlined by Ellis (2002, 234), would certainly be useful. He lists the main characteristics of such activities as follows:

1. there is an attempt to isolate a specific linguistic feature for focused attention;
2. the learners are provided with data which illustrate the targeted feature and they may also be supplied with an explicit rule describing or explaining the feature;
3. the learners are expected to utilize intellectual effort to understand the targeted feature;
4. misunderstanding or incomplete understanding of the grammatical structure by the learners leads to clarification in the form of further data and description/explanation; and
5. learners may be required (although this is not obligatory) to articulate the rule describing the grammatical structure.

This attention to form must be modified for our language situation to refer specifically to forms of the two language systems. However, given the socio-linguistic complexity which exists (see section 1.1 for details and sections 6.3.2 and 6.3.3 for discussion), students must also come to know the contexts which are appropriate for their use. Antwi (2015) develops a working definition of language awareness for application to the Creole language situation. She takes Carter's (2003, 64) definition as the "development in learners of an enhanced consciousness of and sensitivity to language functions and forms", to aptly capture language awareness, and for the purposes of her study on the syntactic awareness of seventh-grade Jamaican students adapts it to refer to sensitivity to the forms and functions of JC and JE. She continues:

> If the learners of a language do not have this "sensitivity" and knowledge of the way a language is supposed to function then ultimately they will not fully acquire the language. He [Carter 2003, 65] further illustrates that L[anguage]A[wareness] also comes about on an emotional level for the learner, which in turn comes through "enhanced noticing" and "consciousness raising". This will be the true test of LA in the Jamaican context. At the end of their schooling, students should be able to notice differences between the two languages and be aware of the functions and formal rules of the lan-

guages. Not only should they know functions but they should be able to have a deeper level of understanding of how the language works. (Antwi 2015, 15)

Tomlinson (2003, 252) termed this relationship between language and social context critical language awareness. It is an awareness of "the ways in which language represents the world and reflects and constructs power relations" (ibid). Incorporating this knowledge of the functions of language(s) is important in a Creole language situation.

The application of a language awareness approach to language education in a Creole-speaking environment, whether this exists in the native territories or in the diaspora, is not new. Addressing issues surrounding African American Vernacular English (AAVE) speakers learning English in a US context, Wheeler, Cartwright and Swords (2012, 417) discuss the ways in which dialects, or language varieties spoken by learners, interfere with reading comprehension. The ways in which varieties differ in sound, vocabulary and grammar cause decoding accuracy to be compromised, and it becomes important for the teachers when assessing the reading of such students, to distinguish between reading errors resulting from lack of phonics knowledge, for instance, and those resulting from transfer from the variety spoken by the student. A student may already have basic decoding skills, but may read words as they sound in her variety (p. 419). In order to distinguish dialect difference from reading error, teachers must have systematic knowledge of the varieties spoken by their students. Armed with an ability to reliably distinguish reading error from dialect influence, the authors recommend bi-dialectal approaches to the teaching of Standard English to vernacular speakers, using contrastive analysis to alert them to structural differences between the varieties, then leading them to code-switch, choosing the appropriate language variety to fit the setting (p. 421).

Kachru (2006, 31) suggests that a starting point is to legitimize code-mixing and CS, and to exploit them for effective teaching, by encouraging language awareness as a methodologically sound practice in language teaching, not only in the United States but in many contexts where world Englishes are spoken alongside local varieties.

Nero and Ahmad (2014, 3) propose the use and study of vernacular Englishes in knowledge construction within school settings. This is a pedagogy that makes language itself in its totality the central focus of study, that is, its forms, functions, as well as its links to culture, identity and power (p. 51). The approach involves teachers themselves reflecting in a detailed way on their own attitudes towards and identities with language(s) and having a linguistically informed

understanding of language, language variation and language ideologies, allowing them to engage the vernacular in the classroom, and to confront their own
and students' possible biases and misconceptions concerning language (p. 15).

Within the Caribbean context, the Language Materials Workshop (LMW)
Primary Language Arts programme was created and developed by Don Wilson,
Dennis Craig and Hyacinth Campbell and first published for use in Jamaican
primary schools in 1978. The *Teacher's Book* accompanying the year one, term
one material explains (p. 2) that there are three ways in which the differences
between the child's spoken language and the language she has to learn to read
are addressed in the programme. First, the *avoidance strategy* seeks to ensure
that, initially, the material the child meets contains only those words and grammatical structures that are shared in the two language systems. Structures existing in written English but not in the child's language are then introduced "in a
gradual manner, one by one".[23] The third strategy addresses how the second is
to be handled: before the child is asked to read the new structure, it should be
introduced in meaningful speech contexts (*Controlled Talk*).

Jennings (1996, 140) indicates that the significance of the commissioning
of the LMW materials by the Ministry of Education lay in the fact that it represented the first implementation of the ministry's policy to use locally developed
materials wherever possible, and Bryan (2014a, 8) lauds the series as having
"formed the backbone of the reading and language arts material available to
Jamaican primary school children for nearly thirty years".

Craig continued in his career to formalize methods appropriate for the successful acquisition of English by Creole-speaking children. He made a clear
case for the use of language awareness in a classroom of what he came to call
Creole-influenced vernacular speakers, or CIVs (1999). He indicates that the
lexical overlap between the vernacular and the official language tends to cause
structures which are close to the official language but Creole-influenced, to be
perceived as identical to structures belonging to the official language (2006,
236). Recall the example of contracted forms in English, where the English
"He's gone" is perceived as being identical with "He gone" (section 5.5). This
leads Craig (ibid.) to conclude: "Because of the perception difficulty, key English
grammatical elements such as [this] . . . cannot be acquired merely by interaction with English speakers or immersion into English. The learner has to be
induced to focus attention deliberately on those elements, vocalize and write
them, then form habits of using them."

Linguistic insights, then, provide the material for deliberate focus in the
classroom. As Bryan (2014b, 25) puts it, language teachers require "sound linguistic understanding of the child's mother tongue in addition to the target

language" and an orientation towards being lifelong language learners. This is teacher language awareness, TLA (Andrews 2003). TLA is not the same as teacher language proficiency. Instead it is the ability to demonstrate knowledge of language from the learner's perspective, said to be the equivalent to subject matter knowledge for teachers in other disciplines (Murray and Christison 2011, 69). With the metalinguistic means by which to speak about differences and similarities between the two languages, teachers will be in a position to have a good understanding of the language of the children they teach, and the "likely Creole-influenced difficulties they might encounter" (Bryan 2014b, 24). It is in this way that linguistics can serve educators.

Winer (2006, 107) indicates that today, "by and large, progressive Caribbean educators are increasingly using the Language Awareness approach", and some textbooks, such as Simmons-McDonald, Fields and Roberts (1997), are grounded in the approach.

In considering how best to present information about grammar in the language classroom, Pollard (2001, 105) suggests, following Fotos (1994), that formal instruction in grammar be merged creatively with communicative language teaching. She advocates that in the teaching of English in Jamaica and other communities where there is an English-lexified Creole, there be a place for simple descriptions of the L1 alongside grammars of English. These descriptions will allow the teacher to guide elicitation of sentences which illustrate a particular point of grammar, for instance. Subsequent visual representation of those sentences on the blackboard will help to underline their accurate usage (Pollard 2001, 101). Poetry and prose passages, as well as examples previously identified from students' own compositions, will allow for extensive observation of the language in use by students, for discovery of the rule and eventual internalization of it, along with the ability to express it in their own words (p. 103).

Between Two Grammars, the title of Bryan's 2010 book, aptly captures the linguistic status of speakers in a Creole-speaking environment. That linguistic space may be said to be characterized, in the terms used in this book, by the weaving of Creole features with those of the official language, a space within which speakers are caught. The solution is encapsulated in the title of Bryan's chapter 5, which ascribes the role of "making language visible" to language awareness in a Creole-speaking environment. This is done by using the children's intuitions as the basis of the lesson, and building on their existing knowledge. She analyses the components of a grade 5 lesson on pronouns taught by a teacher in rural Jamaica (pp. 91–102). The lesson uses the knowledge of a popular church song as the starting point, and incorporates not only the children's intuitions, but also cultural content and formal discussions of differences between JC and JE pronouns.

A second example of a lesson grounded in language awareness was one on the (linguistic) count–mass distinction,[24] as discussed in section 4.1. The presentation was made to teachers at a primary school in Kingston, and consisted of an explanation of these differences in the form of PowerPoint slides, using the CLAR data to indicate how the distinction is made in JC, and how this differs from JE. For example, in JE, the indefinite 'a' may not be used with a mass noun such as 'milk'. Instead, it must be introduced by a unitizing phrase such as 'a cup of'. In contrast, it is perfectly acceptable in JC for the indefinite to be used, and for the unit therefore to be implied, as in *wahn*$_{INDEF}$ *milk*.

In this way, teachers were equipped with knowledge of the grammatical issue, and provided with an opportunity to practise and internalize the differences. This was followed by a class modelled on Craig's Augmented Language Experience Approach. The class was based on "Our Jamaican Cuisine – The Food We Eat" in Sinanan et al. (2002, unit 16), and began with the eating of a tasty snack, serving as "stimulation", followed by a discussion of its flavours. Portions of the passage from the text were read, and other Jamaican dishes discussed, with an emphasis on vocabulary enrichment and the description of the tastes. Grammatical structures and relevant adjectives were presented. All this was practised through the creation of a recipe for salt fish fritters, with answers to questions incorporating how count nouns are pluralized, and mass nouns measured. As ingredients were added, choice words and phrases were written on the board, for students (participating teachers) to copy. Students were engaged in guided oral reading of the passage, and in word recognition, using the vocabulary journal to record words introduced. Ideally, had time allowed, creative follow-up would perhaps have been in the form of creating an illustration of the finished product, the fritters.

Feedback revealed that the teachers recognized the value of being provided with metalinguistic tools to speak about a grammatical distinction, as well as with the pedagogical tools to pass on the knowledge, translating it into effective classroom practice.

6.5 Concluding Remarks

The CLAR data show that JC is the dominant language of children as they enter the primary school classroom at age 3;0 ± 3 months in Jamaica. We saw that the learning of JE is not simply a matter of learning that number is marked by a morpheme attached to the noun, for instance, or that expressing pastness requires a morpheme attached to the verb. The nominal and verbal systems are fundamentally different in the two languages. That JC nouns are set nouns (see section 4.1) means necessarily that different features will regulate the formation of nominal constructions. Similarly, as an aspect-prominent language, tense marking in JC will necessarily rely on lexical aspectual considerations; as a starting point, the L2 learner must know that there are no default tense interpretations in JE.

Fundamental differences in structure between the languages tend to go unnoticed because of the superficial similarities which exist in pronunciation where correspondences are apparent, as well as similarities in vocabulary due to the large number of shared lexical items. Because of these similarities, there is often confusion concerning the language system to which a particular form belongs, and a belief that similarities exist where, in fact, they do not.

Code-mixing, the natural consequence of languages in contact, is characteristic of normal everyday speech, and therefore also of the input children hear as they acquire their L1. The input is not chaotic, however. The patterns which became apparent in our investigations, show clearly how it is that features associated with each of the languages combine, or (informally) are woven in the speech of the children.

The language of the forms which follow functional categories has been a focus of formal research for decades. We saw that a formal (minimalist) account in terms of satisfying uninterpretable features associated with the language of the functional category is not feasible, since the patterns found allow for the formulation of probabilistic and not absolute or rigid statements.

That there is extreme variation in the input is evident. Alongside this, there is a keen awareness by the children that there are differences between JC and JE, prompted no doubt by what I have called the culture of correction that pervades. It has been said (Irvine 2005; Beckford-Wassink 1999) that it is on the basis of the phonology, particularly, and the lexicon that speakers assess standardness. In support of this, it is reported in the literature that particular forms are stigmatized (for example, JC possessive preposition *fi*), and there are others which are strongly associated with JE (for example, 'the'). It is precisely those forms which predictably tend not to exhibit mixing.

It would appear, then, that it is the interplay of sociological factors and the strong awareness of the differences in pronunciation which determine language choice. Perhaps Grice's pragmatic principle of consistency – Be consistent! – is relevant in language choice.[25]

This may be applied to the classroom in the following way. The correction of speech is commonplace. It may not always reflect a clear knowledge of which variants actually do belong to JE, but it does reflect a certain collective language awareness, and a readiness, perhaps, for more specific knowledge. The existing orientation towards language awareness ought to be capitalized on.

There is good reason for an approach grounded in language awareness to become the choice pedagogy for the language and literacy classroom in a language environment such as that in Jamaica. As Clachar (2005, 325) indicates, such an approach is necessary for all L2 learners, but takes on heightened significance for Creole speakers because of the blurring of the distinction between the L1 and the so-called Standard, and the consequences which this has.

Importantly, Jamaican teachers are at an advantage, being for the large part themselves speakers of JC, as products of the same communities from which their students come, and must themselves be made sufficiently aware of the differences between the two language systems so to be able to explain relevant language structures to them.

To understand the nature of the weave, to have specific knowledge about the language systems and how they work will serve to "make language visible", increase proficiency in JE and success in other areas of the curriculum which depend also on that proficiency.

Appendix 1. The Cassidy-JLU Writing System

The idea behind the writing system is that the same sound is always represented by the same letter or pair of letters.

CONSONANTS

/dʒ/ this sound will always be represented by "j", even if not so in English
   just = *jos*
   danger = *dienja*

/k/ this sound will always be represented by "k", even if not so in English
   kite = *kait*
   call = *kaal*

There is no "q" or "x" in the writing system: "q" is represented as "kw" and "x" as "ks"

SEQUENCES WHICH DON'T EXIST IN ENGLISH:

gy *gyal*
ky *kyaar*
ny *nyam*

OTHER TWO-LETTER SEQUENCES:

ng *ting*
sh *shuga* (think of the sound, not the spelling)
ch *wach* 'watch'

VOWELS – short

a *av* ('have')
e *get*
i *win* (the short vowel)
o *kom* 'come', *bot* 'but' NOTE: when this occurs before "r", it is a bit different (*gorl*, *worl*)
u *gud* 'good', *ful* 'full'

VOWELS – long

Long vowels are represented as double vowels

aa   *haaf*
ii   *biit*
uu   *skuul*

DIPHTHONGS

ai   *laik*
ou   *ous*
ie   *fiesti*
uo   *buot*

NASAL VOWELS

Indicate that a vowel is nasalized by following it with "hn"

waahn   'want'
wan   'one'
wahn   'a'

Source: JLU (Jamaican Language Unit). 2009. *Ou fi rait Jamiekan. Writing Jamaican the Jamaican Way*. Kingston: Arawak.

Appendix 2. The Lexical–Functional Distinction

There is an important distinction in linguistics between lexical and functional categories. Functional categories may include words or parts of words, both of which are referred to as morphemes; they are associated with a grammatical function.

A word is an independent morpheme since it may function on its own; it is known as a free morpheme. Parts of words which are not independent are bound to the word. An example of a bound morpheme is the inflectional ending associated with the past tense, mentioned in the text. This is also called the past-tense morpheme. Inflectional morphemes are not independent morphemes, but function only when attached in JE to the end of the word as suffixes. In JC, there are no bound inflectional morphemes; instead, these grammatical functions are housed in free morphemes. An example of a function word in JC is the past tense *wehn*.

Other function words and morphemes to be considered in this work are associated with the grammatical functions of possession (*fi mi mada* 'my mother's'), (in)definiteness (*di* 'the'), plurality (*di bwai dem* 'the boys'), tense (*did waak* 'walked') and aspect (*a waak* 'is walking').

Lexical categories differ from functional categories in that they are associated not with grammatical function, but with meaning, content or contentful meaning. Nouns, adjectives, verbs and adverbs are considered to be lexical categories. The noun *siit* 'chair, seat', for instance, is associated with the piece of furniture used for sitting, so we say that noun has contentful meaning.

More on Lexical versus Functional Categories

In linguistics, the noun (N), verb (V), adjective (Adj) and the adverb (Adv) are considered to be lexical categories. We can readily identify the meaning of the N *naif* 'knife', or know the event which is referred to by the V *waak* 'walk', for example.

These *content words* may be built into phrases which provide us with a bit more information about the nature of the content. So, for example, we may provide a characteristic of the object (*shaap naif* 'sharp knife') or indicate how the event was executed (*waak faas* 'walk fast'). We say that *shaap* modifies *naif* since it tells us more about *naif*. In a similar way, *faas* modifies *waak*. The noun and all the material which modifies it form a noun phrase, or NP. The noun is said to head the NP, since it determines the class of the phrase to which it builds. Note also that only particular kinds of words, such as an adjective (Adj), may modify the N. So, Adj modifies N and together they form NP. Similarly, the adverb (Adv) *faas* modifies the head V *waak*, and together they form VP. Thus, two lexical phrases, the NP and the VP, have been formed by building more material relevant to the N and the V, respectively.

Structure may continue being built in this way. The lexical NP just formed may itself be used to modify a head which supplies it, not with more information about the nature of its content, but with information such as whether or not it can be identified (definiteness) by the hearer, for instance. It is the function of the definite (*di/i* 'the') or indefinite (*wahn/wan* 'a') articles to indicate definiteness (or indefiniteness). These elements are members of the category *determiner* (D). D and NP together build to a DP.

Continuing the example above, then, *di shaap naif* 'the sharp knife' would be a DP, containing the D *di* and the NP *shaap naif*.

The VP modifies a head which supplies it with information situating it in time (tense). This information is carried by functional tense markers (T) such as past tense *wehn* in JC, appearing before the verb, and by inflections such as the past -ed, attached as an affix to the V in JE. Given this, <u>wehn</u> *waak faas* 'walk<u>ed</u> fast' would be a TP headed by T *wehn* and containing the VP *waak faas*.

The categories D(eterminer) and T(ense) are not lexical, since they do not provide content. Instead, they are functional: they indicate some grammatical function – (in)definiteness or tense – which is relevant to the lexical categories.

Appendix 3. Other Codes Used for Tagging

Category	Code	Meaning	Source (if applicable)/ Comments
Noun-type	&MA	Mass – abstract	Bloom 2002, 89–100
	&MS	Mass – substance	Bloom 2002, 89–100
	&CN	Count – non-object	
	&CG	Count – group	
	&COC	Count object – complex	
	&COS	Count object – simple	
	&COP	Count object – part	
Taxonomy	&BA	Basic	
	&SP	Superordinate	
Verb-type	&VA	Verby-adjective	Baker (2003a, 238–45)
Compound-type	&HE	Error of headedness	Comment: In addition, constituents of compounds are labelled with language codes as in table 1.5.
	&CV	Conventionalized	
	&NV	Novel	
	&LT	Loan (type)	
	&CLT	Creolized loan (type)	
Morphemes	&DP	Derivational prefix	
	&DS	Derivational suffix	
	&IRR	Irregular	
(Affix file)	-AGT	Agentive	
	-PL	Plural	
	-PAST	Past	
	-123S	1st, 2nd or 3rd singular	
	-123P	1st, 2nd or 3rd plural	
	-CP	Comparative	
	-PROGin	Progressive -in	
	-PROGg	Progressive -ing	

Appendix 4. The Type–Token Distinction

It is important to note the distinction between counts of tokens and those of types. A token count provides the number of actual occurrences of words (as in table 3.2), whereas a type count provides a count of the different words which were uttered by the children. Importantly, all variants of the same vocabulary item are counted as one type.

With regard to the counting of types in section 3.1.1, all tokens for all variants 1–7 in (3), that is, all JC as well as JES variants, would also form one type. In this, I am guided by Pearson's (1998) approach to lexical representations by speakers of more than one language. She calls on Chomsky's (1965) definition of a lexical entry as a "sound-meaning pairing" (Pearson 1998, 350). As such, it involves three components: a mental representation for the sound, referred to as a *label*, a second mental representation for the meaning, in the form of a lexicalized concept for the object, event or relation and finally, a link between the two.

For a monolingual, one lexical item will involve one lexical unit, consisting of three components – one label, one lexicalized concept and one link between them. Two lexical items will involve two units, each with three components.

For the speaker of two languages, however, there may be two different labels for the same concept – in our case *aas* and 'horse'. So when learning JE, the child would need to learn the JE label, but the conceptual representation would already have been established with the acquisition of the JC word.

A type is taken here to be a mental representation, regardless of the number of (variations in) labels in both languages. In the case of *aas*, then, we would count all occurrences of all the variants in (3) as one type.

As we saw in the discussion of *chat* in section 3.1.1, there are words, which though pronounced in the same way in both languages, do not share the same mental representation. In all cases, it was the JC meaning only (and not the JE as well) which was intended. Thus, such a word was taken to have one mental representation only, and so counted as one type only.

A type–token count is a ratio of types to tokens, and indicates relative frequency of the use of a type. The larger the ratio, the less repetitive the vocabulary usage (Richards 1987, 201). So, for example, in the case of occurrences of variants of 'horse', there were seven types and eighty-nine occurrences, yielding a type–token count of .079. This is larger than the ratio for the variants of 'dog' – five types and 450 tokens, or 0.011 – suggesting that variants of 'horse' were repeated fewer times.

Type counts are also used as a measure of the richness of a child's vocabulary. I note that the CLAR project is not suited to a determination of vocabulary size, since each child was interviewed for half an hour once a month over a period of six months. This is not considered to be sufficient time spent to assess size of vocabulary. Instead, I look at numbers of types represented in the children's vocabulary in terms of word category membership. This will provide a general guide to the nature of lexical learning. In this regard, it ought also to be borne in mind that the relative use of one word class over another may have been influenced by the type of interactions which the investigators had with the children as well as the play activities in which the children were involved (see section 1.2.2 on methodology).

Appendix 5. SHared Words with Different Meanings

Category	# Tokens	SHared Word	Translation
Adj	1	*fresh*	'fresh' (not salty)
	1	*tikulish*	'it tickles' (not ticklish)
Noun	3	*airish*	'potato'
	2	*baksaid*	'buttocks'
	2	*belch*	'belch' (not crude)
	21	*beli*	'belly' (not crude)
	10	*dish*	'dish' (plate)
	3	*fab*	'detergent' (not a brand)
	241	*fut*	'foot or leg' ("*leg*" not used)
	7	*kid*	'baby animal' (not a child)
	1	*kyuuteks*	'nail polish' (not a brand)
	5	*lasco*	'milk' (not a brand)
	2	*pampaz*	'diapers' (not a brand)
	17	*pan*	'pot'
	77	*rag*	'towel'
	178	*tii*	'drink' (not necessarily tea)
	1	*yuut*	'boy' (not youth)
Verb	44	*bring*	'take'
	1	*chat*	'talk'
	3	*flash*	'make pretty' (not flash)
	3	*kach*	'tie up' (also catch)
	72	*lik*	'hit' (also lick)
	1	*manij*	'achieve' (not manage)
	110	*mash*	'crash' (not mash)
	1	*pich*	'spill' (not pitch)
	38	*pres*	'type on a computer' (not press)
	12	*riich*	'arrive'
	32	*ring*	'dial' (also ring)
	8	*set*	'put'
	10	*stok*	'stab' as present tense

Appendix 6. JConly Words

Category	# Tokens	JConly Word	Translation
Adv	7	*wa mek*	'why' (lit. what makes)
Noun	4	*anansi*	'spider'
	6	*bagi*	'panty'
	4	*bati*	'bottom' ('buttocks')
	13	*briif*	'underpants'
	2	*bula*	'bulla': a rich cake in a small round loaf made using molasses, flour, ginger and nutmeg
	59	*dopi*	'ghost'
	20	*frak*	'dress' (< 'frock' but not used in contemporary JE)
	3	*gyal*	'girl'
	12	*kalalu(u)*	'spinach'
	1	*krep*	'sneakers'
	1	*maka*	'prickle'
	18	*pikni*	'child'
	29	*pus*	'cat' (< 'puss')
	2	*puup*	'bad person'
Verb	4	*bum*	'fall noisily; bounce'
	2	*hala*	'scream' (< 'holler')
	14	*juk*	'stab; inject'
	1	*koch*	'rest on; lean against'
	5	*kraab*	'walk (in a crab-like manner); scratch'
	1	*ruut*	'ruffle'
	3	*shub*	'go; push through'
	20	*tiif*	'steal'
	2	*waid*	'open'
	10	*wain*	'dance; wind'

Appendix 7. List of Plural Fossils Used

# Tokens	JC Word	Translation
9	*antz*	'ant(s)'
17	*biiz*	'bee(s)'
13	*boblz*	'bubble(s)' (band to tie hair)
14	*briekz*	'break-time'
4	*chipz*	'chip(s)'
1	*flitaz*	'fritter(s)'
129	*flouwaz* (+ variants)	'flower(s)'
7	*globz* (1), *glovz* (6)	'glove(s)'
12	*iez/ierz*	'ear(s)'
2	*jiinz*	'jeans'
41	*jingkz* (1), *jringks* (40)	'drink(s)'
222	*kluoz* (206), *klooz* (16)	'clothes'
9	*krakaz*	'cracker(s)'
1	*manaz*	'manners'
36	*panz*	'pants'
40	*piiz*	'pea(s)'
2	*preeyaz*	'prayer(s)'
56	*saks* (47), *soks* (9)	'sock(s)'
3	*setaz*	'curler(s)'
39	*shaatz*	'shorts'
2	*shrimpz*	'shrimp(s)'
312	*shuuz*	'shoe(s)'
4	*siniikaz* (3), *sniikaz* (1)	'sneaker(s)'
18	*sizaz*	'scissors'
17	*slipaz*	'slippers'
3	*snakz*	'snack(s)'
1	*stikaz*	'sticker(s)'
2	*taitz*	'tights'
149	*tiit*	'tooth; teeth'
27	*tingz*	'thing(s)'
16	*waipz*	'baby wipe(s)'

Notes

Chapter 1

1. DON: *mi a go a dakta nou.*
      'I'm going to the doctor now.'
    DON: *"dakter shi iz sik."*
      '"Doctor, she is sick."'
    DON: *no . . . "shii" mi fi se.*
      'No . . . I should say "she".'
2. See section 1.1.2 for discussion.
3. What I call Jamaican English (JE) in this work is more commonly referred to as Standard Jamaican English. The English spoken in Jamaica, however, has not yet been standardized, so the designation "standard" is not adopted here. See section 1.1.2 for discussion.
4. As will become apparent, this work has been inspired by that of, among others, Dennis Craig. Two books published in 2014 were launched in August 2016 by the University of the West Indies Press as a tribute to Craig's contributions to the field. They are *Language Education in the Caribbean: Selected Articles by Dennis Craig*, edited by Jeannette Allsopp and Zellynne Jennings, and *Education Issues in Creole and Creole-Influenced Vernacular Contexts*, edited by Ian Robertson and Hazel Simmons-McDonald. The first contains eight selected articles authored by Dennis Craig; the second contains fifteen articles by contributors who are themselves prominent researchers. Together these books provide a comprehensive account of Craig's work.

5. See sections 1.1.1 and 1.1.3 for a fuller discussion of the continuum.

6. The basic tenets of minimalism are presented in section 2.5.

7. A Google search of *code-weaving* reveals a previous use of the term in a similar sense by Salia (2011), a BA research paper on Facebook conversations in Moroccan.

8. The terms *phonology* and *phonological* are used in this work to include both segment- and pattern-based aspects of sound production, with no distinction made between phonetics and phonology.

9. Thanks to Swithin Wilmot for his contribution, as a historian, to the wording here.

10. Section 2.1 addresses the innate capacity for the acquisition of language, taken to be a uniquely human biological endowment, and section 2.3, the role of input, the language heard, in the acquisition of a language.

11. Plag presented his Interlanguage Hypothesis in a series of four articles published in the *Journal of Pidgin and Creole Languages* in 2008 and 2009.

12. See Winford (1985) and Winer (1993), for instance.

13. I note that the New Testament has been translated into JC, as the first instalment of the translation of the Bible. This has been due to the initiative of the Bible Society of Jamaica, an initiative which has been supported by linguists, and to which they have contributed.

14. We return to this notion of the culture of correction in section 6.3.3, as being an indication that language awareness is not new to our children. It is the language awareness approach to language education that is followed in this work.

15. H-dropping is discussed in section 3.1.

16. Structural weaving is addressed in section 1.1.2, and throughout the work.

17. For an interesting related discussion, see chapter 6, "Black English: Is You Is or Is You Ain't a Language?", in McWhorter (1998, 127–64). As the title suggests, the chapter explores the status of so-called Black English as a language.

18. I note, however, that mutual intelligibility is not definitive, since non-linguistic criteria such as political, national identity, cultural or historical factors may outrank it (see Crystal [2009, 329–35] for discussion).

19. The ICE Corpus may be accessed through their website at http://ice-corpora.net/ice/.

20. Bryan (2010, 2–8) and Winford (1997) trace in some detail the origins and development of the notion of the continuum in Creole studies. The interested reader may wish to refer to these works to supplement this discussion.

21. See, for example, Patrick (1999, 49), who speaks of isolated rural areas as being culturally and linguistically conservative, and who quotes Rickford (1987, 23) as suggesting that rural variants are "characteristically Creole".

22. These are criteria followed in Adger and Smith (2004, 153).

23. Note that this use of /n/ is a regular non-standard English feature.

24. It is the convention in the field of first language acquisition to represent the age of young children in the format YEARS;MONTHS.DAYS. This will be followed throughout.

25. As would be expected, given the language situation outlined in the sections above, the language of the investigators is in fact also characterized by code-mixing. A study of that language is outside the scope of this work.

26. CHILDES is available at http://childes.psy.cmu.edu/.

27. A summary of this writing system is included as appendix 1. It is presented in detail in JLU (2009).
28. See section 3.1 for a comparison of the JE and JC inventories of sounds.
29. There were two files for adjectives (regular; irregular); five files for adverbs (intensifiers; locatives; temporal; wh-; all others); seven files for compounds (N compounds: Adj+N; V+Ptl; Adj+N; N+N; V+N; V compounds; reduplications); two files for determiners (numerals; all others); four files for nouns (nouns; baby forms; plural fossils [see section 4.2.2 for an explanation]; complex nouns); two files for pronouns (wh pronouns; all others); five files for verbs (verbs; auxiliaries; cliticized forms; copulas; modals). All other categories (for example, conjunctions, prepositions) were each in their own files.
30. A notable exception was the coding for compounds: for ease of analysis, these were assigned **cn|** (nouns), **cv|** (verbs), **cadj|** (adjectives), and **cadv|** (adverbs). A similar series beginning with "r" (for example, **rn|**) was created for reduplications.
31. I consider myself to be proficient in JC, though not a native speaker. I was born and raised in Jamaica by a JE-speaking father from Montego Bay and a *dominicana*, born and raised in the United States. For all but four years of my subsequent adult life, I lived and worked in Jamaica, with exposure to and participation in interactions with Jamaicans of varied language backgrounds, including those from Creole-speaking communities.
32. Note that the JC form is *brok*.
33. Though not considered in this work, utterances by investigators and teachers, when present, were also tagged, to allow for later analysis.
34. As indicated in the previous section, the tagging routine would need to be rerun, for instance, when investigating a previously unanalysed construction, or aspect of a construction, for which more fine-grained coding could be necessary.
35. I note that recoding would also be needed for each occurrence of a newly coded item, in the case of total manual tagging.
36. It is common in the field to use the term *type* to refer to each different word used, and *token* for the number of occurrences of a type. See appendix 4 for more on the type–token distinction.

Chapter 2

1. The approach to JC and JE as idealized varieties at either end of the Creole continuum is introduced in section 1.1.1, and discussed in 1.1.2 and 1.1.3.
2. Though highly influential, Krashen's account of consciousness in second language learning has been criticized. Truscott (2014, 142), for example, points out that though the approach is "essentially right", it does not allow for the automatization of consciously learned knowledge: it is the case that explicit knowledge can be internalized.
3. See, for example, Chomsky (1965, 32–34 and 47–59).
4. The 1972 article cited here actually comprised excerpts from a 1971 paper of the same name by Hymes. I do not have access to the original paper.
5. That language learning takes place through imitation and repetition is attributed to the Behaviourist Theory of learning, as applied to language. Introductory language

acquisition texts such as Peccei (2006), Foster-Cohen (1999) or Hoff ([2005] 2009) present these and other theories of language/language acquisition in some detail.

6. These examples are from Radford (2004, 9–10).

7. The interested reader may wish to consult Baker (2001) for what Chomsky (2005, 9) cites as being the most far-reaching approach to understanding what parameters are and how they are organized. Their importance is underlined by Baker's suggestion that they may be organized into a hierarchic structure, with each choice of value setting limits on subsequent choices. See also Baker (2003b).

8. The access hypotheses as they have been called are presented in second-language acquisition textbooks. See, for example, White (2003) for discussion.

9. See Schwartz and Eubank (1996) for discussion of this starting point of non-native grammatical knowledge in L2A, or the initial state as it is commonly referred to. The article serves as an introduction to the journal issue containing three articles each with a different position regarding the extent of transfer, and the initial state.

10. Selinker (1972) was the first to point this out. Interestingly, Elaine Tarone in her opening address at the 2012 conference Interlanguage: Forty Years Later, indicated that this 5 per cent figure was actually a guess made by Selinker, though it has been used since extensively as a given. Her comment appeared in Tarone (2014, 13n8), the conference proceedings.

11. Others such as De Houwer (1990) require that daily exposure to the languages concerned exist from the latest one week after birth, claiming that if AOA is any later, development will necessarily differ from bilingual or monolingual first language development.

12. I note that input interacts not only with AOA but also with numerous other factors in bilingual settings. For example, Tsimpli (2014) considers the role which timing in the L1 development of various phenomena in bilingual children's performance plays, to also be important, and investigates how this interacts with AOA and input. She distinguishes between features acquired early and those acquired late or very late, suggesting that early phenomena are core, whereas later acquired structures involve syntax-external or even language-external resources (p. 283). Oller and Eilers (2002) found effects of socioeconomic status (SES) of parents on the performance of Hispanic bilingual children in school in the Miami-Dade County in the United States, and Hoff (2006, 60–63) considers details of what these associations between SES and children's language might be. See also the discussion which follows here, for a consideration of input affecting outcomes not only with regard to quantity, but also quality. Finally, output is said to interact with input, in that using a language (output) forces the learner to process the language in a way that only hearing (input) does not (Bohman et al. 2010). The result is that a dual language setting has a complex nature (Unsworth et al. 2014, 769).

13. Note that when indicating the languages of the bilingual, it is common to place the native or the more dominant language first.

14. Note that Byers-Heinlein indicates that these results are preliminary. Note also that her methodology did not involve direct observation of parental mixing, but on mixing as reported by parents.

15. Adone (2012, 28) speaks also of the ambiguity of input in Creole-speaking communities, and gives as an example, the omission of functional categories such as tense and determiners. Many can be omitted without causing problems in interpretation, as is

expected with discourse-oriented grammars. She is speaking of first language acquisition, but this ambiguity which is characteristic of a Creole language will mean that in learning an L2 such as JE, children will need to be taught to expect that grammatical relations will be signalled in the syntax.

16. Pragmatics is a field of linguistics which deals with the impact of context of use on language.

17. For this insight, Meisel references a review of the literature in Köppe and Meisel (1995).

18. Cognates are presented as SHared forms in table 1.5 and addressed at some length in 6.3.1.

19. See appendix 2 for an explanation of the distinction between lexical and functional categories.

20. An excellent introduction is also provided by Snyder (2007, 9–13); Snyder's account is then applied by him to child language.

21. That there are two lexicons in operation is in line also with research in cognition. Analyses of the emergence of lexical knowledge and of grammatical structures underlying child utterances have revealed unambiguous evidence that two distinct lexicons are acquired by children even at the one-word stage of simultaneous bilingual development (Meisel [2004] 2006, 98; see also references quoted there).

22. An alternative solution is via a process known as *affix hopping*, the classic solution, where a past-tense affix lowers from T onto V at the point of spell-out. The adoption of one solution over the other is not crucial to the discussion.

23. This assignment is considered *arbitrary*, since there is nothing inherent about a "chair" which would determine its name. This is why, of course, it is named differently in different languages. Interestingly, with regard to this particular lexical item, when one of the CLAR children was told by the investigator sitting on the play mat to "take a seat on the mat", she went for a chair and took it onto the mat so that she could sit down on it.

24. The asterisk preceding a string indicates ungrammaticality.

25. The selection of a complement with certain features, the approach adopted here, is explained in Radford (1997, 67–69). The notation [uN] is adopted from Adger (2003, 67). Radford (pers. comm.) has cautioned, however, that it is not clear, for two reasons, that determiners SELECT a nominal complement. The first has to do with the theoretical approach to the analysis of structure. In a cartographic approach, for instance, adjectives reside in functional projections, then the determiner will SELECT the functional projection, and not the nominal. The approach adopted here, however, is that adjectives are contained in their own projections as adjuncts to the NP, whether adjoined at the phrasal or at the intermediary level; it is the NP which D SELECTS. The second reason Radford offers is that selection as an operation is mere stipulation and so, in principle, it is undesirable. It would be more economical if the requirement were to follow from some other inherent property of D. His suggestion is that there might be uninterpretable number feature on a count noun, for example, which gets valued by a corresponding interpretable feature on D. In this case, this would be agreement (feature valuation and deletion), rather than selection.

26. Thanks go to Andrew Radford, in our early discussions of the data, for suggesting the notion of monolectal and polylectal features; bilectal is my own slight variation, given the language situation in Jamaica presented here.

27. See Radford (2000, 13) for details of the derivation of this utterance.
28. Radford (2000) provides derivations for possessive constructions (pp. 14, 20), subject-verb agreement (pp. 12–14), the progressive (pp. 16–17), tense (p. 16), the infinitive particle 'to' (p. 17), number (pp. 17–20) and case (pp. 11, 20), showing convincingly for each how a grammar without uninterpretable features would operate.

Chapter 3

1. INV: *wa i fan a du?*
           'What's the fan doing?'
   ANN: *it a briiz yu.*
           'It's blowing cool air on you.'
2. We see in section 3.3 that *likl* (and its variants) is the second most frequently used adjective. Interestingly, *lili* 'little' had been used three times by this child in Visit 1, but may have caused him some difficulty in pronunciation, perhaps resulting in the use of *sumaal* as a matter of avoidance. Once mastered, *likl* 'little' was used in the last two visits to the exclusion of *sumaal.*
3. Recall that h-dropping is one of Irvine's (2005) load-bearing variables; see section 1.1.1 for discussion.
4. Interestingly, a phonemic perception study by Whyte (2016) has shown that children ages five and nine in Westmoreland (another western parish in Jamaica) perceive no difference between nonce words with an initial /h/ and those without, indicating that /h/ is not phonemic for them.
5. See section 1.2.3 and, in particular, table 1.5 for details of how language was coded in the lexicon files.
6. See appendix 6 for a listing of all twenty-five JConly words.
7. *Gyal* is arguably a JES form, since it could be said to be derived from English 'girl'. However, all three consultants involved in language code assignments (see section 1.2.3) considered it to be JConly. This is because, perhaps, of the stigma associated with it, and this trend today of using it as a derogatory term.
8. The symbol '&' is used to signal a false start.
9. But see below for a discussion of exceptions to this, where forms with JE segments outnumber their JC counterparts. These forms are presented in table 3.4.
10. Thanks to Silvia Kouwenberg for this insight.
11. Again, thanks to Silvia Kouwenberg for pointing this out.
12. A list of SHared words with different meanings used in the files is included as appendix 5.
13. This count includes JC lexical nouns, verbs, adjectives and adverbs, and excludes all baby forms.
14. But see section 6.3.2 for a discussion of the JE indefinite determiner 'a'.

15. Thanks to an anonymous reviewer for this suggestion, as well as for pointing out that verification would be required from a far larger sample, including adult speech, before making the claim that the data may point towards changing trends.

16. An MLU count is a measure of the development of language. An MLU count may be calculated by counting the total number of morphemes or words in a sample of utterances and dividing that total by the number of utterances being sampled. It is expressed as a percentage. It is considered to be an indicator of the stage the child is at, and is considered far more reliable than age, since it is well known that normally developing children develop at different rates and so reach milestones at very different ages.

17. For a more detailed discussion of derivation, see section 3.4.1.

18. 'Novel' is used here and throughout the chapter to refer to words which do not exist in the adult language, but which have been formed using recognizable word-formation strategies existing in the language. These words are generally readily interpretable.

19. I note that the three age levels investigated by Dhillon (2010) were 1;7 to 2;0, 2;1 to 2;5 and 2;6 to 2;11, with most below the CLAR age range of 2:9–4;2.

20. A gerund is a nominal formed from the present participle form of the verb; for example, 'I love his cooking.'

21. Dhillon's results show strong noun biases for all age groups of English- and Spanish-speaking children, but only for the youngest group of Mandarin-speaking children. Cultural influences are discussed briefly below.

22. This is the result of $(0.71/(0.17+0.12))$ for proportions of types in table 3.6.

23. Note that the noun bias calculation will not be affected by the different categorization of auxiliaries by De Lisser as inflections, and falling therefore under "other", rather than as a subcategory of the category *verb*, since the calculation adds the proportions of verbs and "other".

24. These are nouns which do not have a singular form, and which in JE must be modified by a unitizer or measure phrase. An example is 'a pair of scissors'. In JC, unitizers are not used; instead, a form resembling the JE plural (for example, *flouwaz* 'flower(s)') is used for both the singular and plural. These forms are discussed in some detail in section 4.2.2.

25. The gerunds used by the CLAR children were *aisnin* 'icing' (3 instances), *baalin* 'crying' (1), and *fiidin* 'feeding' (10).

26. Adverbial modification and its roles in the discourse are discussed in sections 5.2.2, 5.2.3 and 5.2.6.

27. A search for studies on the contribution of adverbs to the lexicon of three-year-olds proved unsuccessful. Interestingly, the widely utilized tool, the Fenson et al. 2006 MacArthur-Bates Communicative Development Inventory (CDI) does not include adverbs as a category at all. Instead, it tests children on their production of twelve "words about time". In addition, some adverbs were included as locations, forming part of the category prepositions and locations; others were considered question words.

All these categories were relegated to the "other" category, along with pronouns, quantifiers, articles (determiners, for us), helping verbs (auxiliaries) and connecting words (conjunctions). Together, they were responsible for a total of only 13.3 per cent of all types produced by the children. The comparable share of these categories among the CLAR children would be 44.8 per cent.

The following categories were excluded altogether from the CDI inventory: focus markers, verbal particles, negators, infinitives and complementizers.

Note that it is accepted that many everyday words are not included in the inventory. Pearson (1998, 354) indicates that it accounts for about one-third of the words known by children with six hundred words or more in their vocabularies, that is, thirty-month-old children, the oldest tested. The value of the test lies in its standardization by number of words. I note also that the CDI is intended as a test of children up to the age of 2;6, younger than the youngest CLAR children.

28. Though the CLAR data are coded for all word categories, allowing for counts such as those included in table 3.7, other categories in the table are not discussed in this work.

29. Thanks to Silvia Kouwenberg for pointing out the cross-categorization which must result from the range of meanings.

30. *Ed* in this case was referring to hair rather than to the doll's head, as suggested by the investigator's chuckle and response: *so yu gwain wash it fa or?* 'so, are you going to wash it for her?' [V1-AN2:l 586]

31. This list of most frequently used adjectives does not include *neks* 'next' or *siem* 'same' which would otherwise have ranked fourth and seventeenth respectively. The top twenty adjectives account for 69.2 per cent of all adjective tokens used by the children.

32. I note that many of the children enjoyed colouring as an activity and opportunities for using colour words would have arisen often; see section 1.2.2 for a discussion of methodology.

Together, colours (16.7 per cent) and dimension (24.9 per cent) adjectives account for over 40 per cent of all adjectives used.

33. Compounding as a word-formation strategy is not discussed in this work, but note that it is a very productive means of filling lexical gaps among the CLAR children, as revealed in Stewart (2010c).

34. See section 1.1 for a brief discussion of Plag's Interlanguage Hypothesis.

35. Note also the difference between how the construction *somting fi spin* would be used in JC and in JE. In JE, it is the object itself which is viewed as spinning, and it would therefore be described as "something that spins". A JE translation of the JC, however, might be "something that should be spun", where *fi* is interpreted as a modal. Thanks to Pauline Christie for pointing out the possibility of this interpretation.

36. I note that this mango seller was in fact a woman, and that it was typical to ignore gender, using *man* to identify the occupations of both men and women.

37. Again, thanks to Pauline Christie for this insight.

38. Note the use of the definite here, as if the goat was present and had been mentioned. See section 4.3.1 for discussion.

Chapter 4

1. SEB: *a mai siit ova yaso ahn fi im siit ova deso.*
         'It's my seat that's over here, and his that's over there.'

2. The importance of common nouns is underlined by their frequency: children used 27,442 lexical nouns (see table 3.7) in their speech; common nouns account for 84.0 per cent of these.

3. A bare NP is a noun phrase which is not accompanied by a determiner such as the article 'the' or 'a'. This interpretation of the data on determinerless nouns was suggested by Andrew Radford (pers. comm.).

4. See Stewart (2007, 2011) for details of the Rijkhoff (2004) claim, and of how this may apply to JC.

5. Rijkhoff (2002, 133) refers to these phrases as *mensural classifiers*.

6. Note that although the definite article does not appear with proper nouns such as *Mieri* in JC, such a noun is considered to be rigidly definite, since the referent it picks out is unambiguously identifiable.

7. Many thanks to Andrew Radford for having suggested this possible interpretation of the data.

8. Interestingly, though there are no instances of this in the child data, the JE inflectional -s is known to attach to *main* 'mine' in adult JC. Under this analysis, the use of the JE plural would be unsurprising given the association of inclusiveness with plurality.

9. This possessive construction includes the JE *main* 'mine'. Other less JE possessive adjectives also use *dem* to mark pluralization, though this is rare (two instances only); for example, ROJ: *me mi put iin mai uon **dem***. 'Let me put mine in.' (lit. make me put in my own INCL) [V3-SMT:l 323-3;2.3].

10. Recall that a JES is a lexical word which may be used by speakers as a variant of a JC word. JES variants may have one or more (but not necessarily all) vowel or consonant segment(s) associated with JE, the language.

11. Note that Brown's criterion for acquisition of target-like use is 90 per cent, that is, in 90 per cent of all possible opportunities for its use. Brown's standard referred to here and elsewhere in this work grossly underestimates what children know, however. This is illustrated in Radford (2006) for possessives (p. 48) and infinitival 'to' (p. 77), where overt manifestations of knowledge of the structures appear long before the 90 per cent target is reached.

12. Interestingly, Messam-Johnson (2017) in a study of the attrition of JC in Curaçao found that the co-occurrence of the JC and English plural morphemes was evident in the speech of all informants, but most characteristic of those who had resided in Curaçao for more than ten years (pp. 120–23). Though she recognizes that such forms would exist in their input, since they did have continued contact with JC as well as with its lexifier, she notes that members of her group of informants verifying JC forms (her verification group) did accept the so-called double-plural, but rejected it three times more than they accepted it.

13. Recall that the plural morpheme is represented orthographically in this work using 'z', even when it is actually pronounced as [s].

14. Thanks to Christian Mair (pers. comm.) for this suggestion.

15. For more details on functional versus lexical categories, see appendix 2.

16. The referent is the object in the world which the noun phrase (specifically, the noun) distinguishes.

17. Lyons (1999) also characterizes definites in terms of inclusiveness and uniqueness. Inclusiveness is relevant to definiteness in the case where reference is to the totality of objects in the case of a plural NP, and to the mass, in the case of a mass noun such as 'sand'. We saw in section 4.2 that Inclusiveness provides the link between plurality and definiteness through the *di . . . dem* construction, where *di* is the marker of definiteness and *dem*, that of inclusiveness. In the case of singular nouns, uniqueness indicates that there is just one object satisfying the description. For example, as there is only one sun, this is readily identified KIM: *kom out a i son!* ('come out of the sun') [V1-CLA:l 521-3;0.27].

18. I note that these views are contrary to the early claims of Bickerton (1975, 1981, especially) and Givón (1981) that typical Creole uses of the indefinite differ from those attested in their lexifier languages. See Kennedy (2012, 46–51) for an outline of the Bickerton/Givón analyses of Creole article systems, and how these differ from the approach to definiteness/specificity taken there, and adopted in this work.

19. My thanks to Kathryn Shields-Brodber for providing this reference.

20. An alternative translation of *a* in this utterance could be the preposition 'to'. It is taken to be the focus marker, however, since in the immediately ensuing conversation, the preposition was omitted in a non-focused context – *no, mi no go riva* ('No, I haven't been to the river'). Regardless of interpretation, definiteness has been expressed in the absence of the definite article.

21. In these examples, the symbol * indicates an ungrammatical sequence.

22. I note again that such a language situation is quite different from that of the CLAR children.

23. Two of the six occurrences are *bi* 'be', for example, *wen im bi a man …* 'when he is a man …', one is *woz* 'was' and the other three are a form of the first person with the copula, for example, *aim a raitor* 'I'm a writer.'

24. A corrected form is signalled by the symbol &.

25. For a discussion of dominant versus non-dominant languages, see section 6.2.

26. Patrick (2004, 223) refers to *uon* as "the emphatic or contrastive possessive adjective". I follow Patrick's classification on the basis that in these constructions, if it does not appear, the noun is understood. We may say that it is 'gapped'. In (54), for instance, GAB is referring to the mirror which she had just used.

27. Adam achieved the 90 per cent mark at age 3;2, Sarah at 3;1, and Eve, generally showing early acquisition of morphemes, at age 2;2.

28. The term has been used at least since Halliday (1975) to refer to words used consistently in different contexts with the same meanings, but which are of the child's creation, and may only be marginally related to the adult language heard. As the child grows, her own created language cannot serve her growing communicative needs, and, moving into the adult language, she abandons the creations.

29. It was used as subject and object pronouns also by children from St Ann, Clarendon and St Thomas.
30. The JES *kooz* is considered to be a child form, where the consonant cluster *kl* is reduced to *k*. Cluster reduction is a universal trend in child language acquisition. It involves the simplification of a sequence of more than one consonant by deleting one or more of those consonants, and is common in all positions of the word, due, at least in part, to the lack of maturity of the muscles associated with pronunciation.
31. It is not at all clear that SHared nouns ought to be included in the count, with significance seemingly attached to that. They have been included in this count on the basis that they are at least potential JC forms, since the words do exist in regular JC speech. That the children know that they also exist in JE cannot be claimed with any certainty.
32. No pronouns were classified as SHared.

Chapter 5

1. KAR: *a wait mi did av.*
         'It's a white one that I had.'
2. Comrie's seminal works (1976 on aspect and 1985 on tense) are strongly recommended for further reading on these topics.
3. An alternative analysis would be for the affix to be lowered onto V at spell-out. This is known as affix hopping. See an account in Radford (2004, 65–66).
4. Lengthening of the vowel is not always obvious or readily apparent. Note that transcriptions were not phonetic, but orthographic.
5. Indications are that it is used far earlier than this. See Stewart (2010b) for examples.
6. See the discussion of lexical aspect in section 5.2.6.
7. Thanks to Pauline Christie (pers. comm.) for this insight concerning the effect which the use of the verb has on the location of the action in time.
8. Thanks to Silvia Kouwenberg (pers. comm.) for sharing her take on the construction.
9. Durrleman-Tame (2008, 15) argues for two pre-verbal *don* markers, the marker of completedness, and also an adverbial, translated as 'already', indicating that a sentence such as *im don nyam i* is ambiguous, with possible interpretations of both 'he (or she) finished eating it' and 'he (or she) already ate it'. Ambiguity is considered here to be resolved given stress: when stressed, it is the lexical verb; when unstressed, it is the perfective marker.
10. I note that utterances presented by De Lisser (2015, 101) as making use of completive aspect *don* are here considered to be lexical verbs. An example is *Manski don iit fi ar aredi*, translated by her as 'M already finished eating hers (completely)'. In any case, there were only twenty-two occurrences by five children and twenty-one by one child.
11. Pauline Christie (2003) points out that contrary to what Patrick states, DeCamp (1971b, 357) mentions only *a* and not *da*.
12. This translation was suggested by Pauline Christie, given the presence of the progressive aspect marker *a*.

13. Silvia Kouwenberg notes that the relevant issue here may not be finiteness at all, since *a* marks aspect, not tense. She references Papiamentu, where pre-verbal *ta* may appear in direct perception complements with a progressive interpretation. If this is the case, *a* +V may simply be a gerund in these environments as it is in JE.

14. This was pointed out by Pauline Christie.

15. Dahl (1999) outlines characteristics of aspect-prominent languages.

16. Every finite verb bears tense, though a tensed verb need not be overtly marked for tense. In that case, following the generative approach, tense is still accounted for in the Syntax, represented by a null marker (Ø), to indicate that it is expressed. Zero-marking is an alternate characterization for what I referred to earlier as the bare verb.

17. Thanks to Pauline Christie for this explanation.

18. Recall, also, that all six subjects in De Lisser (2015) were from western Jamaica, so that it may be expected that there would be some use of the variant *wehn*.

19. Silvia Kouwenberg offered this suggestion.

20. In keeping with its general approach to language, over-regularization is said in a generative approach, to be the result of the child internalizing the rule for past-tense formation, but over-applying the rule to irregular verbs.

21. This description of the auxiliary followed by the main verb is based on an analysis which houses the auxiliary in T. T then selects VP containing the V. The auxiliary is within the verbal domain, of course, but not housed within VP.

22. This has been discussed in section 1.1; cf. the Ministry of Education's 2001 Language Policy; Bailey (1966), DeCamp (1971b); and more recently, publications such as Bryan (2010) and Nero (2014).

23. The choice of -in or -ing is not considered to characterize a speaker as being a JC or a JE speaker, and so is not factored in here. Both variants exist in both languages. Indeed, -in(g) does not appear as one of the ten load-bearing oppositions proposed by Irvine (2005) as signalling an (in)ability to speak JE. As might be expected, 75.7 per cent of the inflections used were -in.

24. In JE, the construction 'THE SUBJECT is the one doing the GERUND' exists, but it is unlikely that this was the children's intended construction, and would be an inappropriate reading, given the contexts.

25. In Myers-Scotton's terminology, languages are referred to as the matrix language (ML), or the language considered to be dominant – in this case, the L1 – and the other as the embedded language (EL).

Chapter 6

1. INV: *wa dat niem?*
           'What's that called?'

   %com: pointing to a big sun.

   SHA: *soni wedor.*
           'Sunny weather.'

INV: *soni wedor?*
       'Sunny weather?'

DON: *dat tiicha se.*
       'That's what Teacher calls it.'

2. See table 4.1 for a listing of environments where the omission of the article is ungrammatical in JE, but allowed in JC.

3. See, for example, Bernardini and Schlyter (2004) and Yip and Matthews (2006).

4. Recall that inter-sentential CS (code-switching) is that from one sentence to the next in discourse, while intra-sentential code-switching is switching within a sentence. See section 2.4 for discussion.

5. This may mean that the sentence might have been longer; it is also possible that the indistinct words were not JESs.

6. See Schlyter (1993) on quantitative and qualitative criteria for determining a weaker language.

7. See sections 1.2.3 and 3.1.1 on SHared forms.

8. Recall that nouns constitute the most used category, accounting for 46 per cent of all tokens and 71 per cent of all types used by the CLAR children. See section 3.2 and, in particular, table 3.6. The type count of 690 applies only to common nouns.

9. Reference here is to formal *lexical* transfer, involving false cognates, unintentional lexical borrowing, or coinage of a new word by blending two or more words from different languages.

10. The ensuing discussion assumes some prior knowledge of minimalism, so a review of section 2.5 before proceeding may be useful.

11. Andrew Radford points out also that if a determiner carries an interpretable language feature, [+ACR], for instance, it would presumably require that it value an [uACR] feature on other items, including any adjectives which modify the noun, and any adverbs which may modify those adjectives. However, the likelihood of AGREE applying to an adverb is remote, since the category is *inert*. In any case, this would make for a very complex system of (un)interpretable features, inconsistent with minimalist economic principles. A further problem with the language feature, as he points out, is that interpretable features must be interpreted at both the semantic and the phonological interfaces, and it is unclear what those interpretations would be for a feature such as [ACR].

12. See section 4.4 for a discussion of the differences in possessive constructions in JE and JC. With regard to focus constructions, these are common in JC, and used extensively (over two thousand instances) in statements and questions by the CLAR children. They consist of the focus marker *a* followed by the focused element, which may be a verb, an NP, a PP or an adjectival predicate. There is no focus marker in JE, though phrases may be focused in an it-cleft (It is + focused phrase + that …) or pseudo-cleft (focused phrase + is what …) construction.

13. In both JC and JE, *fi* and 'to', so-called infinitive particles are integral parts of the Infinitive which is considered to consist of particle+V. They do not introduce the infinitive, but together they form it. This contrasts with the infinitive in French or Spanish, for instance, which are single words referring to forms of the verb. Many thanks to Pauline Christie for having pointed this out.

14. Chunk learning is common cross-linguistically. As Andrew Radford has pointed out, *wanna* and *gonna* are treated by some as indivisible items in standard varieties of English.

15. Note that each different function qualifies the form to be considered a separate word in the JC lexicon.

16. Andrew Radford suggested the pre-theoretical phrase "sociolinguistically confused", more in keeping, perhaps, with the notion of blurred boundaries.

17. This is as suggested by Lacoste (2012, 31).

18. Again, many thanks to Andrew Radford for guidance. His thoughts concerned specifically sociophonological and pseudo-Gricean principles, both of which have laid the foundation for conclusions reached here. A note follows on H. Paul Grice. He was a philosopher. The basis of Gricean pragmatics is the cooperative principle which states "Make your conversational contribution such as is required, at the stage at which it occurs, by the accepted purpose or direction of the talk exchange in which you are engaged" (Grice 1975, 45, as cited in Chapman 2005, 102). Chapman (2005) provides a broad overview of the Gricean model.

19. Laaha and Gillis (2007) report on the results from the "Cross-linguistic Project on Pre- and Protomorphology in Language Acquisition", a project aimed at investigating the early phases of morphological development in a sample of eleven different languages that show important typological variation (from the preface).

20. See section 3.4.1 on derivational affixation, 4.2.1 on the plural -s in JE, 4.4.2 on the possessive -s, 5.4.1 on the JE past tense -ed and 5.4.2 on agreement in the JE progressive construction. Though concord with regular verbs was not addressed in this work, I note that there was no use of the JE present tense -s for the third-person singular.

21. Whether implicit knowledge can be gained through explicit noticing has been debated in the field. This is defended in Schmidt (2010), who distinguishes between *noticing* as a technical term limited to the conscious registration of specific instances of language which have been attended to, and *understanding*, a higher level of awareness that includes generalizations across instances. Schmidt proposes that noticing is necessary for second language acquisition, and that understanding is facilitative but not required.

22. Craig (2006, 231–36) provides syllabus resources (SRs) for use by the teacher. SR-1, for example, summarizes basic morphological and syntactic contrasts between what he calls internationally accepted English (IAE) and English-based, Creole-influenced vernaculars (CIVs).

23. The rationale for this approach is compatible with the approach taken here to the composition of the lexicon of speakers in a Creole context. See, in particular, discussions on SHared forms (introduced in section 1.2.3, discussed in section 3.1.1 and throughout) and appendix 4 for Pearson's (1998) take on lexical representations by speakers of more than one language.

24. The linguistic component of this lesson was prepared and presented by the author, and the educational application by Dr Yewande Lewis-Fokum, a colleague in the School of Education at the University of the West Indies, Mona.

25. Thanks to Andrew Radford for this insight.

References

Abney, Steven. 1987. "The English Noun Phrase in Its Sentential Aspect". PhD dissertation, Massachussets Institute of Technology.

Aboh, Enoch O. 2015. *The Emergence of Hybrid Grammars: Language Contact and Change.* Cambridge: Cambridge University Press.

Aboh, Enoch O., and Umberto Ansaldo. 2007. "The Role of Typology in Language Creation: A Descriptive Take". In *Deconstructing Creole,* edited by Umberto Ansaldo, Steve M. Matthews and Lisa Lim, 39–66. Amsterdam: John Benjamins.

Acquaviva, Paolo. 2008. *Lexical Plurals: A Morphosemantic Approach.* Oxford: Oxford University Press.

Adger, David. 2003. *Core Syntax: A Minimalist Approach.* Oxford: Oxford University Press.

Adger, David, and Jennifer Smith. 2004. "Variation and the Minimalist Program". In *Syntax and Variation: Reconciling the Biological and the Social,* edited by Leonie C. Cornips and Karen P. Corrigan, 149–78. Amsterdam: John Benjamins.

Adger, David, and Peter Svenonius. 2011. "Features in Minimalist Syntax". In *The Oxford Handbook of Linguistic Minimalism,* edited by Cedric Boeckx, 27–51. Oxford: Oxford University Press.

Adone, Dany. 2012. *The Acquisition of Creole Languages: How Children Surpass Their Input.* Cambridge: Cambridge University Press.

Alleyne, Mervyn C. 1971. "Acculturation and the Cultural Matrix of Creolization". In *Pidginization and Creolization of Languages,* edited by Dell Hymes, 169–86. Cambridge: Cambridge University Press.

———. 1980. *Comparative Afro-American: An Historical Comparative Study of English Based Afro-American Dialects of the New World.* Ann Arbor, MI: Karoma.

Andersen, Roger W. 1978. "An Implicational Model for Second Language Research". *Language Learning* 28:221–82.

———. 1990. "Papiamentu Tense-Aspect, with Special Attention to Discourse". In *Pidgin and Creole Tense-Mood-Aspect Systems*, edited by John Victor Singler, 56–96. Amsterdam: John Benjamins.

Andrews, Stephen. 2003. "Teacher Language Awareness and the Professional Knowledge Base of the L2 Teacher". *Language Awareness* 12 (2): 81–95.

Anschutz, Arlea. 1997. "How to Choose a Possessive Noun Phrase Construction in Four Easy Steps". *Studies in Language* 21 (1): 1–35.

Antwi, Jessie. 2015. "Student Language Awareness: An Exploratory Study of Language Awareness among Jamaican High School Students and the Relation to Their Proficiency in English". M.Phil thesis, University of the West Indies, Mona.

Bailey, Beryl. 1966. *Jamaican Creole Syntax: A Transformational Approach*. Cambridge: Cambridge University Press.

Bailey, Nathalie, Carolyn Madden and Stephen D. Krashen. 1974. "Is There a 'Natural Sequence' in Adult Second Language Learning?" *Language Learning* 24:235–43.

Baker, Mark. 2001. *The Atoms of Language*. New York: Basic Books.

———. 2003a. *Lexical Categories: Verbs, Nouns, and Adjectives*. Cambridge: Cambridge University Press.

———. 2003b. "Linguistic Differences and Language Design". *Trends in Cognitive Sciences* 7:349–53. http://www.rci.rutgers.edu/~mabaker/papers%20to%20add/Language-diffs-TICS.pdf.

Beckford-Wassink, Alicia. 1999. "Historic Low Prestige and Seeds of Change: Attitudes toward Jamaican Creole". *Language in Society* 28:57–92.

Belazi, Hedi M., Edward J. Rubin and Almeida Jacqueline Toribio. 1994. "Code Switching and X Bar Theory: The Functional Head Constraint". *Linguistic Inquiry* 25 (2): 221–37.

Bernardini, Petra, and Suzanne Schlyter. 2004. "Growing Syntactic Structure and Code-Mixing in the Weaker Language: The Ivy Hypothesis". *Bilingualism, Language and Cognition* 7 (1): 49–69.

Bhat, D.N. Shankara. 1999. *The Prominence of Tense, Aspect and Mood*. Amsterdam: John Benjamins.

Bickerton, Derek. 1975. *Dynamics of a Creole System*. Cambridge: Cambridge University Press.

———. 1981. *Roots of Language*. Ann Arbor, MI: Karoma.

Bloom, Paul. 2002. *How Children Learn the Meanings of Words*. Cambridge, MA: MIT Press.

Bobyleva, Ekaterina. 2013. *The Development of the Nominal Domain in Creole Languages: A Comparative-Typological Approach*. Utrecht, the Netherlands: LOT.

Bohman, Thomas M., Lisa M. Bedore, Elizabeth D. Peña, Anita Mendez-Perez and Ronald B. Gillam. 2010. "What You Hear and What You Say: Language Performance in Spanish-English Bilinguals". *International Journal of Bilingual Education and Bilingualism* 13 (3): 325–44.

Bornstein, Marc H., Linda R. Cote, Sharone Maital, Kathleen Painter, Sung-Yun Park, Liliana Pascual, Marie-Germaine Pêcheux, Josette Ruel, Paola Venuti and Andre Vyt. 2004. "Cross-Linguistic Analysis of Vocabulary in Young Children: Spanish, Dutch, French, Hebrew, Italian, Korean, and American English". *Child Development* 75 (4): 1115–39.

Brandt, Deborah. 2001. *Literacy in American Lives*. Cambridge: Cambridge University Press.

Brimo, Danielle, and Kenn Apel. 2011. "The Effects of Syntactic Awareness and Syntactic Knowledge on Reading Comprehension". American Speech-Language-Hearing Association Convention. San Diego, California. www.asha.org/Events/convention/handouts/2011/Brimo-Apel.

Britton, James. 1982. "Writing to Learn and Learning to Write". In *Prospect and Retrospect: Selected Essays of James Britton*, edited by G.M. Pradl, 94–111. Montclair, NJ: Boynton Cook.

Brown, Roger. 1973. *First Language*. London: Allen and Unwin.

Bryan, Beverley. 2010. *Between Two Grammars: Research and Practice for Language Learning and Teaching in a Creole-Speaking Environment*. Kingston: Ian Randle.

———. 2014a. "'English Is an Arena, Not a Subject': Language Learning and Teaching in Post-Independence Jamaica". In *Lectures on Language Education: A Monograph*, edited by Beverley Bryan, 2–32. Kingston: School of Education, University of the West Indies.

———. 2014b. "Dennis Craig and Language Education". In *Education Issues in Creole and Creole-Influenced Vernacular Contexts*, edited by Ian Robertson and Hazel Simmons-McDonald, 15–28. Kingston: University of the West Indies Press.

Byers-Heinlein, Krista. 2009. "Characterizing Bilingual Input: A Self-Report Measure of Language Mixing by Bilingual Parents". Poster presented at the annual Boston University Conference on Language Development, Boston, November 2009.

Cain, Kate. 2007. "Syntactic Awareness and Reading Ability: Is There Any Evidence for a Special Relationship?" *Applied Psycholinguistics* 28:679–94.

Cantone, Katja F. 2007. *Code-Switching in Bilingual Children*. Dordrecht: Springer.

Cantone, Katja F., and Natascha Müller. 2008. "*Un Nase* or *una Nase*? What Gender Marking within Switched DPs Reveals about the Architecture of the Bilingual Language Faculty". *Lingua* 118:810–26.

Carlisle, Joanne F. 1995. "Morphological Awareness and Early Reading Achievement". In *Morphological Aspects of Language Processing*, edited by Laurie Beth Feldman, 189–209. Hillsdale, NJ: Lawrence Erlbaum Associates.

———. 2004. "Morphological Processes That Influence Learning to Read". In *Handbook of Language and Literacy. Development and Disorders*, edited by C. Addison Stone, Elaine R. Silliman, Barbara J. Ehren and Kenn Apel, 318–39. New York: Guilford Press.

Carter, Ronald. 2003. "Language Awareness". *English Language Teaching Journal* 57 (1): 64–65.

Caselli, Maria Cristina, Elizabeth Bates, Paola Casadio, Judi Fenson, Larry Fenson, Lisa Sanderl and Judy Weir. 1995. "A Cross-Linguistic Study of Early Lexical Development". *Cognitive Development* 10:159–99.

Catts, Hugh W., Suzanne M. Adlof and Susan Ellis Weismer. 2006. "Language Deficits in Poor Comprehenders: A Case for the Simple View of Reading". *Journal of Speech, Language, and Hearing Research* 49 (2): 278–93.

Chapman, Siobhan. 2005. *Paul Grice: Philosopher and Linguist*. Hampshire, UK: Palgrave Macmillan.

Chard, David J., and Shirley V. Dickson. 1999. "Phonological Awareness: Instructional and Assessment Guidelines". http://www.ldonline.org/article/6254/.

Chaudenson, Robert. 2001. *Creolization of Language and Culture*. New York: Routledge.

Chomsky, Noam. 1957. *Syntactic Structures*. The Hague: Mouton.

———. 1965. *Aspects of the Theory of Syntax*. Cambridge, MA: MIT Press.

———. 1994. "The Golden Age Is in Us: Noam Chomsky Interviewed by Alexander Cockburn". *Grand Street* (Fall): 170–76. http://chomsky.info/19940622/.

———. 1995. *The Minimalist Program*. Cambridge, MA: MIT Press.

———. 1998. "Minimalist Inquiries: The Framework". *MIT Working Papers in Linguistics* 15.

———. 1999. "Derivation by Phase". *MIT Occasional Papers in Linguistics* 18.

———. 2005. "Three Factors in Language Design". *Linguistic Inquiry* 36 (1): 1–22.

———. 2007. "Approaching UG from Below". In *Interfaces + Recursion = Language? Chomsky's Minimalism and the View from Syntax-Semantics*, edited by Henk van Riemsdijk, Jan Koster and Harry van der Hulst, 1–29. Berlin: Mouton de Gruyter.

Christie, Pauline. 1986. "Evidence for an Unsuspected Habitual Marker in Jamaican". In *Focus on the Caribbean*, edited by Manfred Gorlach and John Holm, 183–90. Amsterdam: John Benjamins.

———. 2003. *Language in Jamaica*. Kingston: Arawak.

Clachar, Arlene. 2005. "Creole English Speakers' Treatment of Tense-Aspect Morphology in English Interlanguage Written Discourse". *Language Learning* 55 (2): 275–334.

Clark, Eve V. 1993. *The Lexicon in Acquisition*. Cambridge: Cambridge University Press.

———. 2003. *First Language Acquisition*. Cambridge: Cambridge University Press.

Clark, Eve V., and Berman, Ruth A. 1984. "Structure and Use in the Acquisition of Word Formation". *Language* 60 (3): 542–90.

———. 1987. "Types of Linguistic Knowledge: Interpreting and Producing Compound Nouns". *Journal of Child Language* 14:547–67.

Clyne, Michael. 1987. "Constraints on Code-Switching: How Universal Are They?" *Linguistics* 25:739–64.

Colorado, Colorín. 2007. "Using Cognates to Develop Comprehension in English". http://www.colorincolorado.org/educators/background/cognates/.

Comrie, Bernard. 1976. *Aspect: An Introduction to the Study of Verbal Aspect and Related Problems*. Cambridge: Cambridge University Press.

———. 1985. *Tense*. Cambridge: Cambridge University Press.

Costa, Albert. 2005. "Lexical Access in Bilingual Production". In *Handbook of Bilingualism. Psycholinguistic Approaches*, edited by Judith F. Kroll and Annette de Groot, 308–25. Oxford: Oxford University Press.

Costa, Albert, Alfonso Caramazza and Nuria Sebastian-Galles. 2000. "The Cognate Facilitation Effect: Implications for Models of Lexical Access". *Journal of Experimental Psychology: Learning, Memory, and Cognition* 26:1283–96.

Costa, Albert, Michele Miozzo and Alphonso Caramazza. 1999. "Lexical Selection in Bilinguals: Do Words in the Bilingual's Two Lexicons Compete for Selection?" *Journal of Memory and Language* 41:365–97.

Craig, Dennis R. 1971. "Education and Creole English in the West Indies". In *Pidginization and Creolization of Languages*, edited by Dell Hymes, 371–91. Cambridge: Cambridge University Press.

———. 1980. "Language, Society and Education in the West Indies". *Caribbean Journal of Education* 7 (1): 1–17.

———. 1999. *Teaching Language and Literacy: Policies and Procedures for Vernacular Situations*. Georgetown, Guyana: Education and Research Associates.

———. 2006. *Teaching Language and Literacy to Caribbean Students: From Vernacular to Standard English*. Kingston: Ian Randle.

Crystal, David. 2009. *How Language Works: How Babies Babble, Words Change Meaning and Languages Live or Die*. New York: Penguin.

Cummins, Jim. 2009. "Pedagogies of Choice: Challenging Coercive Relations of Power in Classrooms and Communities". *International Journal of Bilingual Education and Bilingualism* 12 (3): 261–71.

Dahl, Östen. 1985. *Tense and Aspect Systems*. Malden, MA: Blackwell.

———. 1999. *The Prominence of Tense, Aspect and Mood*. Amsterdam: John Benjamins.

Deacon, S. Hélène, and John R. Kirby. 2004. "Morphological Awareness: Just 'More Phonological'? The Roles of Morphological and Phonological Awareness in Reading Development". *Applied Psycholinguistics* 25:223–38.

DeCamp, David. 1961. "Social and Geographical Factors in Jamaican Dialects". In *Proceedings of the Conference on Creole Language Studies* (Creole Language Studies, no. 2), edited by R.B. LePage, 60–84. London: Macmillan.

———. 1968. "The Field of Creole Language Studies". *Studia Anglica* 2:29–51.

———. 1971a. "Introduction: The Study of Pidgin and Creole Languages". In *Pidginization and Creolization of Languages*, edited by Del Hymes, 13–45. Cambridge: Cambridge University Press.

———. 1971b. "Towards a Generative Analysis of a Post-Creole Speech Continuum". In *Pidginization and Creolization of Languages*, edited by Del Hymes, 349–70. Cambridge: Cambridge University Press.

DeGraff, Michel. 1996. "Review of *Temps et Aspects en Créole Seychellois: Valeurs et Interferences*, by Suzanne Michaelis" *Journal of Pidgin and Creole Languages* 11 (1): 121–37.

———. 2005. "Morphology and Word Order in 'Creolization' and Beyond". In *The Oxford Handbook of Comparative Syntax*, edited by Guglielmo Cinque and Richard Kayne, 293–372. Oxford: Oxford University Press.

De Houwer, Annick. 1990. *The Acquisition of Two Languages from Birth: A Case Study*. Cambridge: Cambridge University Press.

De Lisser, Tamirand Nnena. 2015. "The Acquisition of Jamaican Creole: The Emergence and Transformation of Early Syntactic Systems". PhD dissertation, University of Geneva.

Devonish, Hubert. 2003. "Language Advocacy and 'Conquest' Diglossia in the 'Anglophone' Caribbean". In *The Politics of English as a World Language*, edited by Christian Mair, 155–77. Amsterdam and New York: Rodopi B.V.

Devonish, Hubert, and Karen Carpenter. 2007. "Full Bilingual Education in a Creole Language Situation: The Jamaican Bilingual Primary Education Project". *SCL Occasional Paper*, no. 35.

Devonish, Hubert, and Kadian Walters. 2015. "The Jamaican Language Situation: A Process, Not a Type". In *Globalising Sociolinguistics: Challenging and Expanding Theory*, edited by Dick Smakman and Patrick Heinrich, 223–32. New York: Routledge.

Dhillon, Rajdip. 2010. "Examining the 'Noun Bias': A Structural Approach". *Proceedings of the 33rd Annual Penn Linguistics Colloquium: University of Pennsylvania Working Papers in Linguistics* 16 (1): 51–60.

Di Sciullo, Anna Maria, Pieter Muysken and Rajendra Singh. 1986. "Government and Code-Mixing". *Journal of Linguistics* 22 (1): 1–24.

Dixon, R.M.W., and Alexandra Y. Aikhenvald. 2004. *A Cross-Linguistic Typology*. Oxford: Oxford University Press.

Döpke, Susanne. 1996. "The Weaker Language in Simultaneous Bilingualism: Why It Is Not Like L2". http://www.bilingualoptions.com.au/consTXTL2.pdf.

Dressler, Wolfgang. 2010. "A Typological Approach to First Language Acquisition". In *Language Acquisition across Linguistic and Cognitive Systems*, edited by Michèle Kail and Maya Hickman, 109–24. Amsterdam: John Benjamins.

———. 2012. "On the Acquisition of Inflectional Morphology: Introduction". *Morphology* 22:1–8.

Durrleman-Tame, Stephanie. 2008. *The Syntax of Jamaican Creole: A Cartographic Perspective*. Amsterdam: John Benjamins.

Eisenbeiß, Sonja. 2000. "The Acquisition of the DP in German". In *The Acquisition of Syntax: Studies in Comparative Developmental Linguistics*, edited by Marc-Ariel Friedemann and Luigi Rizzi, 27–62. Singapore: Pearson.

———. 2010. "Production Methods in Language Acquisition Research". In *Experimental Methods in Language Acquisition Research*, edited by Elma Blom and Sharon Unsworth, 11–34. Amsterdam: John Benjamins.

Ellis, Rod. 2002. "Does Form-Focused Instruction Affect the Acquisition of Implicit Knowledge? A Review of the Research". *Studies in Second Language Acquisition* 24 (2): 223–36.

Epstein, Richard. 2002. "The Definite Article, Accessibility, and the Construction of Discourse Referents". *Cognitive Linguistics* 12 (4): 333–78.

Fantini, Alvino E. 1985. *Language Acquisition of a Bilingual Child: A Sociolinguistic Perspective (to Age Ten)*. Clevedon, UK: Multilingual Matters.

Fenson, Larry, Philip S. Dale, J. Steven Reznick, Elizabeth Bates, Donna J. Thal, Stephen J. Pethick, Michael Tomasello, Carolyn B. Mervis and Joan Stiles. 1994. "Variability in Early Communicative Development". *Monographs of the Society for Research in Child Development* 59 (5): 1–185.

Fenson, Larry, Virginia Marchman, Donna J. Thal, Philip S. Dale, Steven Reznick and Elizabeth Bates. 2006. *The MacArthur-Bates Communicative Development Inventories User's Guide and Technical Manual*. 2nd ed. Baltimore, MD: Brookes.

Ferguson, Charles A. 1959. "Diglossia". *Word* 15:325–40.

Fernald, Anne, and Hiromi Morikawa. 1993. "Common Themes and Cultural Variations in Japanese and American Mothers' Speech to Infants". *Child Development* 64 (3): 637–56.

Flege, James E. 1999. "Age of Learning and Second-language Speech". In *Second Language Acquisition and the Critical Period Hypothesis*, edited by David Birdsong, 101–32. Hillsdale, NJ: Lawrence Erlbaum Associates.

Foster-Cohen, Susan H. 1999. *An Introduction to Child Language Development*. London: Longman.

Fotos, Sandra. 1994. "Integrating Grammar Instruction and Communicative Language Use Through Grammar Consciousness-Raising Tasks". *TESOL Quarterly* 28 (2): 323–51.

Foursha-Stevenson, Cassandra, and Elena Nicoladis. 2011. "Early Emergence of Syntactic Awareness and Cross-Linguistic Influence in Children's Judgments". *International Journal of Bilingualism* 15 (4): 521–34.

Frawley, William. 1992. *Linguistic Semantics*. Hillsdale, NJ: Lawrence Erlbaum Associates.

Gardner-Chloros, Penelope 1995 "Code-Switching in Community, Regional and National Repertoires: The Myth of the Discreteness of Linguistic Systems". In *One Speaker, Two Languages: Cross Disciplinary Perspectives on Code-Switching*, edited by Leslie Milroy and Pieter Muysken, 68–89. Cambridge: Cambridge University Press.

Gathercole, Virginia C. Mueller. 1997. "The Linguistic Mass/Count Distinction as an Indicator of Referent Categorization in Monolingual and Bilingual Children". *Child Development* 68 (5): 832–42.

Gawlitzek-Maiwald, Ira, and Rosemarie Tracy. 1996. "Bilingual Bootstrapping". *Linguistics* 34:901–26.

Gee, James Paul. 2015. *Literacy and Education*. New York: Routledge.

Gentner, Dedre. 1982. "Why Nouns Are Learned before Verbs: Linguistic Relativity versus Natural Partitioning". In *Language Development*. Volume 2: *Language, Thought and Culture*, edited by Stan A. Kuczaj, 301–34. Hillsdale, NJ: Lawrence Erlbaum Associates.

Gentner, Dedre, and Lera Boroditsky. 2003. "Individuation, Relativity, and Early Word Learning". In *Language Acquisition and Conceptual Development*, edited by Melissa Bowerman and Stephen C. Levinson, 215–56. Cambridge: Cambridge University Press.

Giancaspro, David. 2013. "L2 Learners' and Heritage Speakers' Judgments of Code-Switching at the Auxiliary-VP Boundary". In *Selected Proceedings of the 16th Hispanic Linguistics Symposium*, edited by Jennifer Cabrelli Amaro, Gillian Lord, Ana de Prada Pérez and Jessi Elana Aaron, 56–69. Somerville, MA: Cascadilla.

Givón, Talmy. 1981. "On the Development of the Numeral 'One' as an Indefinite Marker". *Folia Linguistica Historica* 2 (1): 35–53.

Goddard, Cliff. 2009. "A Piece of Cheese, a Grain of Sand: The Semantics of Mass Nouns and Unitizers". In *Kinds, Things and Stuff*, edited by Francis Jeffry Pelletier, 132–65. Oxford: Oxford University Press.

Gooskens, Charlotte, and Renée van Bezooijen. 2006. "Mutual Comprehensibility of Written Afrikaans and Dutch: Symmetrical or Asymmetrical?" *Literary and Linguistic Computing* 21 (4): 543–57.

Gough, Philip B., and William Tunmer. 1986. "Decoding, Reading, and Reading Disability". *RASE: Remedial and Special Education* 7:6–10.

Grant, Anthony. 2012. "Bound Morphology in English (and Beyond): Copy or Cognate?" In *Copies versus Cognates in Bound Morphology*, edited by Lars Johanson and Martine Robbeets, 99–122. Leiden: Koninklijke Brill NV.

Grice, Paul. 1975. "Logic and Conversation". In *Syntax and Semantics 3: Speech Acts*, edited by Peter Cole and J.L. Morgan, 41–58. New York: Academic Press.

Grosjean, François. 1989. "Neurolinguists, Beware! The Bilingual Is Not Two Monolinguals in One Person". *Brain and Language* 36:3–15.

———. 2001. "The Bilingual's Language Modes". In *One Mind, Two Languages: Bilingual Language Processing*, edited by Janet L. Nichol, 1–22. Malden, MA: Blackwell.

———. 2008. *Studying Bilinguals*. Oxford: Oxford University Press.

Halliday, M.A.K. 1975. *Learning How to Mean: Explorations in the Development of Language Development*. London: Edward Arnold.

Harley, Trevor A. (1995) 2014. *The Psychology of Language: From Data to Theory*. 4th ed. London: Psychology Press.

Hawkins, Eric W. 1984. *Awareness of Language: An Introduction.* Cambridge: Cambridge University Press.

Hawkins, Roger. 2004. "The Contribution of the Theory of Universal Grammar to Our Understanding of the Acquisition of French as a Second Language". *French Language Studies* 14:233–55.

Hoff, Erika. (2005) 2009. *Language Development.* 4th ed. Belmont, CA: Wadsworth.

———. 2006. "How Social Contexts Support and Shape Language Development. *Developmental Review* 26:55–88.

Honey, John. 1998. "Sociophonology". In *The Handbook of Sociolinguistics*, edited by Florian Coulmas, 92–106. Malden, MA: Blackwell.

Hornstein, Norbert. 1990. *As Time Goes By: Tense and Universal Grammar.* Cambridge, MA: MIT Press.

Hyltenstam, Kenneth, and Niclas Abrahamsson. 2005. "Maturational Constraints in SLA". In *The Handbook of Second Language Acquisition*, edited by Catherine J. Doughty and Michael H. Long, 539–88. Malden, MA: Blackwell.

Hymes, Dell. 1972. "On Communicative Competence". In *Sociolinguistics: Selected Readings*, edited by John Bernard Pride and Janet Holmes, 269–93. Harmondsworth: Penguin.

Ihsane, Tabea, and Genoveva Puskas. 2001. "Specific Is Not Definite". *Generative Grammar in Geneva* 2:39–54.

Imai, Mutsume, Etsuko Haryu, Hiroyuki Okada, Lianjing Li and Jun Shigematsu. 2006. "Revisiting the Noun-Verb Debate: A Cross-Linguistic Comparison of Novel Noun and Verb Learning in English-, Japanese-, and Chinese-Speaking Children". In *Action Meets Word: How Children Learn Verbs*, edited by Kathy Hirsh-Pasek and Roberta Michnick Golinkoff, 450–76. Oxford: Oxford University Press.

Irvine, G. Alison. 2005. "Defining Good English in Jamaica: Language Variation and Language Ideology in an Agency of the Jamaican State". PhD dissertation, University of the West Indies, Mona.

James, Carl. 1996. "A Cross-Linguistic Approach to Language Awareness". *Language Awareness* 5 (3 and 4): 138–48.

Jarvis, Scott, and Aneta Pavlenko. 2007. *Cross-Linguistic Influence in Language and Cognition.* New York: Routledge.

Jennings, Zellynne. 1996. "Curriculum Change Strategies: The Impact on West Indian Education". In *Education in the West Indies: Development and Perspectives 1948–1988*, edited by Dennis R. Craig, 136–58. Kingston: Institute of Social and Economic Research, University of the West Indies.

Jia, Gisela. 2003. "The Acquisition of the English Plural Morpheme by Native Mandarin Chinese-Speaking Children". *Journal of Speech, Language and Hearing Research* 46:1297–311.

Jiménez, Robert T., Georgia Earnest García and P. David Pearson. 1996. "The Reading Strategies of Bilingual Latina/o Students Who Are Successful English Readers: Opportunities and Obstacles". *Reading Research Quarterly* 31 (1): 90–112.

JLU (Jamaica Language Unit). 2009. *Writing Jamaican the Jamaican Way.* Kingston: Arawak.

Kachru, Yamuna. 2006. "World Englishes and Language Education". In *Dialects, Englishes, Creoles, and Education*, edited by Shondel J. Nero, 19–37. New York: Routledge.

Kennedy, Michele M. 2012. *Quantification in Jamaican Creole: The Syntax and Semantics of evri ('every') in Interaction with Indefinites*. LinCom Studies in Pidgin and Creole Linguistics 11. Muenchen: LinCom Academic.

Kiczkowiak, Marek. 2014. "Native English-Speaking Teachers: Always the Right Choice?" https://www.britishcouncil.org/voices-magazine/native-english-speaking-teachers-always-right-choice.

Kirby, John R., S. Hélène Deacon, Peter N. Bowers, Leah Izenberg, Lesly Wade-Woolley and Rauno Parrila. 2012. "Children's Morphological Awareness and Reading Ability". *Read Writ* 25:389–401.

Kirby, Susannah. 2014. "Major Theories in Acquisition of Syntax Research". In *The Routledge Handbook of Syntax*, edited by Andrew Carnie, Yosuke Sato and Daniel Siddiqi, 426–45. New York: Routledge.

Klibanoff, Raquel S., and Sandra R. Waxman. 1998. "Preschoolers' Acquisition of Novel Adjectives and the Role of Basic-Level Kind". In *Proceedings of the 22nd Annual Boston University Conference on Language Development*, edited by Annabel Greenhill, Mary Hughes, Heather Littlefield and Hugh Walsh, 442–53. Sommerville, MA: Cascadilla.

———. 2000. "Basic Level Object Categories Support the Acquisition of Novel Adjectives: Evidence from Preschool-Aged Children". *Child Development* 71 (3): 649–59.

Köppe, Regina, and Jürgen Meisel. 1995. "Code-Switching in Bilingual First Language Acquisition". In *One Speaker, Two Languages: Cross Disciplinary Perspectives on Code-Switching*, edited by Leslie Milroy and Pieter Muysken, 276–301. Cambridge: Cambridge University Press.

Kouwenberg, Silvia. 2011. "Linguistics in the Caribbean: Empowerment through Creole Language Awareness". *Journal of Pidgin and Creole Languages* 26 (2): 387–403.

Kouwenberg, Silvia, and John Singler. 2011. "Pidgins and Creoles". In *The Cambridge Handbook of Sociolinguistics*, edited by Rajend Mesthrie, 283–300. Cambridge: Cambridge University Press.

Krashen, Stephen D. 1977. "Some Issues Relating to the Monitor Model". In *On TESOL '77: Teaching and Learning English as a Second Language: Trends in Research and Practice*, edited by H.D. Brown, C.A. Yorio and R.H. Crymes, 144–58. Washington, DC: TESOL.

———. 1981. *Second Language Acquisition and Second Language Learning*. New York: Prentice-Hall.

———. 1982. *Principles and Practice in Second Language Acquisition*. New York: Prentice-Hall.

Kroll, Judith F., Susan C. Bobb and Zofia Wodniecka. 2006. "Language Selectivity Is the Exception, Not the Rule: Arguments against a Fixed Locus of Language Selection in Bilingual Speech". *Bilingualism: Language and Cognition* 9:119–35.

Kroll, Judith F., Cari A. Bogulski and Rhonda McClain. 2012. "Psycholinguistic Perspectives on Second Language Learning and Bilingualism: The Course and Consequence of Cross Language Competition". *Linguistic Approaches to Bilingualism* 2 (1): 1–24.

Kroll, Judith F., Paola E. Dussias, Cari A. Bogulski and Jorge R. Valdes Kroff. 2012. "Juggling Two Languages in One Mind: What Bilinguals Tell Us about Language Processing and Its Consequences for Cognition". In *Psychology of Learning and Motivation*, edited by Brian Ross, 229–62. Vol. 56. San Diego, CA: Elsevier.

KU. 2015. "Phonological Awareness Skills Test". University of Kentucky *Special Connections*. http://www.specialconnections.ku.edu/~specconn/page/instruction/ra/case/caseb/pdf /caseb_scene1_2.pdf.

Kuo, Li-jen., and Richard C. Anderson. 2006. "Morphological Awareness and Learning to Read: A Cross Language Perspective". *Educational Psychologist* 41 (3): 161–80.

Laaha, Sabine, and Steven Gillis, eds. 2007. *Typological Perspectives on the Acquisition of Morphology*. Antwerp Papers in Linguistics 111. Antwerp: University of Antwerp.

Lacoste, Véronique. 2012. *Phonological Variation in Rural Jamaican Schools*. Amsterdam: John Benjamins.

Lalla, Barbara, and Jean D'Costa. 1990. *Language in Exile: Three Hundred Years of Jamaican Creole*. Tuscaloosa, AL: University of Alabama Press.

Lardière, Donna. 2004. "Knowledge of Definiteness Despite Variable Article Omission in Second Language Acquisition". In *Proceedings of the 28th Annual Boston University Conference on Language Development*, edited by Alejna Burgos, Linnea Micciulla and Christine E. Smith, 328–39. Somerville MA: Cascadilla.

———. (2008) 2010. "Feature Assembly in Second Language Acquisition". In *The Role of Formal Features in Second Language Acquisition*, edited by Juana Liceras, Helmut Zobul and Helen Goodluck, 106–40. Hillsdale, NJ: Lawrence Erlbaum Associates.

Larsen-Freeman, Diane. 1975. "The Acquisition of Grammatical Morphemes by Adult ESL Learners". *TESOL Quarterly* 9:409–30.

Lefèbvre, Claire. 1996. "The TMA System of Haitian Creole and the Problem of Transmission of Grammar in Creole Genesis". *Journal of Pidgin and Creole Languages* 11 (2): 231–311.

———. 1998. *Creole Genesis and the Acquisition of Grammar: The Case of Haitian Creole*. Cambridge: Cambridge University Press.

LePage, Robert B., and Andrée Tabouret-Keller. 1985. *Acts of Identity: Creole-Based Approaches to Language and Ethnicity*. Cambridge: Cambridge University Press.

Lewis, Yewande. 2010. "Literacy in Elementary School in Jamaica: The Case of the Grade Four Literacy Test". PhD dissertation, University of Iowa.

Lyons, Christopher. 1999. *Definiteness*. Cambridge: Cambridge University Press.

MacSwan, Jeff. 1999. *A Minimalist Approach to Intrasentential Code-Switching*. New York: Garland.

———. 2000. "The Architecture of the Bilingual Language Faculty: Evidence from Intrasentential Code Switching". *Bilingualism: Language and Cognition* 3 (1): 37–54.

———. 2006. "Code-Switching and Grammatical Theory". In *Handbook of Bilingualism*, edited by Tej K. Bhatia and William C. Ritchie, 283–311. Malden, MA: Blackwell.

———. 2014. "Programs and Proposals in Codeswitching Research: Unconstraining Theories of Bilingual Language Mixing". In *Grammatical Theory and Bilingual Codeswitching*, edited by Jeff MacSwan, 1–33. Cambridge, MA: MIT Press.

MacWhinney, Brian. 2000a. *The CHILDES Project: Tools for Analyzing Talk*. 3rd ed. Hillsdale, NJ: Lawrence Erlbaum Associates.

———. 2000b. *The CHILDES Project: The Database*. 3rd ed. Hillsdale, NJ: Lawrence Erlbaum Associates.

Mair, Christian, and Véronique Lacoste. 2012. "A Vernacular on the Move: Towards a Socio-linguistics of Mobility for Jamaican Creole". *Cahier de Linguistique* 38 (1): 87-110.

Malabonga, Valerie, Dorry M. Kenyon, Maria Carlo, Diane August and Mohammed Louguit. 2008. "Development of a Cognate Awareness Measure for Spanish-Speaking English Language Learners". *Language Testing* 25 (4): 495–619.

Marcus, Gary F. 1996. "Why Do Children Say 'breaked'?" *Current Directions in Psychological Science* 5 (3): 81–85.

Maslen, Robert J.C., Anna L. Theakston, Elena V.M. Lieven and Michael Tomasello. 2004. "A Dense Corpus Study of Past Tense and Plural Overregularization in English". *Journal of Speech, Language and Hearing Research* 47 (6): 1319–33.

McLaughlin, Barry. 1984. *Second Language Acquisition in Childhood*. Vol 1: *Preschool Children*. Hillsdale, NJ: Lawrence Erlbaum Associates.

McWhorter, John. 1998. *Word on the Street: Debunking the Myth of a "Pure" Standard English*. New York: Basic Books.

Meade, Rocky. 2001. *Acquisition of Jamaica Phonology*. Amsterdam: Holland Institute of Generative Linguistics/Netherlands Graduate School of Linguistics.

Meisel, Jürgen M. 1989. "Early Differentiation of Languages in Bilingual Children". In *Bilingualism across the Lifespan: Aspects of Acquisition, Maturity, and Loss*, edited by Kenneth Hyltenstam and Loraine K. Obler, 13–40. Cambridge: Press Syndicate of the University of Cambridge.

———. (2004) 2006. "The Bilingual Child". In *The Handbook of Bilingualism*, edited by Tej K. Bhatia and William C. Ritchie, 91–113. Malden, MA: Blackwell.

———. 2007. "The Weaker Language in Early Child Bilingualism: Acquiring a First Language as a Second Language?" *Applied Psycholinguistics* 28:495–514.

———. 2011. *First and Second Language Acquisition: Parallels and Differences*. Cambridge: Cambridge University Press.

Messam-Johnson, Trecel. 2017. "Attrition of a Creole: The Syntactic Effects of the L2 Acquisition of Papiamentu on Jamaican Creole". PhD dissertation, University of the West Indies, Mona.

Miller, Errol. 2015. "Educational Reform in Independent Jamaica". OAS Educational Portal of the Americas.http://www.educoas.org/portal/bdigital/contenido/interamer/bkiacd/interamer/Interamerhtml/Millerhtml/mil_mil.htm#.

Ministry of Education, Youth and Culture, Jamaica. 2001. *Language Education Policy*. Kingston: Ministry of Education, Youth and Culture.

———. 2006. *Literacy 1-2-3 Manual Accompanying the Language Education Curriculum for Grades 1 through 3*. Kingston: Ministry of Education, Youth and Culture.

Montrul, Silvina. 2005. "Second Language Acquisition and First Language Loss in Adult Early Bilinguals: Exploring Some Differences and Similarities". *Second Language Research* 21 (3): 199–249.

Morales, Alexandra. 2011. "The Role of the L1 in the Acquisition of English Articles by Spanish-Speaking Children". In *Proceedings of the 11th Generative Approaches to Second Language Acquisition Conference* (GASLA), edited by Julia Herschensohn and Darren Tanner, 83–89. Somerville, MA: Cascadilla.

Mufwene, Salikoko. 1986. "Number Delimitation in Gullah". *American Speech* 61:33–60.

———. 2001. *The Ecology of Language Evolution*. Cambridge: Cambridge University Press.

Müller, Natascha. 1994. "Gender and Number Agreement within DP". In *Bilingual First Language Acquisition: French and German Grammatical Development*, edited by Jürgen M. Meisel, 53–88. Language Acquisition and Language Disorders, no. 7. Amsterdam: John Benjamins.

Murphy, M. Lynne. 2010. *Lexical Meaning*. Cambridge: Cambridge University Press.

Murray, Denise E., and MaryAnn Christison. 2011. *What English Language Teachers Need to Know*. Volume 1: *Understanding Learning*. New York: Routledge.

Muysken, Pieter. 1981. "Creole TMA Systems: The Unmarked Case?" In *Generative Studies on Creole Languages*, edited by Pieter Muysken, 181–99. Dordrecht: Foris.

———. 1995. "Code-Switching and Grammatical Theory". In *One Speaker, Two Languages: Cross Disciplinary Perspectives on Code-Switching*, edited by Lesley Milroy and Pieter Muysken, 177–98. Cambridge: Cambridge University Press.

———. 2000. *Bilingual Speech: A Typology of Code-Mixing*. Cambridge: Cambridge University Press.

———. 2008. *Functional Categories*. Cambridge: Cambridge University Press.

Myers-Scotton, Carol, and Janice L. Jake. 1995. "Matching Lemmas in a Bilingual Language Competence and Production Model: Evidence from Intrasentential Code Switching". *Linguistics* 33:981–1024.

———. 2001. "Explaining Aspects of Code-Switching and Their Implications". In *One Mind, Two Languages: Bilingual Language Processing*, edited by Janet L. Nicol, 84–116. Malden, MA: Blackwell.

Nagy, William E., and Anderson Richard C. 1984. "How Many Words Are There in Printed School English?" *Reading Research Quarterly* 19 (3): 304–30.

Nero, Shondel. 2014. "*De Facto* Language Education Policy through Teachers' Attitudes and Practices: A Critical Ethnographic Study in Three Jamaican Schools". *Language Policy* 13 (3): 221–42.

———. 2015. "Language, Identity, and Insider/Outsider Positionality in Caribbean Creole English Research". *Applied Linguistics Review* 6 (3): 341–68.

Nero, Shondel, and Dohra Ahmad. 2014. *Vernaculars in the Classroom: Paradoxes, Pedagogies, Possibilities*. New York: Routledge.

Nicoladis, Elena, and Fred Genesee. 1997. "Language Development in Preschool Bilingual Children". *Journal of Speech Language Pathology and Audiology* 21 (4): 258–70.

Nicoladis, Elena, Jianhui Song and Paula Marentette. 2012. "Do Young Bilinguals Acquire Past Tense Morphology Like Monolinguals Only Later? Evidence from French-English and Chinese-English Bilinguals". *Applied Psycholinguistics* 33:457–79.

Oller, D. Kimbrough, and Rebecca E. Eilers. 2002. "An Integrated Approach to Evaluating Effects of Bilingualism in Miami School Children: The Study Design". In *Language and Literacy in Bilingual Children*, edited by D. Kimbrough Oller and Rebecca E. Eilers, 22–40. Clevedon, UK: Multilingual Matters.

O'Neill, Daniela K. 1996. "Two-Year-Olds' Sensitivity to the Parent's Knowledge when Making Requests". *Child Development* 67:659–77.

Owens, Robert. 2001. *Language Development: An Introduction*. Boston: Allyn and Bacon.

Paradis, Johanne. 2011. "The Impact of Input Factors on Bilingual Development: Quantity versus Quality". *Linguistic Approaches to Bilingualism* 1 (1): 67–70.

Patrick, Peter. 1999. *Urban Jamaican Creole: Variation in the Mesolect*. Amsterdam: John Benjamins.

———. 2002. "Modelling Synchronic Variation: The (Post-) Creole Continuum". MS, University of Essex.

———. 2004. "Jamaican Creole Grammar". In *Handbook of Varieties of English*. Vol. 2: *Morphology and Syntax*, edited by Bernd Kortmann, Kate Burridge, Rajend Mesthrie, Edgar W. Schneider and Clive Upton, 201–33. Berlin: Mouton de Gruyter.

———. 2007. "Jamaican Patwa (Creole English)". In *Comparative Creole Syntax*, edited by John Holm, and Peter L. Patrick, 127–52. London: Battlebridge.

———. 2009. "Number Marking in Jamaican Patwa". Talk given at the Eighth Creolistics Workshop, Giessen, Germany, April 2009. http://privatewww.essex.ac.uk/~patrickp/papers/NumberMarkingJamaicanPatwaGiessen09.pdf.

Patterson, Janet L., and Barbara Zurer Pearson. (2004) 2012. "Bilingual Lexical Development, Assessment, and Intervention". In *Bilingual Language Development and Disorders in Spanish-English Speakers*, 2nd ed., edited by Brian A. Goldstein, 113–29. Baltimore, MD: Brookes.

Pearson, Barbara Zurer. 1998. "Assessing Lexical Development in Bilingual Babies and Toddlers". *International Journal of Bilingualism* 2 (2): 347–72.

Peccei, Jean Stilwell. 2006. *Child Language: A Resource Book for Students*. New York: Routledge.

Petersen, Jennifer. 1988. "Word-Internal *Code-Switching* Constraints in a Bilingual Child's Grammar". *Linguistics* 26:479–93.

Pinker, Steven. 1995. "Language Acquisition". In *An Invitation to Cognitive Science*. 2nd ed., edited by Lila R. Gleitman and Mark Liberman, 135–82. Cambridge, MA: MIT Press.

Place, Silvia, and Erika Hoff. 2011. "Properties of Dual Language Exposure That Influence Two-Year-Olds' Bilingual Proficiency". *Child Development* 82 (6): 1834–49.

Plag, Ingo. 2006. "Morphology in Pidgins and Creoles". In *Encyclopedia of Language and Linguistics*, 2nd ed., edited by Keith Brown, 304–8. San Diego, CA: Elsevier.

———. 2008. "Creoles as Interlanguages: Inflectional Morphology". *Journal of Pidgin and Creole Languages* 23 (1): 109–30.

———. 2009. "Creoles as Interlanguages: Word Formation". *Journal of Pidgin and Creole Languages* 24 (2): 339–62.

Pollard, Velma. 2001. "'A Singular Subject Takes a Singular Verb' and Hypercorrection in Jamaican Speech and Writing". In *Due Respect: Papers on English and English-Related Creoles in the Caribbean in Honour of Professor Robert Le Page*, edited by Pauline Christie, 97–107. Kingston: University of the West Indies Press.

———. 2002. "The Role of Jamaican Creole in Language Education". Popular Series Paper, no. 2. Society for Caribbean Linguistics.

Poplack, Shana. 1993. "Variation Theory and Language Contact". In *American Dialect Research*, edited by Dennis R. Preston, 251–86. Amsterdam: John Benjamins.

———. 2004. "Code-Switching". In *Soziolinguistik: An International Handbook of the Science of Language*, 2nd ed., edited by Ulrich Ammon, Norbert Dittmar, Klaus J. Mattheier and Peter Trudgill, 589–96. Berlin: Mouton de Gruyter.

Postal, Paul M. 1966. "A Note on 'Understood Intransitively'". *International Journal of American Linguistics* 32:90–93.

Radford, Andrew. 1990. *Syntactic Theory and the Acquisition of English Syntax*. Malden, MA: Blackwell.

———. 1997. *Syntax: A Minimalist Introduction*. Cambridge: Cambridge University Press.

———. 2000. "Children in Search of Perfection: Towards a Minimalist Model of Acquisition". MS, University of Essex.

———. 2004. *English Syntax: An Introduction*. Cambridge: Cambridge University Press.

———. 2006. "Children's English: Principles-and-Parameters Perspectives". MS, University of Essex.

———. 2016. *Analysing English Sentences*. 2nd ed. Cambridge: Cambridge University Press.

Radford, Andrew, and Joseph Galasso. 1998. "Children's Possessive Structures: A Case Study". MS, University of Essex.

Reichenbach, Hans. 1947. *Elements of Symbolic Logic*. New York: Macmillan.

Richards, Brian. 1987. "Type/Token Ratios: What Do They Really Tell Us?" *Journal of Child Language* 14 (2): 201–9.

Riches, Caroline, and Fred Genesee. 2006. "Literacy: Cross-Linguistic and Cross-Modal Issues". In *Educating English Language Learners: A Synthesis of Research Evidence*, edited by Fred Genesee, Kathryn Lindholm-Leary, William Saunders and Donna Christian, 64–108. Cambridge: Cambridge University Press.

Rickford, John. 1985. "Standard and Non-Standard Attitudes in a Creole Continuum". In *Language of Inequality*, edited by Nessa Wolfson and Joan Manes, 145–60. Berlin: Mouton.

———. 1987. *Dimensions of a Creole Continuum*. Stanford: Stanford University Press.

Rijkhoff, Jan. 2002. "Verbs and Nouns from a Cross-Linguistic Perspective". *Rivista di Linguistica* 14 (1): 115–47.

———. 2004. *The Noun Phrase*. Oxford: Oxford University Press.

Ringbom, Håkan. 1987. *The Role of the First Language in Foreign Language Learning*. Clevedon, UK: Multilingual Matters.

———. 2001. "Lexical Transfer in L3 Production". In *Cross-Linguistic Influence in Third Language Acquisition: Psycholinguistic Perspectives*, edited by Jasone Cenoz, Britta Hufeisen and Ulrike Jessner, 59–68. Clevedon, UK: Multilingual Matters.

SABER Country Report. 2013. *Jamaica. Early Childhood Development*. World Bank. http://wbgfiles.worldbank.org/documents/hdn/ed/saber/supporting_doc/CountryReports/ECD/SABER_ECD_Jamaica_CR_Final_2013.pdf.

Salia, Rachel. 2011. "Between Arabic and French Lies the Dialect: Moroccan Code-Weaving on Facebook". BA thesis, Columbia University.

Sandhofer, Catherine, and Linda B. Smith. 2007. "Learning Adjectives in the Real World: How Learning Nouns Impedes Learning Adjectives". *Language Learning and Development* 3 (3): 233–67.

Schaeffer, Jeannette. 1997. "Direct Object Scrambling in Dutch and Italian Child Language". PhD dissertation, University of California, Los Angeles.

Schaeffer, Jeannette, and Lisa Matthewson. 2005. "Grammar and Pragmatics in the Acquisition of Article Systems". *Natural Language and Linguistic Theory* 23:53–101.

Schiffrin, Deborah. 1998. *Approaches to Discourse*. Malden, MA: Blackwell.

Schlyter, Suzanne. 1993. "The Weaker Language in Bilingual Swedish-French Children". In *Progression and Regression in Language: Sociocultural, Neuropsychological, and Linguistic Perspectives*, edited by Kenneth Hyltenstam and Åke Viberg, 289–308. Cambridge: Cambridge University Press.

Schmidt, Richard. 1990. "The Role of Consciousness in Second Language Learning". *Applied Linguistics* 11 (2): 129–58.

———. 2001. "Attention". In *Cognition and Second Language Instruction*, edited by Peter Robinson, 3–32. Cambridge: Cambridge University Press.

———. 2010. "Attention, Awareness, and Individual Differences in Language Learning". In *Proceedings of CLaSIC 2010, Singapore, December 2–4*, edited by Wai Meng Chan, Seo Won Chi, Kwee Nyet Lin, Johanna Istanto, Masanori Nagami, Jyh Wee Sew, Titima Suthiwan and Izumi Walker, 721–37. Singapore: National University of Singapore. http://nflrc.hawaii.edu /PDFs/SCHMIDT%20Attention,%20awareness,%20and%20individual%20differences.pdf.

Schwartz, Bonnie D., and Lynn Eubank. 1996. "What Is the L2 Initial State?" *Second Language Research* 12 (1): 1–5.

Schwartz, Bonnie D., and Rex A. Sprouse. 1996. "L2 Cognitive States and the Full Transfer Full Access Model". *Second Language Research* 12 (1): 40–72.

———. 2007. "Linear Sequencing Strategies or UG-defined Hierarchical Structures in L2 Acquisition? A Reply to Meisel". In *Phrasal and Clausal Architecture: Syntactic Derivation and Interpretation*, edited by Simin Karimi, Vida Samiian and Wendy K. Wilkins, 295–318. Amsterdam: John Benjamins.

Sebba, Mark. (2009) 2012. "On the Notions of Congruence and Convergence in Code-Switching". In *The Cambridge Handbook of Linguistic Code-Switching*, edited by Barbara E. Bullock and Almeida Jacqueline Toribio, 40–57. Cambridge: Cambridge University Press.

Selinker, Larry. 1972. "Interlanguage". *IRAL: International Review of Applied Linguistics* 10:209–30.

Shields, Kathryn. 1989. "Standard English in Jamaica: A Case of Competing Models". *English World-Wide* 10 (1): 41–53.

Simmons-McDonald, Hazel, Linda Fields and Peter Roberts. 1997. *Writing in English: A Course Book for Caribbean Students*. Kingston: Ian Randle.

Sinanan, Roma, Uriel Narinesingh, Ian Attong and Clifford Narinesing. 2002. *Rainbow Readers: A Jamaican Reading Series, Grade 3*. Claxton Bay, Trinidad: Royards Educational Books.

Slabakova, Roumyana. 2009. "Features or Parameters: Which One Makes Second Language Acquisition Easier, and More Interesting to Study?" *Second Language Research* 25 (2): 313–24.

Smith, Carlota. 1997. *The Parameter of Aspect*. Dordrecht: Kluwer.

Smith, Linda B., Susan S. Jones and Barbara Landau. 1996. "Naming in Young Children: A Dumb Attentional Mechanism?" *Cognition* 60:143–71.

Snow, Catherine E., Susan Burns and Peg Griffin, eds. 1998. *Preventing Reading Difficulties in Young Children*. Committee on the Prevention of Reading Difficulties in Young Children, National Research Council. Washington, DC: National Academies Press.

Snyder, William. 2007. *Child Language: The Parametric Approach*. Oxford: Oxford University Press.

Spradlin, Kenton Todd, Juana Liceras and Raquel Fernández Fuertes. 2003. "Functional-Lexical Code-Mixing Patterns as Evidence for Language Dominance in Young Bilingual Children: A Minimalist Approach". In *Proceedings of the 6th Generative Approaches to Second Language Acquisition Conference (GASLA 2002)*, edited by Juana Liceras, Helmut Zobl and Helen Goodluck, 298–307. Somerville, MA: Cascadilla.

Stewart, Michele M. 2007. "Aspects of the Syntax and Semantics of Bare Nouns in Jamaican Creole". In *Noun Phrases in Creole Languages: A Multi-faceted Approach*, edited by Marlyse Baptista and Jacqueline Guéron, 383–99. Amsterdam: John Benjamins.

———. 2010a. "The Emergence of Determination in the Speech of Two-Year-Olds in Urban Kingston". Paper presented at the Society for Pidgin and Creole Linguistics Conference held in conjunction with the 84th Annual Meeting of the Linguistic Society of America, Baltimore, Maryland, January 2010.

———. 2010b. "Jamaican Creole alongside Standard Jamaican English in the Speech of Two-Year-Olds from Urban Kingston". *Caribbean Journal of Education* 32 (2): 177–201.

———. 2010c. "When Three-Year-Old Jamaican Children Don't Know the Word". Paper presented at the Society for Caribbean Linguistics 18th Biennial Conference, Barbados, August 2010.

———. 2011. "The Expression of Number in Jamaican Creole". *Journal of Pidgin and Creole Languages* 26 (2): 363–85.

Tardif, Twila, Susan A. Gelman and Fan Xu. 1999. "Putting the 'Noun Bias' in Context: A Comparison of English and Mandarin". *Child Development* 70 (3): 620–35.

Tarone, Elaine. 2014. "Enduring Questions from the Interlanguage Hypothesis". In *Interlanguage: Forty Years Later*, edited by ZhaoHong Han and Elaine Tarone, 7–26. Amsterdam: John Benjamins.

Tomlinson, Brian. 2003. "How Would You Define Language Awareness?" In Rod Bolitho, Ronald Carter, Rebecca Hughes, Roz Ivanic, Hitomi Masuhara and Brian Tomlinson. 2003. "Ten Questions about Language Awareness". *English Language Teaching Journal* 57 (3): 251–59.

Torgesen, Joseph K., Ann W. Alexander, Richard K. Wagner, Carol A. Rashotte, Kytja K.S. Voeller and Tim Conway. 2001. "Intensive Remedial Instruction for Children with Severe Reading Disabilities: Immediate and Long-Term Outcomes from Two Instructional Approaches". *Journal of Learning Disabilities* 34 (1): 33–58, 78.

Trudgill, Peter. 2011. *Sociolinguistic Typology: Social Determinants of Linguistic Complexity*. Oxford: Oxford University Press.

Truscott, John. 2014. *Consciousness and Second Language Learning*. Clevedon, UK: Multilingual Matters.

Tsimpli, Ianthi Maria. 2014. "Early, Late or Very Late? Timing Acquisition and Bilingualism". *Linguistic Approaches to Bilingualism* 4 (3): 283–313.

Unsworth, Sharon. 2016. "Quantity and Quality of Language Input in Bilingual Language Development". In *Bilingualism across the Lifespan: Factors Moderating Language Proficiency*, edited by Elena Nicoladis and Simona Montanari, 103–21. Berlin: Mouton de Gruyter.

Unsworth, Sharon, Froso Argyri, Leonie Cornips, Aafke Hulk, Antonella Sorace and Ianthi Tsimpli. 2014. "The Role of Age of Onset and Input in Early Child Bilingualism in Greek and Dutch". *Applied Psycholinguistics*. 35 (4): 765–805.

Uriagereka, Juan. 2000. *Rhyme and Reason: An Introduction to Minimalist Syntax*. Cambridge, MA: MIT Press.

Valdman, Albert. 1981. *Haitian Creole-English-French Dictionary*. Bloomington: Indiana University, Creole Institute.

Valera, Salvador 2006. "Conversion". In *Encyclopedia of Language and Linguistics*, 2nd ed., edited by Keith Brown, 172–75. San Diego, CA: Elsevier.

Vásquez-Carranza, Luz Marina. 2010. "Cross-Linguistic Influence Evidenced in Possessive Constructions: A Study with an English-Spanish Simultaneous Bilingual Child". *Káñina: Revista de Artes y Letras de la Universidad de Costa Rica* 34 (1): 147–67.

Vendler, Zeno. 1967. *Linguistics in Philosophy*. Ithaca, NY: Cornell University Press.

Vintenko, Marina. 2016. "Language Awareness in Primary Schools in Jamaica". Master's thesis, Albert-Ludwigs-Universität Freiburg.

Walters, Kadian. 2016. "'I got what I wanted but how did they make me feel?': The Anatomy of Linguistic Discrimination in a Diglossic Situation". PhD dissertation, University of the West Indies, Mona.

Wheeler, Rebecca, Kelly B. Cartwright and Rachel Swords. 2012. "Factoring AAVE into Reading Assessment and Instruction". *Reading Teacher* 65 (5): 416–25.

White, Linda. 2003. *Second Language Acquisition and Universal Grammar*. Cambridge: Cambridge University Press.

Whyte, Tina. 2016. "Jamaican Children's Perception of English Sounds". MPhil thesis, University of the West Indies, Mona.

Wilson, Don, Dennis Craig and Hyacinth Campbell. 1978. *Language Materials Workshop Teacher's Book: Year 1 Term 1*. Kingston: Heinemann Educational (Caribbean).

Winer, Lise. 1993. *Trinidad and Tobago*. Amsterdam: John Benjamins.

———. 2006. "Teaching English to Caribbean English Creole-Speaking Students in the Caribbean and North America". In *Dialects, Englishes, Creoles, and Education*, edited by Shondel J. Nero, 105–18. New York: Routledge.

Winford, Donald. 1985. "The Concept of 'Diglossia' in the Caribbean Creole Situations". *Language in Society* 14:345–56.

———. 1993. *Predication in Caribbean English Creoles*. Amsterdam: John Benjamins.

———. 1997. "Re-examining Caribbean English Creole Continua". *World Englishes* 16 (2): 233–79.

———. 2001. "A Comparison of Tense/Aspect Systems in Caribbean English Creoles". In *Due Respect: Papers on English and English-Related Creoles in the Caribbean in Honour of Professor Robert LePage*, edited by Pauline Christie, 155–83. Kingston: University of the West Indies Press.

Yang, Suying, and Yue Yuan Huang. 2004. "The Impact of the Absence of Grammatical Tense in L1 on the Acquisition of the Tense-Aspect System in L2". *IRAL: International Review of Applied Linguistics in Language Teaching* 42:49–70.

Yip, Virginia, and Stephen Matthews. 2006. "Assessing Language Dominance in Bilingual Acquisition: A Case for Mean Length Utterance Differentials". *Language Assessment Quarterly* 3 (2): 97–116.

———. 2007. *The Bilingual Child: Early Development and Language Contact*. Cambridge: Cambridge University Press.

Youssef, Valerie. 1991a. "Variation as a Feature of Language Acquisition in the Trinidad Context". *Language Variation and Change* 3:71–101 .

————. 1991b. "The Acquisition of Varilingual Competence". *English World-Wide* 12:87–102.

————. 1993. "Children's Linguistic Choices: Audience Design and Societal Norms". *Language in Society* 22:257–74.

Zapata, Angie, and Audra K. Roach. 2011. "Professional Book Reviews: Movement in Literacy: New Directions in Multilingual, Multicultural, Multinational, and Multimodal Literacy Studies". *Language Arts* 88 (4): 310–11.

Zdorenko, Tatiana, and Johanne Paradis. 2008. "The Acquisition of Articles in Child Second Language English: Fluctuation, Transfer or Both?" *Second Language Research* 24 (2): 227–50.

Zobl, Helmut, and Juana Liceras. 1994. "Review Article: Functional Categories and Acquisition Orders". *Language Learning* 44 (1): 150–80.

Index

CPSIA information can be obtained
at www.ICGtesting.com
Printed in the USA
LVOW03s1839071117
555379LV00001B/201/P